The Pastoral Epistles:
1–2 Timothy, Titus
An Exegetical and Contextual Commentary

India Commentary on the New Testament

The Pastoral Epistles:
1–2 Timothy, Titus

An Exegetical and Contextual Commentary

Graham Simpson

FORTRESS PRESS
MINNEAPOLIS

The Pastoral Epistles
1–2 TIMOTHY, TITUS
An Exegetical and Contextual Commentary
by
Graham Simpson

INDIA COMMENTARY ON THE NEW TESTAMENT
Series Editors
Venkataraman B. Immanuel, Brian C. Wintle, and C. Bennema

ISBN: 978-1-5064-3799-6
eISBN: 978-1-5064-3839-9

First edition 2012 Primalogue Publishing Media.
Copyright © 2012 Graham Simpson

COVER ART & TYPESETTING
George Korah
Primalogue Publishing
WWW.PRIMALOGUE.COM

TO THE MEMORY OF

Elvie Simpson
20.5.1922 - 5.3.2011

Contents

Titus

Foreword

Commentaries are useful, often necessary, when one wants to engage with the biblical text at a deeper level and understand the richness of its message. The New Testament, for example, was originally written in the Greek language, about 2000 years ago, in cultures very different to our own. A commentary aims to bridge these gaps and explain the fullness of God's original message for today's world. Unfortunately there is no Indian commentary series available in India—most commentary series come from the West. Although many Western commentaries are undoubtedly invaluable, they are written for a Western audience and often expensive. This realization gave birth to the idea of a distinct commentary series for India.

We thus gladly introduce the unique India Commentary on the New Testament (ICNT). The ICNT series aims to give a well-informed exposition of the meaning of the text and relevant reflections in everyday language for today's Indian context. The intended audience is the theological seminary or bible college, both students and faculty. However, the commentaries are also suitable for pastors and lay people with an interest in theology. The commentaries are culturally-rooted and the various applications relating to culture, society and religious life will help those involved in cross-cultural evangelism and mission work. There is no direct equivalent of the ICNT and hence this will be the first Indian commentary series serving India, and hopefully the entire subcontinent—India, Nepal, Bangladesh and Sri Lanka.

The ICNT series has seven distinctive features:

Indian: the commentaries are written by Indians or those who live in India, and reflect Indian thought and practice;

Exegetical: they explain the text section-by-section (rather than verse-by-verse) in its original first-century socio-historical context ('meaning then'), and interact with Indian sources;

Contextual: they will contextualize and apply the text for today's Indian context ('meaning now');

Scholarly: they are written by excellent Ph.D. New Testament scholars;

Accessible: they are written in everyday language;

Evangelical: the theological perspective is evangelical with scope for various persuasions;

Affordable: they are published in India to keep them affordable.

The ICNT aims at a high level of 'Indianness' in two ways. First, in the exegetical part, the author will attempt to identify the Indian sources available, so that the commentaries as a whole will provide a comprehensive bibliography of Indian (biblical) sources. Second, in the contextual part (called 'Reflections'), the author must address exclusively today's Indian context. The end result is an evangelical, affordable commentary series written by academics in everyday language, providing a well-informed meaning of the text and practical reflections for modern India.

The Series Editors,
Babu Immanuel Venkataraman (Associate Professor of New Testament, TCA College, Singapore)
Brian Wintle (ATA Regional Secretary, India)
Cornelis Bennema (Associate Professor of New Testament, SAIACS, Bangalore)

Preface

The two letters to Timothy and the letter to Titus are together known as the Pastoral Epistles (hereafter PE). This description was first attributed to D.N. Berdot (1703) and made popular by P. Anton (1726), and has been commonly used for the last 300 years, even if its usefulness has been questioned.[1] The description relates to the fact that all three letters are addressed to people (Timothy and Titus) who exercise pastoral ministry, with instructions about their duties.

My first experience of New Testament teaching in a theological seminary was a brief introduction to the PE which I taught at Moore Theological College in Sydney in 1977. I have at various other times taught the PE, most recently for students doing the Serampore Master of Theology course, and in church ministry have had the privilege of preaching on these letters many times. So the PE have become reasonably familiar friends over a long period of time. Against this background I have been delighted to be asked to contribute this commentary to the present series.

In my earlier years the scholarly consensus was strongly against the opinion that Paul was the author of these letters, though this non-Pauline approach was never a unanimous view. The earlier consensus has been challenged by less sceptical views presented in many of the more recent substantial works on the PE. These matters are dealt with more fully (though not in detail) in the introductory chapter of this book, but suffice it to say here that this commentary proceeds on the basis of Pauline authorship against a background of a period of ministry following his release from the imprisonment recorded in Acts 28.

The PE occupy a corner of the NT which seems to have largely disappeared from sight in the Indian church. In the introduction it is noted how few Indian contributions have been made to the scholarly study and explanation of these letters. They also do not normally have a major place in the curricula of our theological courses. And furthermore passages from the PE only occasionally appear in the liturgical calendars of the mainline churches as readings for Sundays or major festivals. Under these circumstances it is likely that few theological graduates finish their studies with a passion to study and use these letters in their ministry, and that even fewer church members know much more than one or two familiar texts from the PE. Perhaps they are seen as having little

[1] For example, by Towner, *Timothy-Titus* (2006), 88-89.

or nothing to offer theologically (and certainly they can hardly compete at this level with the Gospel of John or the major letters of Paul). Perhaps too from the viewpoint of ecclesiastical practice they are regarded as relics of a distant age and of little relevance to the life of the church in India today.

It will be seen that I have a radically different assessment of the value of the PE and my hope is that this modest commentary will (if I may be permitted to reapply the metaphor of 2 Timothy 1:6) help to rekindle the flame of interest in these letters and lead to their more effective use in the churches of India.

This series is based on the text of the New Revised Standard Version (NRSV). Thus, where words of the text are quoted (in italics) it can be assumed they are from the NRSV unless otherwise indicated. Significant use has also been made of other versions, especially the New International Version (NIV). Considerable effort has been made to explain and comment on differences among the translations. A teacher or pastor is often asked which is the 'best' translation, but all translations involve interpretation of the text, which makes it foolish to choose one version and claim it as the best, let alone insist that it is always correct.

Biblical references are given according to standard patterns: e.g., 2 Timothy 3:16, or, where appropriately abbreviated, 2 Tim. 3:16. If only 3:16 is given, it is to be assumed that the passage is from the book being commented on. Thus, within the commentary on 2 Timothy, 3:16 means 2 Timothy 3:16, whereas in the commentary on 1 Timothy, 3:16 would mean 1 Timothy 3:16.

In the footnotes commentaries on the PE are cited by the author's name and abbreviated title, other books with full bibliographical detail. Where an author has two published commentaries (as with Guthrie and Towner), the publication date is added to avoid confusion.

My thanks are due to Dr Cornelis Bennema and Dr Brian Wintle in their role as series editors, and to Indian friends who have offered constructive comment on the reflection sections of the book, Dr J Jeyaseelan Kanagaraj (Danishpet, Tamil Nadu), Reverend Benjamin Christian (Bengaluru), and especially Dr Ivan Satyavrata (Kolkata). Naturally, the author is solely responsible for the book in its final form.

Finally I take the opportunity to express my gratitude to my mother, to whose memory this book is dedicated, whose own commitment to Christ and the cause of the gospel has encouraged me to pursue opportunities of ministry even in distant places, without ever hinting that I have neglected my duty to the family at home. Her sacrifices in this regard are here gratefully acknowledged. It is a matter of regret that by a matter of only a few months she did not live long enough to see the book published.

Graham Simpson

Abbreviations

BDAG   W. Bauer, *A Greek Lexicon of the New Testament and Other Early Christian Literature*, originally translated into English by W.F. Arndt and F.W. Gingrich, 3rd edition fully revised by F. Danker (2000). The abbreviation BAGD, still used in many recent NT commentaries, applies to the 2nd edition.

NA^{27} The 27th edition of the Nestle-Aland edition of the Greek New Testament.

NASB   New American Standard Bible.

NEB   New English Bible.

NIV   New International Version.

NKJV   New King James Version.

NRSV   New Revised Standard Version.

NT   New Testament.

OT   Old Testament.

PE   Pastoral Epistles.

TNIV   Today's New International Version.

UBS^4 The 4th edition of the United Bible Societies edition of the Greek New Testament.

Introduction

Authenticity

One issue which may have contributed to the minor role of the PE in India is the question of authenticity. Are these letters really written by Paul, as each one of them claims in the opening statement? In some scholarly circles it is assumed without need for further debate that the PE are not the writings of Paul. Where this assumption has been accepted, it is almost inevitable that the PE will be seen as having only a minor place in the NT canon and in the life of the contemporary church.

The assumption is based on a number of significant observations about the PE. There are four main areas of argumentation: the *ecclesiastical structures* (which are thought by many to reflect a more developed and institutionalized pattern than was possible in the lifetime of Paul, especially the strong emphasis on authority and tradition which is likewise claimed to be contrary to Paul's normal approach), matters of *theology* (not only the false teaching which is opposed by the author, which is often regarded as characteristic of a later period, but also the positive teaching of the PE which emphasizes supposedly non-Pauline themes, such as godliness, and fails to reflect other genuine Pauline themes, such as a living expectation of the near arrival of the end), the *historical situation* (it is difficult to fit the circumstances assumed by the PE into the framework of the Acts narrative), and the *language problem*. It can immediately be said that the first two are extremely subjective, for on matters of church life and organization, Paul's theological expression, and the nature of the false teaching, what some may think inappropriate for Paul or reflecting a later period may seem to others to be not at all inappropriate for Paul or out of place in his lifetime. The other two items (the historical situation and the problem of the language of the PE) will be dealt with later. Details of all these arguments must be sought in larger works than the present one.

Whatever weight these arguments may be thought to have (by some much but by others not so much), it has come to be accepted in some circles as an assured result of modern scholarship that the PE were not written by Paul. However, if one lives long enough one learns that the 'assured result' of one generation of scholars is often subsequently questioned, and this is certainly the case here. Though one can name works of fairly recent times where a negative conclusion about Pauline authorship is accepted, such as the commentaries of Dibelius and Conzelmann (1972) and Hanson (1982), and the studies of Young (1994) and Davies (1996), there is an equally impressive list of scholars who accept the Pauline origin of the PE. Here one may mention the commentaries of Fee (1988), Guthrie (1990), Knight (1992), Mounce (2000), Johnson (2001), Towner (2006) and Witherington (2006), and from earlier decades Hendriksen (1957) and Kelly (1963). Marshall (1999), more cautiously, may be added to this list. Witherington makes a fascinating observation when he asks: "Why is it that the majority of Pauline scholars who have *not* done a detailed study of these documents or written a scholarly commentary on the Pastoral Epistles in the last fifty years think that these letters are post-Pauline, while the majority of scholars who *have* written such commentaries are either open to the possibility or are convinced that these letters do indeed go back to Paul in some form or fashion?"[2] Whatever conclusion one might wish to draw from this observation, it is clearly not possible to regard the issue as finally settled in favour of non-Pauline authorship and post-Pauline date.

Historical Circumstances

This has already been mentioned as a major problem area. Where do the PE fit historically? This question is equally urgent whatever position one takes on the date and authorship of the PE. As Dibelius and Conzelmann say,[3] it is not enough to assert that the PE were not written by Paul nor from the early period of the church's existence. One must also offer a plausible description of the situation in which they do fit.

---

[2] Witherington, *Commentary*, 50-51.
[3] See, for example, Dibelius and Conzelmann, *Pastorals*, 154.

The essence of the problem is that it is quite difficult to fit the circumstances of the PE into the Acts framework.[4] To take a clear example, 2 Timothy has Paul under arrest in Rome, anticipating death as the outcome, a situation rather different from the positive picture of the circumstances of Paul's imprisonment at the end of Acts. Even if one can be persuaded that it is the same imprisonment in both documents, the circumstances presupposed by the rest of the PE do not fit with the Acts account (namely the details of Paul's apparently recent activity in Ephesus, Crete and elsewhere). To some the entire picture is a fabrication (even if they allow the possibility of some 'Pauline fragments' embedded in the PE), though even if so it is still necessary (following Dibelius and Conzelmann) to offer an explanation of the situation and circumstances of the later age in which the PE were allegedly produced. This however is precisely what is absent from works typical of those who accept pseudonymity. Young says, "The provenance of the Pastorals is unknown ... they emerge into the life of the church during the second century."[5] Hanson is only slightly less vague when he says, "They must be written to a group of Pauline churches. We know that it was in Asia Minor that monepiscopacy first evolved, and large parts of Asia Minor were Paul's mission field. Most scholars therefore conclude that the Pastorals were written in Asia Minor, perhaps specifically in Ephesus."[6]

In contrast, it is reasonably suggested that the PE can be explained as the product of Paul's later ministry, following his release from the imprisonment which Acts 28 records. Such a period of ministry is supported by the positive picture of Acts 28 (with no hint of impending disaster for Paul), by the possibility that Paul exercised a ministry in Spain (in line with Paul's own hope expressed in Rom. 15:23-24, 28 and possibly supported by the reference to Paul's ministry to "the limit of the west" in a late first century document [*1 Clement* 5:7]), and by the evidence of the PE themselves (if one is able on other grounds to accept

---

[4] However, this is not impossible when one recognizes that the book of Acts is not a complete account of Paul's movements. Johnson points out that eight of the twelve years of Paul's ministry between 50 and 62 are dealt with by Acts in four verses: 18:11, 19:10, 24:27, 28:30 (Johnson, *Timothy*, 61). For a brief description of proposals that try to fit the circumstances of the PE within the Acts framework, see Towner, *Timothy-Titus* (2006), 12-14.

[5] Young, F., *The Theology of the Pastoral Letters* (Cambridge: Cambridge University Press, 1994), 142.

[6] Hanson, *Pastorals*, 14.

them as Pauline). There can be no absolute proof that this reconstruction is correct. The point is simply that it is *possible* and in the eyes of many *plausible* that Paul was released after his first Roman imprisonment, travelled to Spain (perhaps only briefly and possibly without much lasting fruit to show for his labours there),[7] then back to the Aegean region with travel and ministry in the Ephesus area and the island of Crete, before being arrested in the course of this activity and taken back to Rome for another trial and his probable execution. Without a narrative framework such as Acts provides for part of Paul's earlier ministry, it is hardly surprising that one cannot give a confident account of the details, or reconstruct a detailed itinerary, or know in which order (on this reconstruction) the PE were written. Some scholars (Marshall and Witherington, for example) arrange their commentary with Titus first, followed by 1 Timothy. The only point that is clear is that 2 Timothy, in which Paul expects his trial to result in his death, is the last of the three, if we take the PE at face value and attribute them to Paul. In the present commentary 1 Timothy is treated first, before Titus, without implying an opinion which one may have actually been written first, with 2 Timothy in its appropriate position as last of the three.[8]

One aspect of the historical context which has been brought out in some of the recent literature is the social setting of the PE and the indications of rhetorical structure and rhetorical devices which are used in the PE. To discuss all of this adequately would require a much larger book than this present commentary, which seeks to take such matters into account in explaining the text without often referring to them specifically. Discussion of these elements is one of the highlights of Witherington's commentary.

The Language of the Pastorals

The last of the main obstacles to accepting the letters' own claim to be written by Paul is the language question. Four main aspects of the

---

[7] On the basis of references in the prison epistles, Fee understands that Paul changed his plans and did not visit Spain (Fee, *Timothy-Titus*, 4).

[8] The order 1 Timothy, Titus and 2 Timothy is also followed by Knight, Fee and Mounce. Titus, 1 Timothy and 2 Timothy is followed by Marshall and Witherington. Others are content to follow the NT book order of 1 Timothy, 2 Timothy and Titus (Barrett, Kelly, Hanson, Guthrie, Towner).

problem can be identified. (a) The *hapax legomena* of the PE (that is, words used in the PE but nowhere else in the NT). (b) Other words in the PE which are found in other NT writings though not in the letters generally accepted as Pauline. (c) Pauline words or groups of words missing from the PE. (d) Grammatical and stylistic differences between the PE and the other Pauline letters. Naturally we are referring here to *Greek* language, and so it is not possible to discuss the technicalities of this subject in this commentary.

Several responses can be made to these observations. One is that the same writer does not always use the same range of vocabulary each time he or she takes up the pen. Among Paul's undisputed letters there are significant differences between, say, 1 Thessalonians and Galatians (one could choose almost any pair of Paul's letters). Different vocabulary is appropriate for different topics and different circumstances, and in any case a writer or speaker's preferred manner of expression often changes over the years. It is certainly possible that many of the distinctive linguistic features of the PE can be explained in these terms.[9]

However, this is not an entirely satisfactory or convincing explanation. In spite of every allowance which may be made on the basis of such considerations, when one reads the Pauline letters in Greek one is still left with the feeling that the person who wrote the PE is not the same person who wrote Romans, 1 Corinthians and other letters. Some further explanation is needed.

The Role of Luke

A frequent suggestion is that Paul used the services of an amanuensis, not merely a secretary recording Paul's dictated words but someone with a more creative role in the composition of the PE. One version of this approach which has appeared from time to time is that Luke had a major role in their production. Wilson's monograph[10] promotes this thesis though he was not the first to make the suggestion; his view is that the PE were the work of Luke from a later period after Paul's death.

More recently Witherington has revived the suggestion of Luke's involvement, though in a different form to Wilson's. For Witherington

---

[9] See the appendix in Guthrie, *Pastorals* (1990), 224-240.
[10] S.G. Wilson, *Luke and the Pastoral Epistles* (London: SPCK, 1979).

Luke is the writer but within Paul's lifetime and with Paul as the authority behind the writing. He agrees with Moule's assessment: "Luke wrote all three Pastoral Epistles. But he wrote them in Paul's lifetime, at Paul's behest, and in part (but only part) at Paul's dictation."[11] Witherington's own summary is that "the voice is the voice of Paul, but the hand is the hand of Luke. In some places these letters sound almost like Pauline dictation, especially in spots 2 Timothy, but in various places they sound much more like Luke."[12] At many points throughout his commentary Witherington convincingly draws attention to details which support this proposal, and the reader who is interested in this matter is encouraged to work through Witherington's commentary carefully.

If accepted, this proposal retains Pauline authorship in a meaningful sense while satisfactorily accounting for the differences in language in comparison with the other letters of Paul.

The Problem of Pseudonymity

If the PE were not in fact written by Paul, they must be regarded as pseudonymous, that is, falsely claiming a well-known author in order to gain acceptance or added authority. It is often claimed that pseudonymity was a common device in the ancient world, among Christians and non-Christians alike, that it was readily recognized and accepted by the intended audience, and that therefore there was no attempt to deceive. With these assumptions the PE are regarded by many as productions by a later 'Paulinist' (perhaps using some genuine fragments from Paul's own writings) who wrote with a view to commend Paul and to apply his teaching to a later generation. However, all of these claims can be challenged, and are helpfully discussed in some of the recent commentaries.[13]

Whether or not pseudonymity was generally seen as an acceptable practice, there are in any case major problems in considering the PE as such. The inclusion of the personal notes and comments (often seen as genuinely Pauline even by those who reject Pauline authorship in general) can hardly have any purpose other than to deceive, an implication which many or most Christians today will find unacceptable in canonical NT books. There are many other points which

---

[11] C.F.D. Moule, "The Problem of the Pastoral Epistles: A Reappraisal," *Bulletin of the John Rylands Library* 47 (1965), 434.

[12] Witherington, *Commentary*, 60.

[13] See, for example, Witherington, *Commentary*, 23-38.

fit much better within the period of Paul's lifetime than at a later time.[14] Topics sometimes regarded as evidence of a later date, such as patterns of ministry and other aspects of ecclesiastical organization, are in fact often better explained as evidence of an early stage of development and appropriate to the later years of Paul's lifetime. As noted above, supporters of pseudonymity and a later date can provide only the vaguest of suggestions about the origin and setting of the PE. They seldom attempt to explain why the alleged author bothered to write three letters (not one), nor to suggest who 'Timothy' and 'Titus' could possibly represent in the life of the churches of a later period.

Granting the possibility of Paul's release from his first Roman imprisonment and a further period of ministry, and granting also the possibility of Luke's involvement (as explained above), the PE are much more satisfactorily interpreted as coming from late in Paul's lifetime and addressed to Timothy at Ephesus and Titus in Crete with the authority of Paul himself. Though there remain many uncertainties, there seems little to be gained from any alternative approach. The theory of later date and pseudonymous authorship creates as many problems as it solves.

Literature on the Pastoral Epistles

One of the aims of this commentary series is to interact with all the relevant works of Indian scholarship. In the case of the PE very little has been written. In a search of the volumes of *New Testament Abstracts*, a comprehensive record of books and articles on every aspect of NT studies, the author has discovered only two scholarly articles on the PE written by an Indian or published in India in the 33 years between 1978 and 2010.[15] M. Gnanavaram's published thesis on wealth and poverty in the NT contains comments on parts of 1 Timothy 6, and there may be material hidden in other similar works which are not specifically focused on the PE. I apologize to the author of any such book whose work I have not been able to locate.

Only four commentaries of Indian origin are known to the present author. M.R. Robinson (1962), of the North India United Theological College, Saharanpur, U.P., wrote in the Christian Students' Library series, with careful exegesis and an occasional example taken from

---

[14] Details of such points may be found in the larger commentaries, such as Kelly, Mounce, Towner (2006) and Witherington.

[15] By K. Luke on 1 Timothy 3:16, and S. Stanislas on the use of military and athletic metaphors in the PE. See the bibiliography for details of these articles.

Indian church or society. Naturally it is now somewhat out of date. Another is by A.P. Carleton (1964), written during his service with the Oxford Mission to Calcutta, but not published in India and without any obvious India focus. The other two were published in 2008, one in the Dalit Bible Commentary series, where the focus is on issues relevant to the Dalit communities. Though these issues arise from the text, the text itself is not dealt with in any detail (the commentary material on the PE occupies only 40 pages and about one-third of this space is occupied by the full text of the PE). The other is by John Mathew, a pastor of the Indian Pentecostal Church of God. This is a useful popular-level commentary with brief verse by verse comment, though not surprisingly critical issues are not dealt with and alternative interpretations of difficult passages are usually ignored.

Two volumes of the Asia Bible Commentary Series are devoted to the PE, on 1 Timothy by P. Trebilco and S. Rae (2006) and on 2 Timothy and Titus by the same authors and C. Caradus (2009). These are high quality commentaries. In keeping with the series in general, they make occasional reference to issues of Asian interest but the authors are all from New Zealand and only one of them, Simon Rae, appears to have had direct experience of life in an Asian country (in his case Indonesia). There is no direct reference to Indian contexts.

There are several other books of south Asian origin, popular-level studies rather than serious works of scholarship. The books by P. Chandapilla (on Titus) and A. Fernando, a Sri Lankan (on 1 Timothy), take the text seriously but are limited by their chosen focus on leadership (which is certainly not the only theme of the PE). In another book on Christian leadership, P.M. Malkhani includes brief comments on passages from the PE. The book by P. Haagen, a foreign missionary based in Gujarat, is the published version of addresses on 2 Timothy given at the Nilgiri Hills Convention in 1963; despite its size (only 67 pages) it contains many helpful exegetical insights. No doubt there is other material of a mostly devotional nature in the magazines and news letters of different churches and organizations in India, but no attempt has been made to survey this in a systematic way.

The pages of *New Testament Abstracts* reveal that scholarly interest in the PE is very much alive and well in other parts of the world. Admittedly there is a disproportionate amount on 1 Timothy 2:8-15 (on the status and roles of women), but much has also been written on other passages in the PE. This healthy interest in the PE is well illustrated by the introductory bibliographies provided by Mounce, with 21 pages of closely printed lists of commentaries and general items, in addition to separate bibliographies on each passage at appropriate points throughout the commentary.

Surveys of international scholarship are provided in the full-scale commentaries and need not be repeated here. In addition mention may be made of Marshall's useful 1997 and 2006 survey articles. Against this wider background it must be admitted that India has failed to participate in the lively study of these letters by the international scholarly community and this may be considered a challenge to a younger generation of Indian scholars.

Bibliographical details about all the items mentioned above are given in the bibliography which follows.

Bibliography

This is by no means a complete bibliography but includes the commentaries used in the preparation of this book and several monographs of a mainly general nature (as distinct from studies with a narrower focus), as well as items for which an Indian origin or at least some Indian or south Asian connection can be claimed. The latter are marked with an asterisk.

Barrett, C.K., *The Pastoral Epistles* (New Clarendon Bible; Oxford: Clarendon Press, 1963)

* Caleb, S.M., et al., *Dalit Bible Commentary, New Testament, Volume 9: The First & Second Letters of Paul to Timothy, The Letter of Paul to Titus, The Letter of Paul to Philemon, The First & Second Letters of Peter, The Letter of James, The Letter of Jude, The First, Second & Third Letters of John* (New Delhi: Centre for Dalit/ Subaltern Studies, 2008); S. Caleb & M. Daniel have written the commentary on 1 Timothy, and M. Daniel 2 Timothy and Titus as well as an introductory essay on the PE

* Carleton, A.P., *Pastoral Epistles: A Commentary* (World Christian Books No. 51; London: Lutterworth, 1964)

* Chandapilla, P., *Christian Leaders and Leadership* (Bombay: GLS, 1978)

Davies, M., *The Pastoral Epistles* (Sheffield: Sheffield Academic Press, 1996)

Dibelius, M. and H. Conzelmann, *The Pastoral Epistles* (Hermeneia; Philadelphia:

Fortress, 1972); translated by P. Buttolph and A. Yarbro from the fourth German edition of 1966

Fee, G.D., *1 and 2 Timothy, Titus* (New International Biblical Commentary; Peabody: Hendrickson, 1984; revised edition 1988; 13th printing 2010)

* Fernando, A., *Leadership Lifestyle: A Study of 1 Timothy* (Wheaton: Tyndale House Publishers, 1985)

* Gnanavaram, M., *Treasure in Heaven and Treasure on Earth: Attitudes towards Poverty and Wealth in the New Testament Communities and in the Early Church* (Delhi: ISPCK, 2008)

Guthrie, D., *The Pastoral Epistles: An Introduction and Commentary* (Tyndale New Testament Commentaries; London: Tyndale Press, 1957; 2nd edition 1990)

* Haagen, P.C., *Second Timothy: A Father's Final Counsel* (Madras: ELS, 1964)

Hanson, A.T., *The Pastoral Epistles* (New Century Bible; Grand Rapids: Eerdmans & London: Marshall, Morgan & Scott, 1982)

Harrison, P.N., *The Problem of the Pastorals* (Oxford: Oxford University Press, 1921)

Hendriksen, W., *I-II Timothy and Titus* (New Testament Commentary; Grand Rapids: Baker, 1957)

Johnson, L.T., *The First and Second Letters to Timothy* (Anchor Bible No. 35A; New York: Doubleday, 2001)

Kelly, J.N.D., *A Commentary on the Pastoral Epistles: I Timothy, II Timothy, Titus* (Black's New Testament Commentaries; London: A & C Black, 1963)

Knight III, G.W., *The Pastoral Epistles: A Commentary on the Greek Text* (New International Greek Testament Commentary; Grand Rapids: Eerdmans & Carlisle: Paternoster, 1992)

* *Leadership in the Church, based on the Pastoral Epistles* (Bangalore: TAFTEE, no date)

Lock, W., *A Critical and Exegetical Commentary on the Pastoral Epistles (I & II Timothy and Titus)* (International Critical Commentary; Edinburgh, T & T Clark, 1924)

* Luke, K., "The Impact of Egyptian Ideas on the Formulation of NT Soteriology," *Biblebhashyam* 14 (1988), 185-194

* Malkhani, P.M., *A Leader in the Making* (Secunderabad: OM Books, 1999)

Marshall, I.H., "Recent Study of the Pastoral Epistles," *Themelios* 23 (1997), 3-29

Marshall, I.H., "Some Recent Commentaries on the Pastoral Epistles," *Expository Times* 117 (2006), 140-143

Marshall, I.H., in collaboration with P.H. Towner, *A Critical and Exegetical Commentary on the Pastoral Epistles* (International Critical Commentary; London & New York: T & T Clark, 1999)

* Mathew, J., *Pastoral Epistles: I & II Timothy, Titus* (Bangalore: Hospital Ministries India, 2008)

Moule, C.F.D., "The Problem of the Pastoral Epistles: A Reappraisal," *Bulletin of the John Rylands Library* 47 (1965), 430-452

Mounce, W.D., *Pastoral Epistles* (Word Biblical Commentary Volume 46; Nashville: Thomas Nelson, 2000)

* Robinson, M.R., *A Commentary on the Pastoral Epistles* (Christian Students' Library No. 27; CLS: Madras, 1962)

* Stanislas, S., "The *Agōn* of the Servant of Christ in the Pastoral Epistles," *Indian Theological Studies* 47 (2010), 73-95

Stott, J.R.W., *The Message of 1 Timothy and Titus* (The Bible Speaks Today; Leicester: Inter-Varsity Press, 1996)

Stott, J.R.W., *Guard the Gospel: The Message of 2 Timothy* (The Bible Speaks Today; Leicester: Inter-Varsity Press, 1973)

Towner, P.H., *1-2 Timothy & Titus* (IVP New Testament Commentary; Downers Grove: InterVarsity, 1994)

Towner, P.H., *The Letters to Timothy and Titus* (New International Commentary on the New Testament; Eerdmans: Grand Rapids & Cambridge UK, 2006)

Trebilco, P. and S. Rae, *1 Timothy* (Asia Bible Commentary; Singapore: Asia Theological Association & Manila: OMF Literature, 2006)

Trebilco, P., C. Caradus and S. Rae, *2 Timothy & Titus* (Asia Bible Commentary; Singapore: Asia Theological Association & Manila: OMF Literature, 2009)

Wilson, S.G., *Luke and the Pastoral Epistles* (London: SPCK, 1979)

Witherington III, B., *Letters and Homilies for Hellenized Christians: A Socio-Rhetorical Commentary on Titus, 1-2 Timothy and 1-3 John* (Downers Grove: IVP Academic & Nottingham: Apollos, 2006)

Young, F., *The Theology of the Pastoral Letters* (Cambridge: Cambridge University Press, 1994)

1 Timothy

1 Timothy 1:1-2

Paul

The introductory words of the letter contain three elements: the name of the writer, the name of the recipient and a word of greeting. This is a standard format in letters of that time, often found in the simplest possible form, such as *Anand to Ashish, greeting*. Paul naturally used this format himself, except that he always expanded each item. Compared to letter styles from the secular world of that day Paul's introductions are longer (sometimes much longer). And among Paul's letters the PE have their own special characteristics.

The first element is the identification of the *author*, stated to be Paul. A brief description of the debate whether Paul was really the author has been given in the introduction to this book. In the remainder of the commentary it will be assumed that Paul was in fact the author.

In other letters Paul associates others with himself in the introductory greeting (most often Timothy, which obviously is not appropriate here in a letter *to* Timothy, but also Silvanus in 1 and 2 Thessalonians, and Sosthenes in 1 Corinthians). But in the PE (as well as Romans, Galatians and Ephesians), Paul mentions his own name alone. In this letter no one else is mentioned in the closing greetings also (unlike most of Paul's letters), and it is possible that he had few if any companions at this point. A different implication which can be drawn from the lack of personal references is that 1 Timothy is written in the style of a *mandatum principiis*, defined as "a letter from a ruler or high official to one of his agents, delegates, ambassador *(sic)*, or governors helping him set up shop in his new post and get things in good order and under control".[16]

As well as his *name* Paul also mentions his *role* as an apostle, which focuses on his authority. An apostle was an accredited representative,

---

[16] Witherington, *Commentary*, 90. See also Johnson, *Timothy*, 140-142.

Paul being a representative of Christ (as 1:1 says). One of the main functions of an apostle was to preach the gospel, and the phrase *apostle of Christ Jesus* could be paraphrased as *preacher of Christ* (Christ being the content of the message). This sense is certainly appropriate a little later, where *apostle* is linked with *herald* (2:7; also 2 Tim. 1:11).

But it is likely that the element of authority is the main focus in 1:1, as further emphasized by the phrase *according to the command of God our Saviour and Christ Jesus our hope*. Paul's apostolic role is not his own idea or his own choosing but derives from God himself and the Lord Jesus Christ. This reminds us of the Damascus road narrative, where Paul, a determined persecutor of the believers, finds his life completely turned around through the appearance of Jesus in glory. This was totally a divine initiative, and Paul remained aware of this for the rest of his life as the basis of his ministry.

The role of Christ in Paul's commission is clear because it was Christ who appeared to him on the Damascus road. But Paul was equally convinced that this was also the commission of God the Father. In other places this is expressed by the word *will* rather than *command* (1 Cor. 1:1, 2 Cor. 1:1, Gal. 1:4, Eph. 1:1, Col. 1:1, 2 Tim. 1:1) but the idea is the same. This may stem from the conviction that the word of the risen and exalted Jesus was equally the word of the Father. The same understanding is seen in one of the Acts accounts of Paul's conversion, where Ananias speaks of Paul's experience as the initiative of *the God of our fathers* (Acts 22:14).

We find the description *apostle* at the beginning of most of his other letters (Philippians, 1 and 2 Thessalonians, and Philemon are the exceptions). It is true that we cannot be sure "how Paul as an older man would address a young man who was his junior colleague",[17] that is, whether he would feel that a certain level of formality was appropriate. Just the same we may think it strange that Paul should find it necessary to sound this note of authority in a letter to his long-time companion and colleague Timothy. It would seem to be necessary only if Timothy has shown signs of being rebellious and disobedient, but there is no hint in the letter of anything like this. In truth it is *not* likely that Timothy needed to be reminded of Paul's apostleship. More probably we have a hint here that the letter has a *hidden audience*; it is not written to Timothy alone

---

[17] Marshall, *Pastorals*, 353.

but to the church in which he exercises leadership.[18] Though the letter is addressed to Timothy, there is a wider audience overhearing (we might say) what Paul is saying to Timothy. It is this wider audience rather than Timothy himself which needs to be reminded of the authority with which a letter like this is written, especially in a context where the Christian message is under threat from false teaching. Paul is reminding the whole church that the message which Timothy is upholding and preaching is a message authorized by God himself and Jesus Christ.

Timothy

The second element of the introduction is the identification of the *recipient*, Timothy, described here as Paul's *child* (not *son* as NIV, which curiously has *son* rather than the correct *child* in the greeting of each of the PE). He is Paul's spiritual child, his child *in faith* (1:2). Information provided by the book of Acts helps us to understand Paul's description here. Timothy's hometown was Lystra (Acts 16:1), one of the towns where Paul preached the gospel during the so-called first missionary journey. Timothy responded positively to the gospel message and believed in Jesus (Acts 14:6-7). Later Timothy travelled with Paul and became his colleague (Acts 16:3, 17:14-15, 18:5, 19:22, 20:3-4, Rom. 16:21, Phil. 2:19, 1 Thess. 3:2, 6). So Paul had known Timothy throughout his spiritual pilgrimage. The word *child* expresses warmth of relationship and *genuine* attests to the depth of Timothy's relationship to Paul; it was much more than a passing acquaintance. Paul knew Timothy well and there was no chance that Timothy was merely pretending. His appreciation of Timothy is expressed in similar terms in verse 18 and 1 Corinthians 4:17.

The phrase *in faith* indicates that this was more than friendship on a normal human level. Most translations have *in the faith*, suggesting something like the Christian religion. But in many references in the PE this word has its fundamental sense of *faith in God through Christ*, and this is the likely sense here.[19] It is not just the fact that Paul and Timothy belong to the Christian community in a general sense that has made their relationship possible, but their common faith in Christ.

---

[18] Fee, *Timothy-Titus*, 35; Mounce, *Pastorals*, 5.

[19] Fee, *Timothy-Titus*, 36; Knight, *Pastorals*, 64; Johnson, *Timothy*, 158-159; Towner, *Timothy-Titus* (2006), 99. It is noteworthy that the word *the* does not occur in the Greek phrase here.

Greeting

The third item in the opening greeting, following identification of the writer and reader, is the actual *greeting* itself (1:2). It can be described as a prayer, or more accurately a wish. The standard greeting in a Greek letter was simply *greeting*. In each of his letters Paul turns the secular *greeting* (Greek *chairein*) into the Christian *grace* (Greek *charis*). This word is at the heart of Paul's message, and we find it again in this chapter (1:14).

The third word in the prayer is *peace*, the standard Jewish greeting (Hebrew *shalom*). The word describes a person's state of harmony with God, and in Paul's usage it must be related to the work of Christ by which this harmony is made possible. This also is used in each of Paul's greetings. So, in the first and the third words of the wish, we find Paul's normal greeting, a mix of the secular (Greek) form and the typical Jewish form, but both invested with Christian meaning.

The other word in the greeting is *mercy*, found in introductory greetings only in the two letters to Timothy.[20] The word is not used anywhere else in 1 Timothy. The related verb is used twice in this chapter (1:13, 16), evidence that the theme of God's mercy was in Paul's mind as he wrote, which may explain why *mercy* is included in the greeting.

It is clear that these three blessings are not new to Timothy. Already he has experienced God's grace, mercy and peace. By implication the wish is that he might have a greater and growing experience of these gifts from God.

God and Christ

It is always instructive to observe how God and Jesus are described. In these two verses there are some particularly interesting points.

To begin, God the Father and Jesus are twice linked, first as the source of Paul's commission to be an apostle (1:1) and then as the source of the grace, mercy and peace which Paul wishes Timothy to experience more fully. Though the Father is nearly always mentioned first (2 Cor. 13:13 is a notable exception), there is no suggestion that there is any superiority or inferiority involved. They are placed on an equal level. This is a remarkable fact, for we need to remember that the first generation of Christians had known Jesus in the flesh, a human being like themselves,

---

[20] It is also used in Galatians 6:16, at a different point of that letter.

and yet very soon they were ascribing to him such an exalted status. The NT clearly points to the reason for this, namely Jesus' resurrection. It is well known that the Bible does not have a fully developed doctrine of the Trinity, but passages like these in which the equality of God and Christ is virtually assumed provide a natural foundation on which that later doctrine was built.

The actual descriptions of God and Christ in 1:1 are also worth noting. God is described as *our Saviour*. This is not a common NT description, though certainly not unknown elsewhere (Lk. 1:47, Jude 25). The concept in John 3:16-17 is that God is the source or initiator of our salvation. Even in Paul's other letters God is presented as the one who saves (1 Cor. 1:21, 1 Thess. 5:9). We are more familiar with Jesus being described as our Saviour, but in the PE the description is equally divided between both. In 1 Timothy, God alone is described as Saviour (also in 2:3, 4:10), though the verb *save* is used of Jesus (1:15).

Here Jesus is described as *our hope*. Only here and in Colossians 1:27 is Christ actually described in these words, but hope is such a basic part of the Christian message (Col. 1:5, 23, Eph. 1:18, 4:4), and linked specifically with Christ in 1 Thessalonians 1:3, that we are not surprised to find Christ described this way. Our hope of eternal life is bound up completely with Christ, and will be fulfilled at his second coming (Tit. 2:13). At the same time we notice that this letter speaks of God as the object of our hope (4:10, 5:5, 6:17), another reminder of the ease with which the NT equates God and Christ.

The descriptions in 1:2 are more standard, God as Father and Jesus as Lord, in almost identical wording as we find in the greetings of Paul's other letters.

Reflection: The Authority of Paul for the Indian Church

The letter begins in a typical manner with Paul asserting his position as an apostle of Christ Jesus. It is clear from the way in which Paul conducted his ministry, and in particular from the way in which he wrote, that he considered that he had significant authority. Even writing to Timothy, his long-time friend and colleague, he finds it important to state his authority at the beginning of the letter.

What does this mean in today's context? Even if we accept that Paul had a rightful authority in his own time, does he have the same authority today? There are many who answer this question in the negative. This response is particularly tempting when we find something in Paul which we do not like, or something which is not politically correct, and there may be plenty of material like that even in this one letter (such as the teaching about women, or about Christ as the only way of salvation, or about absolute moral standards). Some may feel that Paul was not an Indian and so what he writes has no authority in the Indian context.

One's response to this sort of question depends on broader theological convictions. The traditional and orthodox position has been that a letter such as 1 Timothy (or any of Paul's letters for that matter) is not just the expression of one man's private opinions, not necessarily better or worse than any other person's views. Rather, because it is the work of an apostle, it carries an enduring authority.

It is most unlikely that when Paul wrote a letter he would have imagined that it would end up becoming part of the Bible, a book regarded as scripture, with an authority equal to the books of what we call the Old Testament. Nevertheless, this is what happened and one of the essential criteria which determined what books should be regarded as belonging to the New Testament was the criterion of apostolicity. This did not necessarily mean direct authorship by an apostle (or else the Gospels of Mark and Luke would never have been accepted) but it does mean that the book preserves the teaching of the apostles. The testimony of the apostles was regarded as foundational, a view expressed in the NT itself (Eph. 2:20, 3:5). It was not that these men had greater gifts of theological cleverness, but simply that they were the authorized and accredited witnesses to the truth about Jesus. This statement is true not only of the earthly companions of Jesus, who after the resurrection received this commission (Lk. 24:46-48), but it is also true of Paul who through the Damascus road experience received the same commission. Paul fully recognized his own unworthiness (1 Cor. 15:9, 1 Tim. 1:12-13). But as the opening words of our letter show, he just as strongly insisted on his own status and role as an apostle, a status not of his own choosing but with a divine origin.

If I reject Paul I not only reject the apostolic witness but also set myself up as an independent authority; or to put it more bluntly, I make the claim that my opinion about Christian truth and the Christian life has just as much authority as that of Paul and the other apostles. It hardly needs to be pointed out what chaos would result if every professing Christian claimed such independent authority. And perhaps it is worth pointing out that chaos is exactly what has overtaken the church in many places where the authority of the apostles (Paul included) has come to be seen as having a limited validity. To view the matter positively, whole-hearted acceptance of Paul's apostolic authority (and indeed the authority of the whole Bible) provides a solid basis for Christian belief and practice which my own personal opinion can never provide.

1 Timothy 1:3-11

Paul, Timothy and Ephesus

Paul says that he left Timothy in Ephesus, with the specific responsibility of dealing with false teachers, while he himself travelled to Macedonia (1:3). The usual way of interpreting this is that Paul and Timothy had been in Ephesus together, Paul leaving while Timothy remained. We ask where this may fit into the narrative of Acts. Acts 20:1 mentions Paul leaving Ephesus on his way to Macedonia but Timothy does not seem to have been with him then. He had been with Paul in Corinth (18:5), but when Paul left Corinth, only Priscilla and Aquila are mentioned as accompanying him (18:18). Timothy next appears as sent (with Erastus) from Asia to Macedonia (19:22) and then as one of the party travelling with Paul to Jerusalem, joining Paul in Troas (20:4-5). There is nothing to suggest that Timothy was in Ephesus with Paul at the time of the riot, and so it is difficult (perhaps impossible) to see how Acts 20:1 can coincide with 1 Timothy 1:3. In fact Acts 19:22 has Paul in Asia (Ephesus) and Timothy leaving for Macedonia, whereas 1 Timothy 1:3 is the opposite (Timothy in Ephesus and Paul leaving for Macedonia). It seems necessary to conclude that Acts 20:1 and 1 Timothy 1:3 refer to two different situations at different times.

Another way of reading our verse is that Paul was going into Macedonia *from somewhere else*, and sent word to Timothy to remain in Ephesus where he was, or that the two men met somewhere else from where Timothy was sent to return to Ephesus and remain there.[21] Thus there are other possible historical reconstructions, but the suggestion made in the previous paragraph seems to be the most natural reading of the statement here.

Ephesus was the capital of the Roman province of Asia (what we now call Asia Minor or the western part of Turkey). As such Paul considered it to be of great strategic value, spending at least two years there (Acts 19:10), during which time the gospel spread to other parts of the province. Later, he had opportunity to address the elders of the church of Ephesus (Acts 20:17-38), warning them of testing times ahead.

---

[21] Something like this last interpretation is favoured by Mounce, *Pastorals*, 17.

Later still he wrote a letter to the Ephesians while he was in prison. Assuming that 1 Timothy reflects a situation later than the period covered by Acts, it appears that Paul was released from prison and continued to exercise oversight over the affairs of the Ephesian church, appointing Timothy to represent him there.

Paul speaks here of going to Macedonia (1:3), the area of northern Greece where churches had been established under Paul's ministry, including Philippi, Thessalonica and Beroea. Without any further information we cannot say exactly why he was travelling there at that time.

Genuine Christian Ministry

It is clear from this letter that Timothy had been given responsibility to direct the affairs of the church of Ephesus. Much is said in the letter about Timothy's character as a leader and the duties which he must fulfil. Though administrative matters are mentioned (e.g., 3:1-13, 5:1-22), his main responsibility was to safeguard the gospel, both by teaching the truth and by opposing false teaching. We will come to the false teaching in the next section, but first let us note Timothy's positive task.

The positive focus of Timothy's task is described as *the divine training that is known by faith* (1:4-5). This is a difficult phrase to translate, as seen by the variations in the English versions. We might paraphrase it as *the proper management of God's household in the context of faith.*

As this paraphrase suggests, the basic idea of the word translated *training* in NRSV is *household management.* Paul's concern is that God's household be managed properly. This, he insists, can only be done in the context of faith, faith on the part of those responsible for such management and the strengthening of faith as the goal to which they seek to lead other members of the household. Faith must be exercised by those who lead and teach, and the growth of faith in the members of the church must be one of the main aims of this task.

1:5 speaks of the aim or goal of Christian teaching and ministry. Paul has already spoken of the instruction given to Timothy (1:3) but the *instruction* mentioned here appears to be the broader instruction which is given to all believers and part of basic Christian teaching.

In contrast to the effect of the work of the false teachers (1:4), the true teacher of God's word desires to see the practical fruit of a changed character in the life of the believer. This result is summed up here as *love*. It has been suggested that in the context of 1 Timothy "mutual love in the church"[22] is what is being emphasized, but if Paul is speaking about the sort of instruction relevant to *all* believers in *any* situation, it will include love towards God and towards all others, and not limited to love for other believers. This is what the basic response of the human heart to the love of God towards us in Christ will involve. The greater our awareness of God's work for us, the more likely it will be that we will show this breadth of love.

The following phrases in 1:5 explain where such love comes from. Three sources are mentioned. The first is a *pure heart*. The heart is the seat of human desires, emotions and intentions. It can be pure or clean only when free from sin. Of course this is an ideal state which will never be fully realized in this life. But the ideal must never be forgotten, and the believer must be reminded that sin renders the heart impure. When we are directed by our sinful (self-centred) impulses our heart cannot be pure and the goal of love (selfless action towards God and others) cannot be achieved.

The second source is a *good conscience*. The heart (as defined above) and the conscience are very similar. But assuming that some distinction is intended here, we may define conscience as that which gives direction to our behaviour. A good conscience gives good and proper direction, telling us what is right behaviour. Whether a conscience is *good* will depend on how it is trained. The conscience is only as effective as what is fed into it. The Christian conscience is fed by the word of God, and this then becomes the standard by which the conscience evaluates right and wrong and guides the behaviour of the believer.

The third source is *sincere faith*. Here faith means much more than the response by which we accept God's gift of salvation. It is continuing trust in God, daily commitment to his way. The NT insists that the *life* of faith is vital, not just the initial response of faith. *Sincere* faith is genuine commitment, not the mere appearance of it; the adjective *sincere* might be translated (very literally) as *unhypocritical*.

These are the three sources necessary for Christian love to be produced, and so we have four characteristics which are the marks of a mature believer: a pure heart, a good conscience, sincere faith and love.

---

[22] Marshall, *Pastorals*, 369.

Love arising from these three sources must be the goal which Timothy and all church leaders should aim for in their ministry.

At the end of this paragraph are several other words and phrases which help us to understand more of the nature of true Christian ministry. In 1:10 Paul refers to *sound teaching*. We will often observe in the PE a strong emphasis on teaching. The same words as we have here are used again in 2 Timothy 4:3, Titus 1:9, 2:1. The word *sound* is literally *healthy*. It is clear from the use of this phrase in 1:10 (note the context of 1:9-10) that teaching in the church is more than instruction in abstract theological truth but includes a strong ethical element. Healthy teaching is not just theologically orthodox but productive of good spiritual health in the lives of believers.

Then in 1:11 he mentions the *gospel*. This is the basis of any work done by Paul, Timothy or any other true Christian minister. The gospel is the standard by which a work can be claimed as Christian. If it is *according to the gospel* it is such, but if not according to the gospel, the opposite is true. The gospel is not a human invention but the gospel *of God*. It reveals his glory and indeed makes it possible for others to share his glory (see Rom. 3:23, 5:2); note TNIV *the gospel concerning the glory of the blessed God*, not just *the glorious gospel* as NRSV. The nature of the gospel gives Christian work a great authority while also bringing a great responsibility on those who are entrusted with specific ministries.

Reflection: Aims in Ministry

If you were to ask a typical church-attending Indian Christian what ministry is all about, the answer would probably include things like conducting the Sunday services and other necessary services in the church, chairing committee meetings, home visitation, attending conferences of the wider church, and possibly other activities. Naturally, the answer will focus on the things which a church member sees their minister (pastor or presbyter) doing.

Someone engaged in ministry in a regular (perhaps full-time) way may also come to see his or her ministry in the same way, that is, as simply a set of functions to perform. But a minister needs to be more reflective than this. This paragraph reminds us that the ministries of different people can have very different outcomes. One possible outcome mentioned here is promoting theological speculation, with no practical benefit for the members of the church. Other possible outcomes in today's context might be preserving the harmony of the Christian community (or sadly the opposite sometimes) and good relations with the communities of other faiths (or the opposite), or the social upliftment of the Christian community. The positive outcome which Paul mentions here focuses on the changed lives of church members, with a focus on love which arises from an inner change of heart and conscience.

A problem faced by those in ministry is that there is always so much urgent work to do that it is often simplest just to do the tasks that come to hand, to be carried along by whatever currents are flowing that day. The currents may lead in good directions but unfortunately the currents may also end up in swamps, with no good outcome. We may hope that no minister intends to produce harmful results, but without strategic planning anything might happen.

There is an old saying that if you aim at nothing, that is exactly what you will achieve. Unfortunately that is not quite true. Ministry will always have a result, and it may easily be a negative result unless there is intentional planning for something specific and positive. One basic aim indicated in 1:5 is to produce love that comes from a pure heart, a good conscience, and sincere faith. Are you brave enough to ask your minister how he or she is planning for this outcome? Or if you are the minister, do you have the courage to ask yourself the same question?

False Teachers and False Teaching

It seems that Paul's earlier prediction about savage wolves attacking the flock (Acts 20:29) had been fulfilled, as Paul now reminds Timothy about his duty to resist false teachers at Ephesus (1:3).

We do not know who these people were, except that they are likely to have been insiders, perhaps even some of the elders of the church.[23] Hymenaeus and Alexander are mentioned in 1:20 as victims of false teaching. Perhaps they had also become teachers of it. Otherwise, the false teachers are vaguely described as *certain men* (not only here in this chapter in 1:3, 6, 19, but also in 4:1, 5:15, 24, 6:10, 21).

We are better informed about their teaching, though again there are many unanswered questions. To some extent it was based on the law of the OT, inasmuch as those men desired to be *teachers of the law* (1:7). However, their emphasis was on *myths and genealogies* (1:4), and their teaching did not promote truth and godliness but *speculations* (1:4) and *meaningless talk* (1:6). The passage clearly says that though they desired to be teachers of the law, they did not understand the law (1:7).

---

[23] This is strongly argued by Fee, *Timothy-Titus*, 7-8, 40.

In seeking to specify the exact nature of the false teaching at Ephesus, some have seen a link with the movement known as Gnosticism. It is not possible to give a simple definition of Gnosticism, for Gnosticism was not characterized by a unified set of beliefs. As the name implies, there was an emphasis on knowledge (Greek *gnosis*), often a secret knowledge which enabled the soul to be released from its imprisonment in the body. God was remote and removed, linked to the created order in an indirect manner only, by a vast series of spiritual beings. Things like *myths*, *genealogies* and *speculations* were certainly characteristic of Gnosticism. Gnostics were also happy to use OT materials for their own purposes. But that is not sufficient evidence to claim that the false teaching at Ephesus was a definite form of Gnosticism, especially as Gnosticism as such is known only from the second century AD and later. Perhaps the most that can be claimed is that tendencies which later came to expression in developed forms of Gnosticism are starting to be seen in the first century (here in the church at Ephesus, but also at Colossae as Paul's letter to that church reveals).[24]

The Law

The false teachers desired to be known as teachers of the law (1:7), no doubt using the law to claim authority for their teaching. But they did not understand the things they were talking about. In other words, Paul is saying, they were not in fact teaching the law at all. The two parallel clauses at the end of this verse, *what they are saying* and *the things about which they make assertions*, are probably saying the same thing, an example of rhetorical emphasis, rather than making different points. If there is a distinction, it is that the second possibly means the *persons* about which they make assertions,[25] but even so the point of the distinction is hardly clear.

The law should be used *properly* (NIV) or *legitimately* (NRSV). The word used here actually means *lawfully* (NASB), which may seem an obvious and unnecessary thing to say (hence the alternate translations in some of our English Bibles). The meaning is probably that the law should be used *as law*, in contrast to being treated as a source of speculations.

---

[24] Discussion of the nature of the false teaching at Ephesus may be found in Mounce, *Pastorals*, lxix-lxxvi; Marshall, *Pastorals*, 40-52; and helpfully summarized more briefly in Knight, *Pastorals*, 11-12.

[25] So Barrett, *Pastorals*, 42.

But in using the law as law one must be aware of a further distinction, between the righteous and the unrighteous person. According to 1:9 the law is *laid down not for the innocent* (NRSV). The literal meaning of the word translated *innocent* is *righteous* (NASB, TNIV). What is the meaning of this statement?

It would be easy to suggest that there is a contradiction with other passages of scripture, and especially other parts of Paul's writings. It can be pointed out that no one is righteous (Rom. 3:10, 20) and that it is the law which helps to make that clear (Rom. 3:9-20). From that perspective the law is relevant to all. But it is important to observe the different contexts in which the law is mentioned. In Romans (and elsewhere, Galatians for example) the focus is on who is acceptable in the sight of God, who needs to be made acceptable, and how a person becomes acceptable; that is, the issue is the way of salvation.

Here in 1 Timothy that is not the subject at all. The subject is the law as such, and the point is that it is the standard by which right and wrong conduct are measured. The law is not needed if a person's life is already characterized by good conduct, that is, if he or she is already righteous in that general sense. The word *righteous* is not a claim to moral perfection but refers to one who is (in general) morally upright (similar to Paul's use of the same word in Rom. 5:7). Such a person does not need the law because their life already follows the requirements of the law. The same is implied again by the last phrase of 1:10, where the point is that those who accept the legitimate teaching of the church will avoid the types of lawless behaviour described in this passage, showing that the requirements of the law have already shaped their lives.

But there are others who do need the law, and these are described in the remainder of 1:9-10. First, there are three pairs of words which present a general picture of godlessness and rejection of God and his requirements. Then follow eight other words which seem to echo several of the Ten Commandments. The fifth commandment is reflected in *those who kill their father or mother*, the sixth in *murderers*, the seventh in *fornicators* and *sodomites*, the eighth in *slave-traders* (or *kidnappers*), and the ninth in *liars* and *perjurers*. (The eighth commandment is about stealing, which the Jewish rabbis interpreted to apply to the stealing of persons, which explains the inclusion of *slave-traders* in the list here, rather than the stealing of property.)²⁶ The way these eight descriptions correspond with these five commandments (even following the same order) can hardly be accidental, and helps to show that when Paul refers in this passage to the law it is specifically the Jewish law, the OT law, which he has in mind and which the false teachers are pretending to teach.

It is these people who need the law to tell them of the error of their ways and to encourage them to repent. This is what it means to use the law *lawfully* (as law), not as the false teachers were trying to use it.

Paul is anxious to insist that the law is good (1:8). People may misuse it, but the problem is not the law itself. He has said in Romans 7:12 (in the context of showing that the law is not responsible for the presence of sin in a person's life) that *the law is holy, and the commandment is holy, righteous and good*. And as we have already noticed, Romans 3:9-20 focuses on the role of the law in revealing human sinfulness, which is the basic point being made here in 1:9-10.

Reflection: Law and Legalism in the Indian Church

The Indian church is often perceived as being highly legalistic. This may be an unfair description of many churches, but this is the prevailing picture of the situation in general.

There is no doubt that the NT rejects a lawless way of life as a Christian option. We are not free to do what we like. The rules (if it is right to call them rules) are that we must aim to please God (1 Thess. 4:1) and to be holy as God is holy (1 Pet. 1:15-16). Here we have standards which provide positive guidelines and at the same time rule out many types of behaviour.

However, it is interesting to observe that apart from basic moral standards the NT does not lay down laws. On the contrary, in situations where we might have thought some sort of law might have been useful, Paul refuses to do such a thing. This is seen, for example, in the disagreement described in Romans 14-15 about what foods can or cannot be eaten by believers. Paul speaks of those who are weak and strong, but does not say one side is right and the other is wrong. He calls for mutual acceptance and tolerance.

Legalism is the attempt to impose rules, to define what is acceptable and unacceptable behaviour. This is an almost irresistible temptation for many churches. It may provide a sense of security for the group and a clear-cut basis

---

²⁶ So Kelly, *Pastorals*, 50; Fee, *Timothy-Titus* 45-46; Marshall, *Pastorals*, 380; Johnson, *Timothy*, 170-171; Towner, *Timothy-Titus* (2006), 128.

on which church discipline can be exercised. We know the limits and can adjust our behaviour accordingly.

Unfortunately such an approach does not produce Spirit-led Christians. In the NT the Holy Spirit is seen as the key to a God-pleasing life. He teaches and guides and transforms the life of the believer. Rules invented and imposed by local church leadership stunt growth and produce conformist Christians who do what they are told for fear of exclusion but who are prevented from experiencing the work of the Spirit. Legalism is a basic lack of trust in the Holy Spirit to do the work he has been sent to do. The Spirit's task is to change the believer from within, exactly the opposite to ecclesiastical laws imposed from without.

Our passage indicates that for a Spirit-filled believer law is not necessary. It is not law but the Spirit who will produce in the believer a God-pleasing life. Where legalism prevails, the Spirit cannot. Which option do we really prefer?

1 Timothy 1:12-17

Paul's Testimony

Paul now gives his personal testimony, his experience of the power, grace and mercy of Christ in his life. In this context Paul's testimony stands in contrast to the false teaching which has been mentioned and condemned, especially because of its misuse of the law, and thus serves to demonstrate the true way of salvation. We can say, therefore, that though in a sense the focus is on Paul, in reality the emphasis is on the gospel which Paul's experience illustrates. In 1:11 Paul has mentioned the gospel of God's glory. His testimony now illustrates the power of the gospel, a reminder to Timothy and the Ephesians not to be diverted from the gospel by the fruitless theological speculations of the false teachers.

The stages of Paul's spiritual pilgrimage are set out in this passage. To put them in chronological order, he moved from (a) being a persecutor (1:13), to (b) being a recipient of mercy (1:13, 16) and of grace (1:14); a saved sinner (1:15) and a believer (1:16); and a recipient of the gift of eternal life (1:16), to (finally) (c) being an appointed servant (1:12).

He begins by expressing his thanks to Christ (1:12), not surprising in the light of his amazing conversion experience. The story of Paul's conversion is well known from the book of Acts (9:1-19, 22:6-16, 26:12-18). Its profound effect on Paul's life is seen by references in his own letters. He does not tell the actual story, but he refers to the experience several times, most clearly in 1 Corinthians 15:8, Galatians 1:13-17 and Philippians 3:4-11, but in many other possible, less direct, references. Here he does not hide the shame of his past but acknowledges that he was *a blasphemer, a persecutor, and a man of violence* (1:13), as again we know from the Acts story (8:1-3, 9:1-2, 22:4-5, 26:9-11). He does not refer to this out of a perverse sense of pride but in order to highlight the wonder of the mercy he has received.

Though in one sense Paul was fully aware of what he was doing (he was trying to destroy the church, as he says in Gal. 1:13), from another perspective he was ignorant (1:13), ignorant of the truth about Jesus and so ignorant of the significance of his actions. He now describes himself as a blasphemer, for he had absolutely rejected the possibility that Jesus was the Messiah and Son of God and he was resisting the purposes of God. But while involved in his persecuting activity he thought the opposite - that the Christians were the blasphemers and that he was upholding the honour of the God of his ancestors. It was because he thus acted ignorantly that he was able to be forgiven. Ignorance did not mean that he was not guilty, but it did mean that his sin was unintentional.

He was, he confesses, the *foremost* of sinners (1:15). The word is literally *first*, as again in 1:16, not in the sense that Paul was the first person to sin or the first person to believe, but as the *worst* of sinners and as the *prime* example of undeserved mercy. The enormity of his sinful opposition to God is also expressed in 1 Corinthians 15:9-10, where again it is the grace of God that he says has changed his life. It is because he is the *first* of sinners (in this sense) that he is also the *first* of believers, the *example* or pattern for others. If God could work such a miracle in such a sinner, he can certainly do the same in the lives of others. If Christ's mercy was shown to Paul, it can certainly be shown to other sinners, who are perhaps not as 'bad' as Paul.

As there was something unique about Paul in his pre-conversion state (so he claims), there was also something unique about the direction which his life took afterwards, for he became the apostle to the Gentiles. He refers to the call to this ministry in 1:12. We often use term *ministry* as one of great dignity and honour. Indeed, Paul himself speaks of the glory and greatness of Christian ministry (as in 2 Cor. 3-4), but ministry is in fact *service*, following in the footsteps of Jesus who came to serve (Mk

10:45). A puzzling aspect of Paul's statement here is that his appointment to Christ's service is connected with being considered *faithful*. We wonder how he could be regarded as faithful *before* he had performed any service, especially as he had been a violent opponent to that point. But Christ considered that he would prove to be faithful. Paul is saying: Christ considered me worth trusting, even when there was no basis for such an assessment from a human perspective. This can be understood as further evidence of his remarkable grace. Finally in this verse we notice the reference to Christ as the one who strengthens Paul. Ultimately, his usefulness in Christ's service was not due to his own faithfulness but to Christ's strength within him.

We have suggested that in his pre-conversion experience and in his apostolic ministry there are elements which may be regarded as unique to Paul. But the second aspect identified above (the second stage of his spiritual pilgrimage) contains experiences common to all believers. We will look at this in the section which follows.

The Christian Experience

We have already observed the different ways in which Paul describes the Christian experience. Much of this focuses on what the believer receives from God or Christ, a fact which reminds us of the divine initiative in our salvation. Without God's action reconciliation with God and spiritual renewal is not possible.

This initiative is first described in this passage in terms of the *mercy* which had been shown to him (1:13). The fact that Paul repeats this in 1:16 suggests his deep consciousness that this was absolutely vital. Without it, nothing would have happened in Paul's life, just as in Ephesians 2:4 it is divine mercy which is required to make the dead alive. A similar word is *grace* (1:14), which expresses the totally undeserved nature of God's work. This grace is not just adequate but overflowing: the verb in 1:14 might be very literally translated *super-abounded*.

Paul considers himself to be the foremost of sinners, but what is now significant is that he is a *saved* sinner. That is the work Christ came to do (1:15). To speak of salvation implies that there is a problem, something from which a person needs to be saved. The fact that Christ's work was to *save sinners* shows that the problem is sin. Before his conversion Paul would not have accepted that this was a problem for him. He may not have claimed moral perfection, but he did claim to be blameless regarding righteousness under the law (Phil. 3:6). He now knows that his previous claim was meaningless. Though he was not aware of his need, the need was there, and now he can gratefully speak of Christ's work as dealing with a problem of which he was the chief example.

That means that he now has the blessing of *eternal life* (1:16). In the PE life can refer to our present experience (as in 4:8). Timothy is urged to take hold of eternal life *now* (6:12). But true life is also viewed as something *future*, for which we *hope* (Tit. 1:2, 3:7). So, it is not easy to say what specific aspect of life is being referred to here (1:16). Perhaps it is left deliberately vague, covering any and every aspect of the new life with which the believer in Christ is blessed, now and in eternity.

We can think of salvation and eternal life as negative and positive expressions of the gospel message. Salvation speaks of deliverance from the problem into which our sin has brought us. It is the removal of what threatens our well-being as humans. On the other hand, eternal life speaks of the positive benefit which comes in place of the previous problem. Both are vital aspects of Christian experience.

Alongside the divine initiative and the blessings available through the gospel, we are also given a clear picture of the expected human response. The first such response is *faith* (1:14). The grace of Christ overflowed together with or accompanied by faith. Faith includes both a trusting acceptance of what God has done in Christ (that is, that this work is relevant to us and effective for our salvation) and the commitment of our life as disciples of Christ. Faith is mentioned again in 1:16, where faith is specifically faith in Christ and the outcome of such faith is eternal life. The essence of eternal life is a restored relationship with God, something which is possible only because our sin has been dealt with. The holy God can have no fellowship with an unforgiven sinner.

Alongside faith is *love* (1:14). There must be a practical outflow in our life of the love which we have experienced. As we have been loved by God, so we express love, first toward God, as a natural and proper response of gratitude to his love, and then also towards others. In Paul's life love had the effect of totally transforming his rejection of Jesus and hatred towards his followers into a total commitment to Jesus and an unreserved identification with his followers.

Faith and love go closely together. They are mentioned together many times in the PE, usually in lists with other Christian virtues, but in 2 Timothy 1:13 in the same phrase as here: *the faith and love that are in Christ Jesus*. The grammar suggests that the two responses are thought of as parts of a single entity, both being *in Christ Jesus*, which means something like *arising from and inspired by the work of Christ and our relationship to him*. Thus, while *faith and love* refer to necessary responses from our side, the little phrase *in Christ Jesus* suggests that even these human responses owe much to Christ and are not possible apart from what he has done for us.

Thus, while the believer has no doubt that nothing is achieved without God's work in Christ on our behalf and God's initiative to apply that work in our life, it is equally true that we have an undeniable responsibility to respond to what has been done for us.

The Person and Work of Christ

In the preceding section we have commented on the divine initiative and the work of God, but when we look at these verses more closely we realize that the focus of 1:12-16 is actually on Christ rather than God the Father.

Christ Jesus is our Lord (1:12), as again in 1:14 where *Lord* refers to Jesus rather than God the Father. Alongside the lordship of Christ is placed the sovereignty of God the Father (1:17), with no contradiction or even tension between the two. Here again (as in 1:1-2) we have the common early Christian testimony to the exaltation of Jesus even to the extent that he is viewed as an equal partner with God the Father. The same exalted status is implied in other ways, for it is Christ whom Paul thanks (1:12), meaning that prayer is directed to Christ, and the reference to Jesus *coming into the world* (1:15) contains at least a strong hint that the man Jesus who was born in Bethlehem and grew up in Nazareth already existed in heaven before his coming to earth.

But the emphasis in these verses is not so much on the person of Christ as his work in the world and his dealings with humanity. So, although he is Lord he did not remain in the glory of heaven but came into the world. This is stated in 1:15 in the first of the five *faithful* or *trustworthy sayings* which we find in the PE (also 3:1, 4:9, 2 Tim. 2:11, Tit. 3:8). These sayings seem to be recognized summaries of some aspect of

Christian truth, statements which already were familiar traditions in the early church. As such the saying is *worthy of full acceptance* by Timothy and all other readers of this letter.[27]

The saying records one of the reasons why Jesus came into the world, namely to save sinners (1:15). As we have already observed in the previous section, alongside the (negative) removal of our problem of which salvation speaks, there is a second aspect of Jesus' work, the (positive) provision of eternal life for those who believe (1:16).

Within this framework specific aspects of Christ's activity are mentioned. Central to Paul's testimony is the *mercy* he has received (1:13, 16). It is not specifically stated that it was Christ who showed him mercy (as distinct from God the Father) but there is little reason to doubt this, especially as Christ is identified as the source of the *grace* which overflowed for Paul (1:14). We also note the reference to Christ's *patience* (1:16). Elsewhere Paul speaks of God's patience or forbearance towards sinners (Rom. 2:4, 3:25, 9:22) but here it is Christ's patience for which Paul expresses gratitude. To Paul Christ had shown *the utmost* (literally *all* or *complete*) patience. Paul's life as the worst of sinners called forth the highest display of patience on the part of Christ. Paul offers no explanation why he should have been treated so generously, except that it provides proof that no one is beyond the scope of Christ's saving work, so long as they are willing to believe in him as Paul did.

One further aspect of Christ's activity is his strengthening presence (1:12). This is mentioned in the context of Paul's call to ministry. Whereas the other three elements of Christ's activity (mercy, grace and patience) focus on Paul's past life up to his conversion, Christ's strengthening work is not only what enabled Paul to respond positively to his initial experience of Christ's mercy but is also part of his present and ongoing experience. We are reminded of the famous statement of Philippians 4:13.

The paragraph concludes with a doxology (1:17), an exclamation of praise directed towards God (the Father), the *King of the ages*.[28] This doxology is similar in many details to the description of God near the end of 1 Timothy (6:15-16). All the attributes mentioned here are included

---

[27] For general discussion of these five sayings, see Marshall, *Pastorals*, 326-330; Mounce, *Pastorals*, 48-49; Towner, *Timothy-Titus* (2006), 143-145.

[28] Mounce, *Pastorals*, 50, suggests that it is addressed to Christ, though his later comments (pages 59-61) imply that it is God who is described.

there also: his sovereignty as King, his immortality, his invisible nature (that is, invisible to the human eye), and his uniqueness. Also in both passages is the recognition that honour rightly belongs to him (here *honour and glory*; in 6:16 *honour and eternal dominion*). This is intended not simply to be a statement of theological truth but a call to believers to give him his rightful honour in their lives.

The doxology as such contains no surprises, but what may be thought surprising is a doxology directed towards God the Father after the focus on Christ in the preceding verses. This tells us that Paul does not draw absolute distinctions between God and Christ. In a sense what Christ does, the Father also does. What comes from Christ comes equally from God, and honour is due to God just as much as Christ. This confirms what we have already seen in this letter about the exalted position of Christ.

1 Timothy 1:18-20

Timothy and His Ministry

At the end of the chapter Paul speaks of *instructions* given to Timothy (1:18). The word is actually *command* (singular not plural), and this is the third time in the chapter that Paul has mentioned a command to Timothy. Previous examples are in 1:3, 5, where also NRSV has *instruct* or *instruction*. Whether Paul is referring to the same command each time is unclear; it may be a coincidence that the same language is used so often in the same chapter. In any case the command here appears to cover most of what the chapter has dealt with. It is a command to Timothy to uphold the gospel: to live it out in his own life (with *faith and a good conscience*, 1:19), to promote it in the lives of others, and to defend it against those who threaten it. This is seen not as a burden imposed on Timothy but as a sacred trust. The verb used here might better be translated *entrust* (instead of *give*), and is closely related to 2 Timothy 1:14 where Paul speaks of what has been entrusted to Timothy (that is, the gospel and gospel ministry).

The ministry which Timothy is now exercising is closely connected with previous *prophecies* made about him (1:18). We do not know what these prophecies might have been, when they came or through whom.[29] Nothing that is said about Timothy in Acts gives us any relevant information. Other possible passages in the PE are 4:14 and 2 Timothy 1:6, which tantalizingly refer to *prophecy* and the *gift* Timothy has received, but without actually filling in the details we may be curious to know. From the present passage itself we can at least draw two important conclusions. (a) Those prophecies provide the foundation for Timothy's ministry and perhaps the specific content of his ministry. What Timothy now does at Ephesus must be *according to* the prophecies. Timothy does not have the right to invent his own ministry but must fulfil the task that has been entrusted to him. (b) That task is a divine commission. Prophecy is not a human mechanism but one of God's ways of speaking to his people. By being reminded of the prophecies Timothy should be encouraged to know that his ministry has divine authority and that he can be assured of divine power to enable him to carry out his ministry.

Paul uses the language of warfare to describe what Timothy is called to do.[30] He must *fight the good fight* (1:18). Again, it is the prophecies which are the inspiration for him to do this. The same military language occurs in 2 Timothy 2:3-4, and similar language (though more to do with an athletic contest than warfare) in 4:10, 6:12, 2 Timothy 4:7. In some other places it is a picture of the Christian life in general (as in 6:12), but here it has a more specific application to the task of leadership in ministry. It vividly shows that Christian service is hard work. If the military metaphor is pressed to the full, we could claim that it is dangerous work - not necessarily physically dangerous (though possibly sometimes so), but certainly emotionally and spiritually dangerous.

The final reference to Timothy in this paragraph comes at the beginning of 1:19, where he is reminded of the importance of *faith and a good conscience*. These two characteristics of the Christian life have already been mentioned together (1:5). As we realize from the remainder of the paragraph, these are not just necessary characteristics of the leader but of every believer. But we must not imagine that the leader is exempt, as if he or she can somehow reach a level of status or importance in life where basic Christian characteristics become unnecessary. (See the next section for further comment on these two characteristics.)

---

[29] See Mounce, *Pastorals*, 70-72 (*Excursus: Prophecies about Timothy*).

[30] On such language, here and elsewhere in the PE, see S. Stanislas, "The *Agōn* of the Servant of Christ in the Pastoral Epistles," *Indian Theological Studies* 47 (2010), 73-95.

Shipwrecked Believers

Sadly, Paul needs to note that not all have accepted the truth of what he has just mentioned. He speaks of some who have rejected this or these. Whether it is faith and a good conscience that have been rejected or a good conscience alone is a question of the interpretation of the Greek grammar. The word is literally *which* (TNIV) and is grammatically singular which may suggest that it refers to the nearer word *conscience* alone. However, it is certainly possible that the pronoun refers to both and that the singular is used because Paul is thinking of faith and a good conscience as a single entity (two parts of the one item).

Whatever the exact interpretation of this point, it seems right to say that these two things, faith and conscience, are closely related, and that in rejecting one you reject the other: rejecting the life of faith (trustful obedience to God) will ruin the conscience, and rejecting the promptings of a God-directed conscience will ruin the possibility of truly living a life of faith.

That this is true is confirmed by the final words of 1:19, where these people are said to have *suffered shipwreck in the faith*. This translation, with the word *the* included, should not be understood to mean that they have merely made some doctrinal mistakes. It is their whole Christian life which is at stake; *the faith* certainly involves the issue of theological truth but also includes their own personal life of faith. NIV brings this out with *shipwrecked their faith*. The metaphor of shipwreck speaks of total disaster and loss, of ruin beyond repair, and again reminds us (like the warfare metaphor of 1:18) that the Christian life can be unpredictable and even dangerous. Those who fail to cultivate the life of faith or who neglect to develop their conscience according to the teaching of God's word are asking for trouble.

As in other passages (such as 1:3, 6) Paul uses the word *some* (1:19) when referring to false teachers or opponents. That is his normal way in the PE of referring to such people, but here he identifies two of them (obviously there were others as well). The two are *Hymenaeus and Alexander*, possibly though not necessarily the same people as false teachers or opponents mentioned elsewhere in the PE: a man called Hymenaeus is mentioned along with Philetus in 2 Timothy 2:17, and Alexander the coppersmith in 2 Timothy 4:14. Exactly who these men were cannot be determined, but that is less important than recognizing that here are people who are well-known (for they need no further description than their names) and who had probably been leaders among the believers either in Ephesus or in some other Christian assembly known to Timothy. It is sobering to be reminded of the possibility of such people falling away from the faith, especially if they had been leaders.

Despite the seriousness of the situation, all is not lost. Paul holds out the possibility of change, for action has been taken *so that they may be trained not to blaspheme* (1:20). Paul does not simply mean that they should come to recognize that they should not have blasphemed in the past, but more particularly that they should not blaspheme in the future. His hope is their repentance and restoration. In this context their blasphemy is the rejection of faith and conscience, or to put it differently, the rejection of God's will and way.

Exactly what action has been taken by Paul is almost impossible to say. It is described as handing them over to Satan (1:20), the same language as is used in 1 Corinthians 5:4-5. We must assume that the action taken is extremely serious, probably not death as in the Acts 5 story of Ananias and Sapphira (who were given no opportunity to change), but possibly exclusion from Christian fellowship and in that sense turning them over to the realm of Satan. Satan is most often seen as God's enemy, but here, while that aspect is not denied, he is presented as God's agent, doing a work which God approves and which is intended to lead to a God-honouring result. That of course is one of the difficulties of this passage, because we are not told in scripture how that might work in reality. As we do not know what handing over to Satan involved in that situation, it would be foolish to try to imitate this in contemporary church life, but at the same time it is clear that church discipline should be taken seriously, and leaders need to pray for great wisdom to act appropriately, not harshly in response to relatively small matters but also not weakly when strong action is needed.

Reflection: Discipline in the Church

It is easy to read quickly the statement about handing over Hymenaeus and Alexander to Satan without pausing to consider the real life situation in which this occurred. There must surely have been much heartache and pain. As we have noted, these two men are mentioned as well-known in the church of Ephesus, quite possibly as leaders, and their excommunication (if we may use this word) would not have happened quietly or have gone unnoticed.

Church discipline is never straightforward and simple. One extreme is never to exercise discipline. Sometimes this approach is necessitated by the relatively weak role of the pastor, whose job is dependent on the goodwill of a powerful group of lay people (perhaps the deacons or the long-term members of the pastorate committee). In this sort of situation the pastor dare not act or even speak against misconduct on the part of the decision-makers in the church. Even when the pastor's position is more secure than this, it is easy to adopt the attitude that the pastor's role is to keep everyone in the Christian community happy or, to express the point in slightly more theological language, that love requires pastoral sensitivity, which may easily be another way of saying that it is acceptable to turn a blind eye to sin.

A different extreme is to take disciplinary action in quite trivial matters. A minority in a pastorate committee might be 'disciplined' for daring to express opinions which are not approved by the majority. Being bold enough to suggest new ideas or to differ from the prevailing views can become a punishable offence. Groups develop their own opinions about what is appropriate dress for men and women, and in some churches, for example, the failure of a woman to wear a white saree or to cover her head can lead to ostracism (not necessarily excommunication in a formal sense but perhaps not much different in practice). To make matters worse this may be connected with personal animosities and a spirit of revenge.

A passage such as 1:19-20 suggests a different attitude. On the one hand, discipline is seen to be sometimes necessary, perhaps a necessary evil but necessary just the same. Keeping the peace at all costs can be presented as a good Christian principle, but there are at least two things more important. One is the health of the church. A church which knowingly tolerates evil in its midst is on the road to spiritual disaster. As Paul says elsewhere, "A little yeast leavens the whole batch of dough" (1 Cor. 5:6, Gal. 5:9). Such a church becomes ineffective as an agent of mission, for the life of the church is observed by outsiders and weaknesses are very quickly noted (see Tit. 2:5, 8, 10).

The other matter of importance is the spiritual health of the individual. It does no one any good to give the impression that the church will tolerate any kind of teaching or behaviour. Here Paul's concern for Hymenaeus and Alexander is expressed in the words "so that they may learn not to blaspheme". The action taken against them is not just punitive but remedial. Paul seeks their rehabilitation, and so should we with any erring members with whom we need to deal.

On the other hand, if discipline is accepted as sometimes necessary, we need to be clear on what grounds it is appropriate to take disciplinary action.

It should not just be a response to trivial matters at the edge of church life. The reference in our passage is to "faith and a good conscience", a phrase which points to things that threaten the very heart of Christian belief and practice. There are major issues in church life in India which are sometimes allowed to pass without comment: false teaching in the pulpit or in home study groups; mismanagement of church funds; addiction to alcohol; long-term legal battles over property. Such things either threaten the faith directly or draw attention away from the church's calling to be the holy people of God, and so undermine the church's witness. Not all these things call for the same sort of response; excommunication is not the only action which can be taken. But they call for some sort of response, and leaders in the church (both local and regional leaders) need to pray for great wisdom to handle these matters in a godly way.

1 Timothy 2:1-7

The Importance of Prayer

Chapter 2 covers several different topics, but it seems that the main focus is on prayer, which is mentioned at the beginning of the chapter and again in 2:8. Other topics which may at first appear to be digressions, such as the saving work of God in Christ (2:4-7) or matters to do with women in church (2:9-15), are actually connected with this same main theme - so it can be claimed, as we will see in the following comments.[31]

The *first* thing Paul wants to talk about is prayer. Of course, this is chapter 2, not chapter 1, and so it is not the first thing in an absolute sense. But, following the general exhortations and warnings of chapter 1, it is the first of the instructions about specific aspects of church life. The meaning of the phrase used here may not simply be first in *order* but also first in *importance*. It is likely that the instructions about prayer are a conscious reaction to the effect of the false teachers. Their work not only produced controversy and division (as indicated in 1:4) but also an elitist view that salvation belonged only to the enlightened who understood the mysteries of the myths and genealogies which could be discovered in the OT. In this atmosphere prayer for others would not have been high on the agenda, and Paul challenges the church to come back to a more godly attitude.

---

[31] Mounce, *Pastorals*, 76, regards the theme as "the universal offer of salvation to all people", with the instructions about prayer serving this concern.

Prayer is described by four different words: *supplications, prayers, intercessions, and thanksgivings*. It is unlikely that the first three are intended to refer to three strictly distinct types of prayer.[32] The second in the list is simply the general word for *prayer*. The other two, *supplications* and *intercessions*, refer to prayers of request, possibly requests regarding oneself and requests for others respectively, but even this distinction is not certain. It is more likely that the three words are simply a means of emphasizing the importance of prayer. The fourth, *thanksgiving*, clearly has a different focus, and is a reminder that prayer is more than asking; it also should include remembering past blessings and answers to previous prayers, and expressing this in gratitude when we pray.

Part of the challenge of prayer is expressed in the last phrase of 2:1. Prayer is to be made *for all people*. This introduces a theme prominent in this paragraph. To pray for *all* is in line with God's interest in *all* (2:4) and Christ's work for *all* (2:6). The false teachers may have been interested only in an elite group, but that is not true of God.

The *all* for whom we must pray include kings and all others in high office (2:2). Earthly rulers make many mistakes and can be criticized for many reasons, as Paul himself knew very well. But the NT urges a mainly positive attitude to our leaders (Rom. 13:1-7, 1 Pet. 2:13-17). Orderly government is a divine institution, and we should pray that our political leaders will be able to fulfil God's intention. Such prayer clearly has a measure of self-interest, for we all benefit from peaceful conditions in society. However, in this context Paul no doubt also has in mind the wider benefits for *all*, not least that the gospel can be more easily spread in conditions of peace and stability. But the gospel is spread not only when external conditions are favourable but also when believers live lives of *godliness and dignity* (2:2). These and related words are found commonly in the PE, and we will consider their meaning more fully later.

Reflection: The Ministry of Prayer

Prayer is mentioned as the first of the matters which Timothy is to deal with in the life of the church at Ephesus (2:1). The words used here cover all kinds of prayer, including requests for oneself, intercession for others, and expressions of

---

[32] Knight's attempt to differentiate produces highly unlikely distinctions (Knight, *Pastorals*, 115). Towner more helpfully sums up the words as describing "every dimension and action of prayer" (Towner, *Timothy-Titus* (2006), 166).

thanks. The context is corporate prayer (that is, what we do in church), though no doubt the same principles are relevant to our private and personal prayers also.

This instruction invites further reflection in the light of actual practice in our churches. It can be suggested that although one hears fervent exhortations on the subject of prayer, the practice of prayer may be deficient in several respects.

Many of the mainline denominations have liturgical prayer built into the structure of the Sunday service. A close study of a typical Lord's Supper service will reveal many prayers covering many matters, such as confession of sin, thanksgiving, expressions of praise in the form of doxology, and intercession for a wide range of issues. This is highly commendable and would surely meet with Paul's approval. Of course, as those of us who come from this sort of ecclesiastical background know very well, it is easy for all these prayers to be recited thoughtlessly (not only by the congregation but even by the officiating presbyter). So the challenge is how to keep these prayers fresh and meaningful, perhaps by occasionally adding a brief and appropriate introduction to a prayer (as long as this also does not become a mere routine of the liturgy) and by including in the intercessions specific points of need (not only the names of the sick and reference to other needs within our immediate community but also specific matters related to current issues in India and indeed the needs of the wider world). Such suggestions are a reminder that even a liturgical service requires careful preparation.

Many other churches do not use liturgical forms. At one level this offers much greater freedom but at the same time much bigger challenges. Here too there is a danger that the same pattern is followed week after week (what might be called a non-written liturgy) and that the pattern will become just as meaningless as a poorly conducted liturgical service. The pattern may be a particular style of prayer (always mass prayer or always silent prayer or always one long pastoral prayer). The pattern may also be a standard and very limited scope for prayer, most probably the immediate concerns of the congregation and family members (sickness, forthcoming examinations, family problems, employment problems) and with little or no recognition that there is a bigger world which is the object of God's love (2:4, Jn 3:16). It is worth remembering that this passage gives instruction to pray for kings and all who are in high position, in India meaning our Prime Minister and other politicians, members of the judiciary, and others with influence in society. This is not the only matter for which we should pray but a reminder of a much broader scope for prayer than may happen in some of our churches.

We may also pause to think about other opportunities for prayer outside the regular Sunday services. Many churches conduct prayer meetings, perhaps even a weekly prayer meeting, but how much time is actually spent in prayer? The temptation is to use a prayer meeting as yet another preaching opportunity, not only because preaching is important but perhaps also because it is easier for one person to prepare a message than to think of creative ways of involving church members in prayer or to plan and prepare material which can be used for prayer in such meetings.

God our Saviour

The immediate focus of the next few verses (2:3-5a) is on God. Though it is possible and tempting to treat this teaching in isolation, the word *this* at the beginning of verse 3 reminds us that this passage should be interpreted within its context. When Paul says *this is good and acceptable*, he may be referring in general to all that has been said in 2:1-2. That is, good governance and Christians living godly and respectable lives (2:2) is good and acceptable to God. But the emphasis now on God's *concern for all* (2:4) perhaps suggests that it is *prayer for all* (2:1) that is particularly in Paul's mind as he writes. In other words, he is now giving a reason why we should pray for *all*, namely that God as Saviour is concerned for all and not just for a select elite.[33]

The description of God as *our Saviour* (2:3) has already occurred at the beginning of the letter (1:1) and we will come across it again (4:10). The following verses here (2:5-6) speak of the ministry of Christ, with a clear allusion to his death on the cross, and so there can be no doubt that when God is spoken of as Saviour, it is spiritual salvation, salvation from sin, which is in mind.

The main question arising from this passage is related to the statement that God wishes all people to be saved. Is this a statement of universalism, that is, that all will in fact be saved? The passage does not *say* that, and, as we will soon see, there is good reason to hold that it does not *mean* that. But, if that is not the meaning, we may ask *why* all will not be saved, if that is God's *wish*. Surely God's will cannot be resisted?

This is not the place to discuss the complexities of a subject like this, which is in the realm of systematic and philosophical theology. But we

---

[33] So Fee, *Pastorals*, 62; Towner, *Timothy-Titus* (2006), 177.

can begin by saying that God desires many things which do not always happen, for the simple reason that God does not always enforce his will. In particular, God does not turn his human creatures into robots, programmed to respond to the buttons which he presses. Here Paul speaks of people *coming to a knowledge of the truth*. This is virtually an expansion of what it means to be saved, and it shows that a human response is needed. Unless and until a person comes to a knowledge of the truth, he or she cannot be saved. So alongside God's will must be set the need for a human response. The thought is remarkably parallel to the well-known John 3:16, where we have God's love for the world expressed in the (apparently irresistible) act of the sending of his Son, together with the requirement that people believe in this Son in order to receive eternal life.

Knowledge of the truth is an important concept in the PE (also in 4:3, 2 Tim. 2:25, 3:7, Tit. 1:1). Truth or knowledge of the truth is often closely linked with faith (see the same references, plus 2:7), and can be regarded as virtually the same as faith. A believer is one who has come to a knowledge of the truth, and vice versa (as in 4:3). To know the truth is to be a Christian. This is not saying that merely an intellectual response is needed, but rather that a real knowledge of the truth produces a life-changing response of trust in God and (conversely) that true faith is not just an emotional response but a response based on sure knowledge.

One Way of Salvation

The statement that there is one God (2:5) can be seen as a reaffirmation of the basic monotheistic Jewish creed, such as we see in Deuteronomy 6:4 (*Hear, O Israel: the Lord our God, the Lord is one*) and confirmed by Jesus in Mark 12:29. However, the emphasis here is not so much on monotheism in contrast to polytheism as on the fact that there is one God for all (rather than separate gods for each nation or ethnic group). In other words, Paul is not launching into a theological defence of monotheism, but continuing his theme that God is Saviour of *all* (a word which is repeated in 2:6). "Since there is only one God and not several, there can therefore only be one way of salvation."[34]

---

[34] Marshall, Pastorals, 429.

It is not just that there is only one God, but also that there is only one mediator between God and humankind, one who is the bridge to link God and man. Paul leaves us in no doubt who this mediator is by naming him (*Christ Jesus*). He also describes him as a *man*. It is not likely that Paul is concerned how to reconcile the divine and human sides of the nature of Jesus (an aspect of later theological debate). The focus here on Jesus as human is more probably linked with the following statement (2:6), which shows that Jesus' fundamental task as mediator was completed during his earthly human life, namely his death on the cross.

Nevertheless, even if it is anachronistic to make Paul a participant in the debates of later centuries, this passage does in fact demonstrate Jesus' suitability to be mediator from a human perspective. He is one of us, and so can represent us. At the same time this does not deny the other side of Jesus' nature. Of necessity a mediator must be in good standing with *both* sides in a dispute. Jesus' suitability to represent God has already been shown in this letter, especially in the assertion of the lordship of Christ and his equal standing with God the Father, as we have observed in 1:1-2 (see also 1:12, 14).

It is assumed here that a mediator is needed, partly because of the nature of God, the great king, the invisible one (1:17). He, the immortal, is inaccessible to mortals. Thus, help is needed if we are to come into his presence. The need of a mediator is also based on the fact of sin as a reality of human life. Sin has created a barrier which must be removed before a positive relation to God can be established. Dealing with the problem of sin has already been mentioned as the purpose of Christ's coming into the world (1:15), and here the solution to the problem is Christ's work as a *ransom* (2:6), his voluntary giving of himself in order to pay the necessary price for our sin to be dealt with. The language of Christ giving himself or being given for our sins is a standard NT description and explanation of the death of Christ (Gal. 1:4, 2:20, Rom. 4:25; see also 1 Cor. 15:3).

We should not overlook the point that this is a ransom for *all*. The effect of Christ's work on the cross is universal and absolute in its scope. No one is in principle excluded. The only ones excluded are those who by their lack of response exclude themselves.

Reflection: One God or Many?

The doxology of 1:17 acknowledges the greatness of the only God, and the same point is made in 2:5 which says there is one God. This raises huge questions in the Indian religious and cultural context. Of course there are many - Muslims for example - who strongly insist that there is only one God, but the majority of our fellow citizens accept the existence of an innumerable collection of gods.

The Christian testimony is a potential source of trouble, for we are taught (from this passage, to take just one example) not simply that we have chosen to direct our worship to one God out of many possibilities but that there is only one God, and that surely is what is taught in these passages (1:17 and 2:5).

One response in Indian Christian circles is virtually to abandon this belief. In some theological circles pluralism is embraced as the appropriate response in the Indian context, and so (on this view) we must not insist that there is only one true God (the God and Father of our Lord Jesus Christ), but must accept that the gods worshipped in different religious systems are all equally valid ways of reaching the goal (however the goal may be defined). This response, theologically fashionable in some circles, is not likely to appeal to the average orthodox church member, and perhaps it is for this reason that those who teach pluralism in the seminary classroom will sometimes preach the biblical doctrine in the church. However, the wider Christian community should be aware of the existence of this unbiblical teaching, and to insist that those who are given the responsibility to lead and preach in the church are those who genuinely hold to the biblical belief that there is one God and that to him alone belong honour and glory for ever and ever.

Of course at a different level religious pluralism is an undeniable fact of Indian society and culture, for it is obvious that there are different religions and that many different gods are worshipped. In such a context there is no place for religious wars which may attempt to wipe out those forms of religious belief and practice which vary from one's own preference and conviction. But in fact the various religious communities of India have learned how to live together despite massive differences of belief. Communal strife seems more often to be the result of political trouble-making rather than a deep-rooted desire in the hearts of ordinary men and women to attack one another. We have learned to accept people's right to their own beliefs, and indeed this is enshrined in the constitution.

So it calls for a very sensitive balance to insist on our right to maintain our own faith and to witness to that faith in a conscientious manner, while at the same time respecting the right of others to hold to whatever form of religious belief and practice they see fit. It is worth remembering that the NT context was just as pluralistic as ours today in India. In that context the followers of Christ had little or no political power and could easily have allowed themselves to be swallowed up into the pluralistic patterns of belief which existed all around them. Instead, they worked out how to maintain an integrity of belief and of life which eventually proved to have enormous power to change an empire. How to live according to the same pattern is the challenge before us in India today.

Paul the Apostle

In many places in the NT we see that it is not enough for Christ to come into the world and to give himself as a ransom for human sin. There must also be proper *testimony* to Christ and what has been achieved through him. John's Gospel is full of the theme of witness (e.g., 1:7, 5:31-40, 21:24). So too at the end of Luke and the beginning of Acts, the apostles are commissioned to bear witness (Lk. 24:46-49, Acts 1:8). And Paul, slightly later, was added to the list of witnesses (Gal. 1:15-16, Acts 22:14-15).

That is the theme which Paul takes up from the end of 2:6, continuing into the next verse. There are three basic points. One is the point already made, that witness is *necessary*. There is not much value in a great event unless news about it is spread. Christ's death was a great event, but it does not have much benefit for a person unless they hear about it - indeed not only hear about the event but also learn its significance. An alternative view of the phrase *attested at the right time* is that it refers to God's witness through the death of Christ rather than subsequent human proclamation about this event.[35] The focus on Paul's ministry in the next verse suggests that human testimony through proclamation is mainly in the author's mind.

The second point is that *true* witness must be given by the *right* people. That seems to be why Paul gives such emphasis to his own ministry, insisting that what he says here is the absolute truth. This was not his own career choice but something to which he was *appointed* (2:7), by the command of God the Father and Christ Jesus (1:1). In this verse

---

[35] It is understood to mean God's testimony by Kelly, *Pastorals*, 64; Fee, *Timothy-Titus*, 66; Mounce, *Pastorals*, 90-91; Witherington, *Commentary*, 216; but human testimony by Marshall, *Pastorals*, 432-433; Towner, *Timothy-Titus* (2006), 186. Knight, *Pastorals*, 123-124, wants to leave it open to include both aspects.

he is not concerned with the authority which an apostle exercised, but with the *role* of an apostle, defined here by the words *herald* and *teacher*. There were others who were promoting different teachings at Ephesus (see 1:3-7), giving witness of a different type and leading people astray. In contrast, Paul insists that his God-given ministry is *in faith and truth*, focusing on and promoting faith and truth. Paul knows, as we know too well today, that not all preaching which professes to be Christian is genuine witness to the gospel of Christ.

A third point here brings us back to a major theme of this whole paragraph. Paul is a teacher of the *Gentiles*, a reminder that God is not God of the Jews only but Saviour of all. That is why Paul was commissioned to be the apostle to the Gentiles. His ministry does not represent an eccentric perspective but reflects God's central concern in sending his Son into the world, namely that the message of salvation should be preached to *all*.

1 Timothy 2:8-15

Men Who Pray

2:8 returns to the theme with which the chapter begins: prayer. The second half of the chapter teaches how men and women should behave in church, beginning with instructions to men. The Greek words for *men* and *women* can refer to men and women generally or to husbands and wives in particular. In this context there is no doubt that it is the general reference that is intended.

The instruction to the men is that they should *pray*. The meaning of this instruction is very simple and obvious, and yet one might wonder how often it is observed, in our churches and in our homes. They are to be careful that they are to be morally fit when they come into the presence of the holy God. They are to *raise holy hands*. It is assumed that standing with uplifted hands was a common posture for prayer, but this is not the point of emphasis. We should not draw the conclusion that this is the only posture, as the NT itself makes clear (e.g., Mk 14:35). Nor is the emphasis on a merely ritual purity, as if ritual washing is necessary before praying. Rather, *holy hands* is a way of referring to a holy life. Before men pray they must confess their sin, or else God will not answer their prayer. And they must not only be right with God but also right with their brothers and sisters, as the phrase *without anger or quarrelling* shows. The uplifted hand can be holy only if one's heart is holy and one's conduct is holy.

All this obviously does not mean that a person must be morally perfect before he prays, but simply that it is futile to expect God to take us seriously if we choose to ignore known sin in our life.

Is Paul saying that only men can pray in church? Is he excluding women? To understand the passage in this way would seem to conflict with a passage such as 1 Corinthians 11:5 which refers to women praying. Of course there are other passages (such as 1 Cor. 14:33-34, and especially verse 12 in this chapter) which speak of a woman remaining silent. Further comments on this subject are made in the following two sections.

Women's Clothing and Ornamentation

In the remaining verses in this passage Paul gives instructions about women. First, he writes about women's clothing and ornamentation (2:9-10). But before we look at his remarks on that subject, there is the question of where the main focus of these two verses really lies. To change from the topic of prayer to the topic of women's ornamentation seems to be very abrupt. There is no obvious reason for suddenly introducing this topic in this context. The likely answer to this issue is that Paul most probably is still speaking about prayer. The sense would be: *and the women [as they pray] should dress* ... In other words the instructions of 2:8-10 all relate to the subject of public prayer, 2:8 dealing with a major hindrance to effective prayer on the part of men and 2:9-10 dealing with a major hindrance to effective prayer on the part of women. This interpretation takes the view that Paul is here assuming (consistent with 1 Cor. 11:5) that there is no problem in principle about women praying in church.

It is not said that it is wrong for a woman to wear good clothing and ornaments. However, both then and now these things can be very expensive. One of the concerns here is extravagant expense, and the proud display of wealth. Another concern is the issue of modesty.[36] Women in church need to be aware of how weak men are and how easily distracted they can be, and, while not making a deliberate effort to be

---

[36] On both of these aspects, see Mounce, *Pastorals*, 114-115.

*un*attractive, to ensure that they avoid every possible accusation of being provocative or seductive. One can be sure that these were specific issues at Ephesus at the time when Paul wrote.

In order to avoid the problems Paul is concerned about, women should wear a different kind of precious ornamentation. Women who practise godliness must put the emphasis on *inner* holiness which produces good works rather than outward ornamentation (2:10). A believing woman's best ornamentation is her good works (see also 1 Pet. 3:3-4). One might suggest that in appearance-conscious societies such as India, this is an important lesson for a believing man also.

Women in the Church

This passage touches on very sensitive issues, particularly for readers for whom women's rights are a major concern, and this makes any attempt to apply what is taught here very risky indeed. But even before reaching the point of application, there is much doubt about what the verses actually mean in their original context. It would be optimistic to think that all the problems can be solved in a brief commentary such as this.[37] The best we can do is to put forward a possible (and hopefully credible) line of interpretation, and leave readers to form their own judgement and to follow up matters of interest in other commentaries.

To a completely objective reader (if there is such a person) the meaning of 2:11-12 may seem quite straightforward: a woman must not teach or exercise authority over a man; she is to learn and not to teach. If on the surface it is so simple, we may well ask: from where does the controversy arise? We can identify several sources of difficulty, and our comments about each of these may suggest a reasonable framework for the interpretation of these difficult verses.

1. What Paul says here is certainly not 'politically correct' in some contemporary circles, not only within extreme expressions of western feminism but also (more relevant to an Indian context) within circles where the oppression of women is a serious concern and where Paul may be seen as supporting the distorted interpretation of Indian cultural norms which justifies the physical, mental and emotional abuse of

---

[37] The comments on 2:11-14 occupy 26 pages in Mounce and in Towner (2006), showing that there is much more to be said than is possible in the present book.

women. Within that sort of context it is natural that there should be resistance to teaching which appears to put women in a second class position.

There can be no doubt that the application of any portion of the Bible needs to be very sensitive to the contemporary context (further comments below will seek to take this factor very seriously). However, the present author's perspective is that today's cultural context cannot be allowed to decide the *meaning* of a passage. What it means is to do with the original situation, and especially what the writer intended the original readers or hearers to understand by his words. How this meaning is to be applied today is an important (indeed vital) question but a separate one.

2.   Focusing on questions of biblical interpretation, concerns have been raised whether this passage contradicts other passages of the NT, not least other passages written by Paul. On the one hand a passage like 1 Corinthians 14:33-34 contains similar teaching, that a woman is not permitted to speak in church but must remain silent. On the other hand, there are references to women praying and prophesying in church (Acts 21:8-9, 1 Cor. 11:5) and to Priscilla (with her husband Aquila) teaching Apollos who was well-versed in the scriptures (Acts 18:24-26). It is interesting to note that this last example happened at Ephesus. The instruction is also given that we are to teach and admonish one another (Col. 3:16), without any gender restriction. Even in the PE the teaching role of women is encouraged (Tit. 2:3-4). So it would seem that in the time of the apostles women did in fact exercise ministries that involved public speaking, including teaching.

The obvious question is whether all this material can be harmonized, or whether it is a reflection of different rules and different standards in different places and at different times (even within the NT era).

It can be reasonably suggested that harmonization is possible which does not violate the meaning of the relevant passages in their different contexts. (a) That women in the NT period were competent to teach and encouraged to teach is clear from the references already given. (b) That this should happen within particular and limited contexts is not stated in so many words but can be inferred from the same references. Thus, the older women (Tit. 2:3-4) are to teach the younger women; it is teaching within a women-only context. The context of Priscilla and

Aquila teaching Apollos was private instruction (the verse says that they took him aside). The prohibition of 1 Timothy 2 and 1 Corinthians 14 is the church gathered for worship (perhaps we could call it the 'formal worship service', despite the risk of anachronism in this description). The context of the reference to teaching one another cannot be specified with certainty but it is likely to be informal (again, at the risk of using modern anachronistic language, a 'home fellowship' context or something comparable).

The instruction of 1 Timothy 2 may have a further limitation. It is possible that it is not an absolute restriction on women teaching in a public setting, but a form of teaching in which authority is exercised. Though the precise meaning of the verb *exercise authority* is debated, it certainly includes the concept of authority, and it may be this specific aspect which Paul is concerned about; that is, not teaching as such, but teaching through which authority and leadership is exercised.[38]

3. Another concern raised by biblical scholars is whether there was something within the context at Ephesus which Paul was specifically addressing. That is not a controversial point, for nearly always we can assume Paul wrote about issues relevant to his readers. However, controversy arises when it is suggested on this basis that what is taught here is necessarily limited in its application to that situation only and cannot have universal relevance. This sort of comment is often made, so much so that it is simply assumed by some writers with little or no justification provided. One piece of evidence that is used is the context of heresy with which Paul is concerned as he writes, and the suggestion is made that the women in that situation were particularly vulnerable to the false teachers and the false teaching, and that is why the prohibition is given here that they must not teach.[39]

To the present writer it seems that this sort of suggestion introduces as many difficulties as it tries to solve. For one thing, it offers a rather patronizing view of women and their intellectual capacity to discern truth and error. It also does not explain why men in general are not prohibited from teaching; after all, it was men, as far as one can judge,

---

[38] For discussion of the crucial Greek verb (*authenteo*) and its relation to the verb *teach*, see Knight, *Pastorals*, 141-142; Marshall, *Pastorals*, 456-460; Mounce, *Pastorals*, 128-130; Towner, *Timothy-Titus* (2006), 220-222.

[39] See, for example, Fee, *Timothy-Titus*, 72-73.

who introduced the false teaching to Ephesus, and the only named false teachers or victims of false teaching are men (1:20, 2 Tim. 1:15, 4:9). Also, it does not explain why women (specifically the older women in Tit. 2:3-4) are actually encouraged to teach.

Another difficulty with the suggestion of a restricted contextual application is 2:13-14. Here Paul turns to the creation account as the basis for the instructions he has just given. In other words he does not base his argument on contextual factors but on much more fundamental reasons, that is on the relation of men and women as established by God at creation.

If the argument of the passage is about order and leadership, we might paraphrase the meaning in this way: God did not create Eve to exercise authority over Adam or to exercise leadership. In fact when Eve did lead, trouble arose. Although Adam also sinned and was equally guilty, it was Eve's action that brought sin into the world. From this Paul has drawn the conclusion that women should not exercise leadership over men, particularly through teaching in the public church context.

The reader of this commentary will need to make up their own mind on this matter. One's conclusion should not be based on the 'I like this interpretation' approach, or on what is congenial within my culture (whether the culture of my society or that of my church). Nor should one be swayed by what is acceptable to modern thinking, for a Bible-believing Christian is committed to accepting the Bible's teaching even when it is not approved by modern trends. The challenge is to discover what the Bible actually does teach, and then to be willing to hold to that teaching, whether popular or unpopular.

One hopes that it does not need to be said that this sort of passage provides no basis for claiming that the male of the species is inherently superior to the female. There is no biblical foundation for that view. Both were made in the image of God (Gen. 1:27); both sinned; and both have equal standing in the family of God as justified sinners (Gal. 3:28). Nor should the passage be used to deny women any sort of church ministry or to allow male leaders to think they have unlimited and uncontrolled authority. Neither of these attitudes can be justified biblically. And finally, there is certainly no basis here for the oppression of women, by their husbands or by anyone else.

The Salvation of Women

The verses just commented on are no doubt the most sensitive and most controversial in the PE, because of their implications for ministry in the church. But 2:15, though not controversial to the same extent, also deals with a potentially very sensitive matter and has actually been described as "among the most difficult expressions in the whole of the Pastorals",[40] perhaps in the whole NT.

A literal translation of the first part of this verse is: *She will be saved through the child-bearing*. From this at least these two questions arise. (a) What kind of salvation is this? Is it spiritual salvation (that is, eternal life) or a different kind of salvation? (b) Which child is in mind? Is it *any* woman's child or could the word refer to a *specific* child?

In response to the first question it is relevant to observe that throughout the PE the language of salvation (whether in the form of a verb or a noun) is applied to what we can call spiritual salvation, with the possible exception of one other passage (see comments on 4:10). That this is the meaning here also is most likely. The suggestion that the words mean *will be brought safely through childbirth*[41] introduces a totally new concept into the passage. Furthermore, this idea has no other scriptural support, and it is not true to experience (many readers, sadly, will be able to think of a godly Christian woman who has *not* survived childbirth).

Regarding the second question, if the phrase *through the child-bearing* refers to any woman's own child, at least two significant problems arise.[42] (a) It seems to suggest that the basis of salvation is something other than faith in Christ, and furthermore that it is different for a woman than a man. (b) It also raises the problem of whether women who do not produce children can be saved. In response to these issues, several suggestions have been offered. (a) The word *through* does not mean *by means of* but *under the circumstances of*. Rather than thinking that their place among the people of God depends on having a public teaching role, women should realize that their proper role is the domestic task of bearing and raising children. However, this proposal suggests an obvious

---

[40] Guthrie, *Pastorals* (1957), 77.

[41] So Guthrie, *Pastorals* (1957), 77-78; Barrett, *Pastorals*, 56-57.

[42] Mathew, *Pastorals*, 38, accepts this interpretation, without addressing the problems raised by this understanding, not least how a woman can be said to be saved in this way.

question: if the point is really that her proper *role* and *ministry* is the bearing of children, why is the language of *salvation* used at all? (b) The statement does not mean that childbearing is *necessary* for *all* women, but simply assumes that this is the normal lot of a woman, perhaps as an objection to some women at Ephesus who were despising this role. This may indeed have been an issue at Ephesus, but again we may wonder why salvation language is used. So, to the present writer neither of these suggestions is convincing.

But it is possible that the phrase does not refer to any woman's child but specifically to Jesus. According to this interpretation Paul is referring here to the prophecy of Genesis 3:15, in which we read the promise of victory over the serpent through the child of the woman. This is often understood as a foreshadowing of the gospel (the so-called *protevangelion*). Although Eve sinned, salvation will be available through the child she (through her distant descendant Mary) would bear. Scholars are significantly divided on this matter,[43] but to the present author it seems to be a possibility worth considering, even if put forward with caution.

The second half of 2:15 has its own difficulties, especially in the words *if they continue*, where the verb has a plural subject *they*. Does the change from singular *she* to plural *they* mask an actual change of subject, possibly from *a woman* (she) to *her children* (they)? Or does it still refer to women, simply changing from a general *she* to a general *they*?

If *they* means the children, the sense is perhaps that a woman's proper role is through the children she bears provided that those children continue as they have (hopefully) begun, that is, by living godly lives (again, understanding this as a general statement, not necessarily applicable to every individual Christian woman). If *they* means the women, the sense is perhaps that salvation depends not just on the historic event of Christ's birth but on appropriating the benefits of Christ and living out the Christian life in practice; or that their proper role is not just to bear children but to live out the Christian life. Of the three

---

[43] The messianic interpretation is favoured by some scholars (Knight, *Pastorals*, 146; Witherington, *Commentary*, 230) but dismissed out of hand by others (Guthrie, *Pastorals* (1957), 78; Marshall, *Pastorals*, 469), though Guthrie takes it more seriously in his later edition (Guthrie, *Pastorals* (1990), 88). Others who reject this view are Fee, *Timothy-Titus*, 75, Mounce, *Pastorals*, 145-146, and Towner, *Timothy-Titus* (2006), 233-236, though with much fuller argumentation.

options presented in this paragraph, only one (the second) clearly relates to a woman's *salvation* and is therefore to be preferred; the other two speak of a woman's *role* and so do not clearly relate to the main issue presented in this verse.

Reflection: Roles of Women in the Church

The last part of chapter 2 is one of the most controversial parts of the Bible, not only because it is difficult to interpret but more especially because it touches on an issue of great sensitivity in the Indian context. In mentioning the Indian context I am thinking not only of traditional cultures where women are expected to be seen but not heard (or sometimes not even seen) but also of a changing India in which the roles and rights of women are being increasingly discussed. So the subject is potentially controversial for two opposite reasons.

The present author's understanding may well cause problems for both of the opposing extremes. On the one hand he believes that there is no absolute prohibition in the NT on women exercising a ministry of teaching; this may give offence to those of a more extreme traditional position in relation to Indian culture. On the other hand he does not believe in the view that all restrictions have been removed and that women can do anything. This position is sometimes supported by a verse such as Galatians 3:28 ("there is no longer Jew or Greek, there is no longer slave or free, there is no longer male and female; for all of you are one in Christ Jesus"), which however does not speak about roles in the church but of spiritual status in Christ. It has been suggested in the commentary that the limitation given in our present passage may be to do with leadership and the exercise of authority in a congregational context. Such an understanding of the passage will almost certainly cause problems in those contexts where women do exercise the ministry of congregational leadership (that is, as senior pastor or equivalent).

The challenge that faces us is how to achieve an appropriate balance. Several factors need to be taken into account. To begin with we may mention basic human rights, which surely rule out any form of oppression (of women or of any other disadvantaged group). Any attempt to justify oppression on the basis of biblical texts is perverse, to say the least, when one considers the huge amount of biblical material which shows God's hatred of oppression. If oppression has become a cultural norm in some segments of Indian society, this needs to be challenged. Nevertheless, the Indian cultural context cannot simply be ignored, and in situations where the gifts and abilities of women (beyond cooking and cleaning) have been ignored, it can hardly be expected that the situation can change overnight. True Christianity (as distinct from a merely cultural Christianity) often challenges what is accepted in the wider society, but this must be done gently and sensitively. (Indeed, this very issue is probably reflected in several NT contexts, as in 1 Corinthians 11 where it may have been a sense of new-found liberty which encouraged some of the women to abandon traditional head-coverings and thus to cause unnecessary offence.)

However, the crucial factor must be the Bible, and here we have the biggest challenge of all. What does the Bible (specifically the NT) permit and indeed encourage in the matter of the ministry of women? As already stated, the author's tentative understanding of our present passage (with which others may not agree) is that leadership of the congregation is not proper. But that does not mean that there are no significant roles for women in church life, or that they should be limited to work among women and children. To this author there seems no reason, for example, why a woman should not be ordained for roles other than congregational leadership, or take her place on her church's preaching roster, or use her theological training to teach in home fellowships or seminars (comparable to Priscilla's role in helping Apollos), or contribute her professional expertise in legal or financial or social or other relevant matters. Some readers will no doubt have different understandings of the situation, but it is important that we all approach the matter from the point of view of what the Bible is understood to teach, rather than adopt an attitude on purely cultural or politically correct grounds or on the basis of personal preference or pragmatism.

1 Timothy 3:1-16

Bishops

This chapter continues the instructions about the good order of the church for which Timothy is responsible. The instructions focus on the qualities required of those who minister in the church - bishops and deacons, as well as women (3:11; we will need to ask to whom exactly this refers). The chapter finishes with a creed-like summary of the truth about Jesus.

The chapter begins with the statement *the saying is sure* (which was used previously in 1:15). The fact that these are the opening words of the chapter may lead us to assume that they introduce the saying that *follows*, that is the saying about the office of bishop being a desirable and worthy one. That is the understanding of most commentators. However, the chapter and verse numbers in our Bible were not part of the original text;

even punctuation marks (such as full-stops and commas) were usually not included in the early manuscripts. So it is possible that *the saying is sure* refers to what has *already* been written, that is the verse about the salvation of women (as understood by the editors of the UBS[4] and NA[27] editions of the Greek text). It is difficult to say. To many readers it may seem that neither saying is especially memorable or inspiring. On the trustworthy sayings in general, see previously on 1:15.

No explanation is given of exactly how the bishop fitted into the ecclesiastical structure of that time. Even to speak of ecclesiastical *structure* may be misleading, for there may not have been formal and rigid structures such as we have today. When we read in these verses about a bishop and his work, we naturally think of the kinds of bishops we know in some of our churches today. A bishop, typically, is a dignitary of the church. Words like authority and status may readily come to mind when we think of the role of a bishop today. With these assumptions it may be hard to put ourselves into the shoes of Timothy and other first-century readers of this letter.

In 3:1 the translation *office of bishop* may be misleading. The Greek has a single word here which could be translated *oversight* or possibly *episcopacy*. The general word *leadership* might even be a possible translation. The emphasis is on the bishop's task. To speak of the *office of bishop* probably suggests the person's status, position or standing in the church. Many Christian people today probably only ever see their bishop as a dignitary and may have little idea what the bishop's work is or should be (apart from sitting on ecclesiastical committees and presiding at confirmation and ordination services). When Paul commends *oversight* as a *noble task*, he is not commending the status value of being a bishop nor the ecclesiastical politics which are sometimes required to obtain the position.

Another assumption today is that it is an honour to be appointed as bishop, the ultimate achievement in an ecclesiastical career. But 3:1, on the contrary, contains a hint that this was not the case at that time, perhaps that some who were competent to do this work saw it as an undesirable responsibility or perhaps that others in the church tended to think less of the bishop than they should have done. The fact that Paul finds it necessary to state that a bishop's work is a *noble task* is at least a hint that some thought the opposite.

Moving beyond what is merely hinted at, we find that the main emphasis of the passage is on the bishop's personal qualities (especially 3:2-3), though there is also some description of the bishop's tasks (end of 3:2 and 3:4-5). The person who holds such a position must be of the highest moral and spiritual character. Only a brief comment on each word or phrase is required. (a) *Above reproach* points to the need for the highest possible moral character. One might feel that it sets an impossibly high standard. Yet, while it is true that no one can ever be above reproach in an absolute sense, it is right that this should be the standard expected of such a leader in the church. (b) *Married only once* suggests that a second marriage after the death of the first wife prohibits a person from the role of bishop. It is maintained by some that this is the sense, based on the ancient attitude that "to remain unmarried after the death of one's spouse or after divorce was considered meritorious, while to marry again was taken as a sign of self-indulgence".[44] But the more common interpretation of this phrase, literally translated *husband of one wife*, is that it emphasizes faithfulness in marriage. It does not prohibit the second marriage of a widower, nor does it mean that a bishop must be married and not single. The point is rather that, on the assumption that a bishop will normally be a married man (the same assumption is seen in 3:4-5), he should be absolutely faithful to his wife. (c) *Temperate* may have a literal sense (restrained in the use of alcohol) or metaphorical (sober in the sense of clear-headed). As a literal reference to alcohol addiction comes at the beginning of 3:3, the metaphorical sense may be preferable here. (d) *Sensible* indicates a life "marked by prudent, thoughtful, self-controlled behaviour".[45] (e) *Respectable* is difficult to distinguish from the previous two, but refers in particular to an orderly and disciplined life. (f) *Hospitable* reminds us that in those days there were few if any respectable hotels where travellers could stay. For the safety and comfort of Christian visitors especially, hospitality was absolutely essential, and the bishop is to set a good example in this. (g) *An apt teacher* draws attention to another of the bishop's roles (on which further comment will be made below).

The list continues in 3:3. (h) *Not a drunkard* may be especially concerned with the bishop's public face, though we should not draw the false conclusion that this permits heavy consumption of alcohol in

---

[44] Kelly, *Pastorals*, 75.
[45] Marshall, *Pastorals*, 478.

private as long as drunken behaviour in public is avoided. Public and private behaviour are inevitably connected, and the words here are in effect a warning about the dangers of alcohol. (i) *Not violent* refers to bullying behaviour, whether expressed in actual physical violence or in more subtle, psychological ways. (j) *Gentle* is the opposite of the preceding, pointing to the characteristic of dealing with others in a respectful, conciliatory manner (not always easy for someone in a position of leadership who cannot simply give in to every request or expectation that comes his way). (k) *Not quarrelsome* represents a single Greek word which basically means someone who does not pick fights with others. (l) *Not a lover of money* needs little explanation but perhaps calls for much honest reflection, for we know how easy is it for someone in authority to misuse their position for personal financial gain.

In 3:4 the list changes from a catalogue of single words or (at the most) short phrases of two or three words to longer descriptions. (m) *How to manage …* Good management of his own household is the next requirement. Here it is not the bishop's relation to his wife which is in view (that has been mentioned in 3:2) but his role as father and control of his children. The last words of the verse are ambiguous. They could refer to the children, meaning that they are to be *respectful in every way* (NRSV), or to the father, meaning that his management of the household must be done *in a manner worthy of full respect* (TNIV).[46] The relevance of this requirement is explained in 3:5, where the church is depicted as a body (of people) which needs care, just as the children in a family.

(n) *Not a recent convert* is a sensible practical requirement, for a recently converted person lacks experience, and experience is needed to be able to handle the authority and power which leadership brings in one form or another. Otherwise he may become *puffed up* (with pride because of his newly discovered importance). The danger is that he may fall into *the condemnation of the devil* (probably meaning *the condemnation reserved for the devil* [TNIV], though *the condemnation pronounced by the*

---

[46] Reference to the children is favoured by Fee, *Timothy-Titus*, 82, Mounce, *Pastorals*, 179, and Witherington, *Commentary*, 238; and to the father by Kelly, *Pastorals*, 78, Marshall, *Pastorals*, 480, Johnson, *Timothy*, 216, and Towner, *Timothy-Titus* (2006), 255-256.

devil is a possible interpretation).[47] As well as this danger, one may suggest positive reasons why a new convert is not an appropriate bishop, for a new convert has not had the time to become a mature believer and well-versed in the scriptures, which are necessary for his task of being an example to others and a teacher of the truth.

(o) Finally, a different dimension is introduced when the wider implications of the bishop's task are considered. He is not only an officer of and in the church but inevitably will be observed and known by outsiders also. It is required that he have (literally) a *good witness* in the eyes of the outsiders. The negative effects of a bad witness are mentioned: *reproach* (justified criticism) and *the snare of the devil* (the trap laid by the devil). We cannot know whether this is only a requirement of the bishop while in office, or whether it is a qualification to be seen in a candidate for this office (meaning that even when he is an ordinary believer, so to speak, he should be known and respected in the wider community). Both are included if the list is a guide to the sort of person to be considered for the role of bishop as well as a checklist of necessary characteristics for those who are already bishops.

The main focus in this paragraph is on the qualities or characteristics required in a bishop, but within the list are some words and phrases which give a glimpse of the bishop's *work*. There are two which may be considered major elements of his work. (a) The requirement that he be *an apt teacher* (3:2) implies that teaching is one of his responsibilities. It has traditionally been true that the bishop has been seen as a defender in his own generation of the truth of the gospel that has been handed down from the apostolic age. (b) He must also be competent *to care for God's church*. This no doubt includes some administration, but the verb is *care for* rather than *administer*. Care suggests something more personal, more focused on the needs of the flock rather than the administration of the property and finances. (c) In addition to these two (which are fundamental and ongoing parts of the bishop's work), he is also to be *hospitable* (though this service may not have been required very regularly or frequently).

In 5:17 Paul mentions elders. When we come to that passage we will observe significant similarities between bishops and elders and will need

---

[47] Knight, *Pastorals*, 164, Mounce, *Pastorals*, 182, and Johnson, *Timothy*, 217, favour the first; and Kelly, *Pastorals*, 79, Marshall, *Pastorals*, 482-483, and Towner, *Timothy-Titus* (2006), 257-258, the second.

to ask whether these are titles of two different ministries or perhaps two titles referring to the same ministry.

Deacons

As with the title or description bishop, deacons are now mentioned without any explanation. Again, we may be tempted to make assumptions based on our own experience. In contemporary episcopal church structures, a deacon is a fairly lowly office, sometimes nothing much more than a preliminary stage prior to ordination as presbyter or priest. In some non-episcopal churches, the deacons are a very significant group of leaders in the local church. There is little information in the NT. The basic meaning of the word is one who does practical service or gives help. In Acts 6:1-6 seven were appointed to do such practical service. But their service was also spiritual service inasmuch as it was necessary for those seven to be filled with the Holy Spirit and with wisdom (Acts 6:3). It is worth noting that the Acts passage does not actually use the word *deacons* to describe the seven. There are few other relevant NT passages. Philippians 1:1 mentions the bishops and deacons of that church; Phoebe (Rom. 16:1) was a deacon of the church of Cenchreae (near Corinth). Our present passage simply assumes that there were deacons in the Ephesus church. But whether or not this was a well-established 'office' or 'order' we cannot say.

Needless to say, Paul is not writing to satisfy our curiosity but to address the needs of that situation where, it appears, the role of a deacon was well-accepted but where care was needed to see that only the right sort of person was admitted to this position. As he writes to Timothy he insists that deacons must be people of good character. Therefore he gives instructions about their personal qualities (3:8), their faith (3:9) and their family (3:12). Just as it is not appropriate for a bishop to be a new convert (3:6), so a deacon must be tested before serving as a deacon (3:10).

Some brief comments may be made about the qualities to be desired in those who hold the position of deacon. (a) The adjective *serious* (NIV *worthy of respect*) appears here for the first time in the PE, though the corresponding noun has been used in 2:2 (of all believers; NRSV *dignity*, NIV *holiness*) and 3:4 (of the bishop, who is to act in a way worthy of *respect*, or his children, who are to respond with proper *respect*). These different translations show that the sense of the word is difficult to express in one simple translation, but a helpful definition is a life of "dignified and serious behaviour that elicits respect from others".[48] (b) *Not double-tongued*. It is not clear whether this means saying one thing and meaning another, or saying different things to different people. In any case the sense is that one is to be straightforward, honest and trustworthy in speech. (c) *Not indulging in much wine* and (d) *not greedy for money* are similar to the qualities required of bishops in 3:3, though expressed in different words.

(e) *Hold fast to the mystery of the faith* (3:9) shows that although (in some churches at least) the deacon may primarily be involved in practical service, he must also be a person of strong theological conviction. This is exactly parallel to the situation regarding Stephen and his colleagues (Acts 6). Though they were appointed to attend to the administration of the assistance to widows, they were required to be *full of the Spirit and of wisdom* (6:3), and two of them (Stephen and Philip) proved to have gifts of much wider application. The word *mystery* does not necessarily mean something confusing and difficult to understand, but in the NT often has the sense of a previously hidden secret which has now been revealed (e.g., Mk 4:11, Eph. 3:3-6). (f) It is necessary that a deacon be *tested* (3:10) before beginning his service as a deacon. We do not know whether a process of formal testing is intended, but in some way a person needs to be approved as one who has the qualities listed in this passage. The task of deacon must never be undertaken lightly or without proper preparation.

After the brief interruption of 3:11, the list of qualifications continues in 3:12 with the same requirements as for a bishop: (g) *faithfulness in marriage* (as in 3:2) and (h) *good management of their household* (as in 3:4).

The word *deacon* itself tells us that the deacon's role was one of service, though the passage says nothing of what type of service in particular. Other than that, the only hint of a deacon's role is contained in the last qualification, namely that some sort of leadership role is included. One suggestion is leadership of a house church,[49] which is certainly possible though unprovable.

---

48 Marshall, *Pastorals*, 489.
49 Marshall, *Pastorals*, 495.

The Women

In the middle of this passage the necessary qualifications for *women* are given (3:11). This probably does not refer to Christian women in general (for the rest of the passage is about qualifications for specific roles in the church) nor to the wives of deacons (for one might ask why the wives of bishops have not similarly been mentioned).[50] The other possibility is female deacons, which would (partly at least) explain why this verse comes in the middle of the passage about deacons; this is the view accepted here.[51]

The first three qualities mentioned here are parallel to the first three for deacons. (a) First, they must be *serious* (the same word as in 3:8). (b) The second is *not slanderers*. Though a different word is used than in 3:8, the general point is the same, namely control of the use of the tongue. (c) Thirdly, they are to be *temperate*. This is the same word as in 3:2, where a metaphorical sense was preferred, but the parallel to the qualifications for deacons suggests a literal sense here, namely self-control (perhaps abstinence?) in the consumption of alcohol. (d) The fourth requirement *faithful in all things* indicates faithfulness, reliability and trustworthiness in the broadest possible sense. If the author is consciously continuing the parallel with 3:8, where the next qualification for deacons is *not greedy for money*, faithfulness in the use of money would be the special point of focus here. In any case that is included in the phrase *in all things*.

The paragraph concludes with a statement about the positive rewards that result from good service (3:13). If 3:11 refers to female deacons, this final statement would apply to both male and female deacons. There is no grammatical reason to limit it to males only.

Two rewards are mentioned. (a) The first is (literally) a *good step*, which has sometimes been understood to mean a step on the ladder of promotion to higher office (though not by recent commentators).[52] But it is much more likely to refer to the value of the work of a deacon in its own right as bringing a *good standing* (NRSV) both in the sight of God and (one might hope) in the sight of one's fellow believers. (b) The second is

---

[50] Knight, *Pastorals*, 170-172, and Mounce, *Pastorals*, 202-205, adopt the second of these two suggestions.

[51] As also by Kelly, *Pastorals*, 83-84; Marshall, *Pastorals*, 492-494; Johnson, *Timothy*, 228-229; Towner, *Timothy-Titus* (2006), 265-266; Witherington, *Commentary*, 241-242.

[52] For this interpretation, see Lock, *Pastorals*, 41.

a *boldness* or confidence in the faith, perhaps through experiencing that Christ's power and presence has enabled the deacon to do things which he or she did not think they were capable of doing.

Reflection: Qualifications for Leadership in the Church

The commentary has indicated some of the uncertainties in understanding exactly to whom Paul was referring when he wrote about the work of oversight. To say the least, one cannot simply assume that they are exactly the same as those who hold the office of bishop in the Indian church. Nevertheless, whatever the ecclesiastical framework of the time (if indeed there was a formal framework at all), the first part of chapter 3 certainly describes people in positions of leadership, meaning spiritual and moral leadership in particular, and to that extent Paul's words provide a model for leadership in any church.

So, even if we cannot make a direct identification between Paul's 'overseer' and today's 'bishop', it is clear that he is talking about people like our modern bishops, district superintendents and presbyters, or, in churches which do not use those particular titles, ministers and pastors. It is worth pausing to ask what sort of people may find themselves in such positions. A number of factors may operate. It may be a person's political power (the number of influential friends he or she has or the finance he controls), the state from which he comes, the ethnic and linguistic group or the family to which he belongs, which determine whether he is considered suitable. When it comes to who is sent for theological training with the longer-term purpose of filling these offices, it may be a matter of whether a person's family is on good terms with the bishop or can raise the necessary finance.

While it can be claimed that most of these criteria play some legitimate role, the risk is that more important criteria can be overlooked. Paul here reminds us what those criteria are. There are two types of criteria. One is good Christian character in a general sense, and involves many matters such as proper sexual behaviour, right attitudes to and right practices in the handling of money, avoiding alcohol addiction, and qualities such as gentleness and lack of conceit that will enable him or her to relate well to others. This criterion is absolutely non-negotiable, and one may hope is normally fulfilled (though sadly one may be able to think of examples of people in leadership in the church who have fallen short in one or more of these basic aspects of Christian character). The other type of criterion is to do with the leader's ability to do the job, and includes matters like ability to teach and ability to manage.

The reality in many of today's churches is that the leaders of tomorrow are today's theological students. The challenge is therefore how to discern those who have the necessary qualities among the (usually) young men and women who apply for admission to India's theological seminaries and Bible schools. To begin with, one might suggest that there needs to be a minimum age. While it is impossible to be certain how a person of any age might behave in the future (for even a 50 year old might do something quite uncharacteristic), this is much more likely to be the case with people whose basic character is still being formed. Only candidates should be considered who have lived long enough for their character to have been observed and assessed. Unfortunately, some students in theological institutions reveal a very poor level of Christian character, but once they have been admitted it is often very difficult to remove them. If for some unavoidable reasons the very young (for example, teenagers) are admitted to theological study, there needs to be a significant period of internship during the course or a probationary period after graduation to allow the opportunity for proper assessment of their character.

Character is not the only criterion, but also the necessary skills to do the job. Naturally, no theological student is likely to have these skills fully developed at graduation, but it is reasonable for the church to expect that the development and testing of basic skills be part of the curriculum, whether formally or informally. Another way of making this point is to say that a theological degree should be much more than merely acquiring another academic qualification. Not only do the theological institutions need to have a balanced focus here but the motivation of applicants needs to be examined as fully as possible so as to weed out those whose main or only interest is to acquire another degree.

Reflection: Special Qualities for Leaders?

We can be tempted to put our church leaders in a special category. At one level that is right and proper. After all they are leaders, who exercise special and vital roles in church life, and, because they are in a sense the public face of the church, higher personal standards are expected of them. In leaders good Christian character is not merely an ideal to aim for in the distant future but something that should be evident in their life now.

At the same time it is worth noting that many of the qualities required of those holding specific offices in the church are the same as for believers in general. Thus, the word translated above reproach (3:2) is used of widows in 5:7. Instructions about self-control in the use of alcohol (3:3, 8, 11) occur elsewhere for other believers (Tit. 2:2-3). Hospitality (3:2) is something which those who are now widows are expected to have shown (5:10). Gentleness

(3:3) is expected of all believers in Titus 3:2, as is the warning against being quarrelsome in the same passage. Love of money (3:3) is to be avoided by all (6:10). Seriousness or behaviour worthy of respect is not only for the deacons (3:8) and the women (3:11) and possibly the bishops (3:4) but is an expected mark of all believers (2:2; see also Tit. 2:2). Slanderous speech (3:11) is condemned elsewhere (Tit. 2:3; see also 2 Tim. 3:3). Behaviour that provides a good testimony to non-believing society around us (3:7) is commended elsewhere (Tit. 2:8).

The obvious conclusion which arises from this is that Christian character is not a special requirement of leaders only. All believers should set themselves the same high standards of morality and ethics, in personal life, their business activities, and all other aspects of life. One reason for this is the testimony of the church to society at large. It was suggested above that leaders are the public face of the church, but that is only partly true. As far as your family, friends, neighbours and business associates are concerned, you are the public face of the church. If there is any difference between leaders and other believers, it may be that leaders are expected to demonstrate Christian character to a higher degree and more consistently, and their mistakes may lead to more serious consequences. But a high standard of character and behaviour is expected of us all.

The Church

Paul anticipates seeing Timothy soon (3:14), though there may be a delay (3:15). We do not know where he was at the time of writing this letter (one ancient tradition says Laodicea, mentioned for example in Col. 2:1 and Rev. 1:11; another tradition says Nicopolis, mentioned in Tit. 3:12), or what his circumstances were which may have caused him to be uncertain about his plans. Whether he comes soon or not, he has written *these instructions* (probably meaning this whole letter) so that Timothy may know what is right conduct within the church (3:15). This statement gives us a hint about the audience for whom the letter was really intended, for it is highly likely that Timothy already knew most if not all of what Paul desired for the church, as he had been Paul's colleague and assistant for many years. Though the letter is addressed to Timothy, it is actually intended for a wider audience, namely the church as a whole. There are some personal words for Timothy (1:18, 4:11-14, 5:23, 6:20, and elsewhere), but even these are intended to be overheard (one might say) by the church as a whole.

The fact that the church knows Paul's instructions to Timothy will serve to remind them of the nature of Timothy's ministry (as given by God and confirmed through his apostle Paul, rather than whatever the church decides their leader should do), and will serve also to keep Timothy accountable.

It is important to observe the importance of the church according to the NT. Some Christian traditions place so much emphasis on the personal salvation of the individual that the significance of the church is easily put aside. It is right to affirm that every individual needs to come into a personal relationship with God, which brings salvation and eternal life. However, God's desire is not only to save me and other individuals but also to build his church. The church is extremely important within God's plan, as the descriptions in this passage (3:15) help us to see.

First, the church is described as *God's household*. It is his family, and God has just as much concern for his family as any earthly father has for his. Members of the church are God's children, which means that we come under his fatherly discipline and also that we are brothers and sisters of one another. Just as in every family there is appropriate and inappropriate behaviour, so too it is necessary to know how one must behave in God's household. The word *behave* covers all aspects of behaviour, not just correct 'religious' behaviour such as the proper way to conduct the liturgy or removing shoes outside the building or similar matters.

Second, it is the church *of the living God*. It belongs to God (rather than the bishop, the pastor, or the church committee) and it is his right to direct the life of the church. The fact that God is the living God tells us that he is present in his church and that we should be very careful not to misbehave within the Christian family.

Third, it is the *pillar and bulwark of the truth*. In part, this is saying that the church is where the truth is preserved and safeguarded. But Paul is not only concerned about correct theology. The emphasis in the present context is on right behaviour. Safeguarding the truth involves proper Christian behaviour. The behaviour of the members of God's family (especially but not only its leaders) needs to be consistent with what is true. Otherwise the truth about God, Christ and the gospel will be obscured.

Summary of the Faith

The final verse of the chapter has been described as a hymn of the early church or possibly a creed.[53] There are other similar statements in the NT which, like the present one, focus on the person and work of Jesus (as in Rom. 1:3-4, 1 Cor. 15:3-5, Phil. 2:6-11, Col. 1:15-20). The way Paul introduces the statement suggests that it was something with which Timothy was already familiar. If that is so, it would have been an accepted part of the church's tradition, used perhaps in worship or for instruction or both.

The six lines of the statement follow the same form (in Greek an aorist passive verb followed by a phrase beginning with the preposition *en* meaning *in*), except for the third line which omits the preposition. This form gives it a rhythmic and poetic feel, making it appropriate for the uses suggested. The exact structure of the poem has been debated by scholars: one stanza with six lines in chronological order or two stanzas of three lines each or three stanzas of two lines each.[54] But these debates are less important than the actual meaning of the phrases.[55]

Though different meanings can be suggested for some of phrases, here is a fairly straightforward paraphrase. (a) Jesus was revealed as man (Jn 1:14). (b) The Holy Spirit provided proof of Jesus through the resurrection (Rom. 1:4) and through his own testimony (Jn 15:26, 16:14). (c) By appearing to angels (after the resurrection) Jesus was seen to be victorious not only on this earth but in the heavenly places too. (d) His victory was proclaimed not only to the Jews but also to many races. (e) People of different races believed in him. (f) He was exalted and is seated at the right hand of God. If one thinks that a chronological sequence is intended,[56] the final statement does not refer specifically to Jesus' ascension but is rather a general statement of Jesus in his exalted state, not focusing on a single event but providing a suitable climax to the creed as a whole.

---

[53] Barrett, *Pastorals*, 64, speaks of a "hymn or creed"; Marshall, *Pastorals*, 499, "confession or hymn"; Mounce, *Pastorals*, 215, "christological hymn"; Towner, *Timothy-Titus* (2006), 276, "Christ hymn". Kelly, *Pastorals*, 89, says "a hymn, not a credal fragment or piece of catechetical material", but Knight, *Pastorals*, 183, allows both possibilities.

[54] For discussion see Marshall, *Pastorals*, 500-504; Mounce, *Pastorals*, 216-218.

[55] Towner observes: "The interests in salvation history, mission and gospel are all detectable no matter how the lines are arranged" (Towner, *Timothy-Titus* (2006), 278).

[56] So Barrett, *Pastorals*, 66.

The first part of 3:16 describes this statement as (literally) *the mystery of godliness* (as in NIV). The first of these nouns has already been used in this chapter (see comments on 3:9), as meaning a truth previously hidden but now revealed to some. To the unbeliever the gospel of Jesus is foolishness which he cannot understand. But the Holy Spirit makes the truth clear to the believer. In addition to references previously given, see Romans 16:25, 1 Corinthians 2:6-10, Ephesians 1:9, Colossians 1:25-27.

We have also previously (in 2:2) come across the word *godliness*. The translation *religion* (NRSV) is not incorrect,[57] but it is too vague to be very helpful. In 6:5 it may have the sense *profession of religion* (in that context a hypocritical profession), but more often it means the *practical expression of religion*, for which *godliness* is a good equivalent. Certainly the context here suggests a focus on the life of the believer, and the TNIV (though expanding the original wording) conveys the sense well: *the mystery from which true godliness springs*.

Reflection: Thinking about the Church

What is the church? The reader may think this is a strange question, especially if he or she has been a Christian all their life. Without trying to give too precise a definition, surely we would say that church is the meeting of members of the Christian community for their weekly worship and perhaps for other activities as well. Some might want to include the church building in their definition.

It is natural for Christians in the Indian context to see a very close link between the church and the Christian community. Hindus have their temples, Muslims their mosques, while the church is the particular possession of the Christian community. Our community is an essential part of our identity as Indians and church (not just the building but the activities of the Christian community) is one aspect of the Christian identity.

So far as it goes there is no problem with that sort of thinking, but from a biblical perspective it does not go far enough. Our present passage is a reminder that the church is not the possession of the Christian community but belongs to God. It is his household and his church (3:15). He is the head of the family (household) and the leader of the community (church). This identifies the criterion which should govern church life. The church does not exist mainly for the benefit of the Christian community but for the glory of God. There are appropriate and inappropriate ways to behave, and such matters are to be decided

---

[57] This is one of the meanings listed in the dictionaries, and is accepted here by Kelly, *Pastorals*, 88-89.

not by us but by God (though of course there are many details which we must work out on the basis of the principles which God has given us in scripture).

We need to remember that the God we worship, the God of the Bible, is not merely one option among many but the only true God (as we have seen in passages in chapters 1 and 2). He and his church do not exist for our benefit but we for his. We have been entrusted with the privilege of being his witnesses in the world in order to bring his world back to him. The church's role is to reflect God to the world, which means that it is vitally important to know how one ought to behave in the household of God.

Church life can easily become the political playground of the Christian community. Sometimes the ordained leadership is guilty of manipulating church affairs so as to reinforce their own status and position, their actions suggesting that the church is their own personal kingdom. Sometimes lay leaders act in a similar way when they lobby for position and influence, not because of concern for the church's spiritual life but to further their own interests. We need to understand how out of place these attitudes and actions really are in "the church of the living God".

1 Timothy 4:1-16

God's Good Creation

We have already observed how important the issue of false teaching is in this letter. From the very beginning (1:3) Paul has found it necessary to mention this subject, identifying one of Timothy's main tasks as resisting false teaching. At the end of the previous chapter (3:15) the church has been described as the *pillar and bulwark of the truth*. Now as we move into chapter 4 the same matter is taken up again.

The first verse links what is happening in the church at Ephesus with warnings previously given. *The Spirit expressly says*: the Spirit has given specific warning. Exactly what this refers to is not clear. We know that Jesus warned about apostasy and the appearance of false prophets (Mt. 24:10-11), though we might have expected Paul to have spoken of *the Lord* rather than *the Spirit* if this is what he is referring to. It could be the warning communicated through Paul in Acts 20:29-30[58] or another word of prophecy of which we have no other knowledge. Whatever it

---

[58] So Mounce, *Pastorals*, 234.

was, Paul appeals to it as an authoritative word which Timothy would have known.

The source of this false teaching is demonic (4:1). Certainly it is being promoted by human agents, and no doubt it was made to appear as attractive as possible, but Paul wants Timothy to know that appearances can be deceptive. It is a case of wolves in sheep's clothing. The teaching which Paul will go on to describe in this paragraph is not just teaching which does not come from God and his word; it is in fact *contrary* to what God has said, and so by definition must derive from sources opposed to God. Presumably Paul would have described any other false teaching which is opposed to the word of God in a similar way.

Demonic as it may be, the false teaching is being spread by human beings, who are described in unflattering terms in 4:2. Hypocrisy and lying are involved. Both concepts speak of deliberate action. These teachers are not accidentally, as it were, teaching what is false. Hypocrisy indicates covering the reality with a mask, presenting a false appearance; they know their teaching is false but they present it as the truth. Lying presents a similar picture. The second half of the verse reinforces the picture, for it suggests that they have silenced their conscience. Their conscience would have warned them about the nature and origin of the nonsense they were teaching, but they have suppressed and deadened their conscience and it is no longer an effective alarm system.

The precise nature of their teaching is summed up in a few words in 4:3. It can be described as *asceticism*, the denial of natural and normal human appetites. Two examples are given: forbidding of marriage and abstention from foods. In the latter case, one presumes that what was intended was abstinence from *some* foods (perhaps foods prohibited by the food laws of the OT or food sacrificed to idols), or abstinence for certain periods under certain conditions; it is obviously not a complete and permanent abstinence (which would amount to suicide).

We may wonder what is the problem which has produced Paul's strong condemnation of these teachings. After all, asceticism has had a long and (often) honourable record in the history of the church. Jesus spoke of marriage being impossible or undesirable for some (Mt. 19:10-12) and Paul's own recommendation to the Corinthians was the state of singleness (1 Cor. 7:8). Why now should he speak in such damning terms about teaching which forbids marriage? We might also think of passages where Paul recommended abstaining from certain foods (Rom. 14:15, 21, 1 Cor. 8:13).

The answer to these questions and the issue here seems to be the compulsory and rigid nature of the prohibitions which the false teachers wanted to enforce. Asceticism as a voluntary practice is one thing, but to make it an absolute demand on all believers is something different and cannot be justified. Similarly, abstinence (whether from marriage or from foods) under certain conditions and for particular reasons is one thing, but to make such demands a general requirement under any and all conditions is not the same. It is likely that at Ephesus a lifestyle involving these sorts of demands was being promoted as the *necessary* way to a higher spirituality, and though this is not actually mentioned in the text it would help to explain why Paul's response is so strong.

Another factor is mentioned as Paul's reason for objecting to what was being taught. The things prohibited (marriage and foods) are all part of God's created order, and as such come under the verdict of *very good* (Gen. 1:31). Marriage, though not in a strict sense a 'created thing', was instituted by God at the very beginning, while Adam and Eve were still in the garden and before the appearance of sin. Though on a strict grammatical interpretation the word *which* in 4:3 refers only to *foods*, it seems unnecessary to limit the remarks of 4:3b-5 to food alone. Paul is attacking teaching which made false assertions about marriage as well as food, and it is likely that he intends his comments in the remainder of the paragraph to refer to both.[59]

While not a necessary part of an ascetic approach to life, asceticism has often been linked with the attitude that the material world is evil and the truly spiritual person will avoid contact with the material as much as possible. On this understanding it is to one's spiritual benefit to reject the material (such as marriage and foods). There may indeed be benefit in ascetic practices, for some people at least, and perhaps for others in a limited way under specified circumstances, but an outright rejection of the material as a necessary part of the true spiritual life for all involves a false view of God's creation.

[59] This is recognized by Knight, *Pastorals*, 190, and Johnson, *Timothy*, 240. To insist on a strict grammatical interpretation is doubtful when one recognizes that the grammar of this sentence is weak (the word *demand* is not in the Greek and has been added by NRSV to complete the sense). In regard to the relative clause beginning with *which*, if Paul intended this clause to refer to marriage as well as foods, it is hard to see what other form of the relative pronoun he could have used.

From the second part of 4:3 onwards Paul goes on to the front foot by presenting a very positive picture of the created order. To begin (4:3b), he claims that the things rejected by the false teachers (marriage and foods) were created by God to be used. Creation is not merely to be observed and admired, but to be received and used. Later (6:17) Paul speaks about the enjoyment of what God has provided. The necessary condition from our side is an attitude of *thanksgiving*, which may mean a *prayer* of thanksgiving, as at meals, but there is no need to limit the thanksgiving to a ritual prayer; what is necessary is a general attitude of thanksgiving. (For a similar point, see 1 Cor. 10:30.) Other people (unbelievers) may have their own different perspectives, but this is the appropriate perspective for *believers*, those who *know the truth*, in this context especially the truth presented in Genesis 1-2 about the goodness of God's creation and his intention that it be used and enjoyed.

Continuing the same theme in 4:4, the same point is made, but this time not with reference only to the issues of marriage and food but to *every* item within God's creation. What God has made is automatically good, and in fact *nothing is to be rejected*, again with the condition of *thanksgiving*. Thus, the positive statement of 4:3 is made even more strongly here by being generalized. This clearly is to be taken as *generally* true, not necessarily absolutely true in every circumstance. There may be contextual factors which can and should limit what one should do or eat (as pointed out in the apostolic decree of Acts 15:19-20, and as illustrated in the situation at Corinth in 1 Corinthians 10:23).

The final verse of the paragraph (4:5) offers an explanation of what *receiving with thanksgiving* means. Paul speaks of the good things of God's creation being *sanctified*. There are two things which bring about this sanctification. One is the *word of God*, which perhaps simply means that scripture has declared the created order to be very good (Gen. 1:31). The second is *prayer*. The Greek word used here more commonly means *intercession*, which hardly fits the context here. The context, rather, suggests a thanksgiving prayer. In a sense that would repeat what has already been said about thanksgiving (4:3-4), but the fresh detail would be that the thanksgiving is expressed in *prayer*, which has not been previously specified (though perhaps implied). These two things (God's specific statement about his creation and the human response of thanksgiving) remove any hint that things belonging to the material created order are in some way evil or harmful. In this way they are set apart for the use which God intended.

Reflection: The Deeper Spiritual Life

The comments on the opening verses of chapter 4 have raised the problem of extra requirements being placed on believers in order that they may come into a deeper experience of the Christian life. In many places in India annual conventions have become a tradition, such as the Maramon Convention, or local forms of the famous English Keswick Convention, or many other conventions arranged by mission agencies for their missionaries and supporters or by other Christian associations. Many can testify of wonderful, life-changing blessing received at such conventions, through the ministry of the word of God, the testimony of God's servants working in the field, and fellowship with believers outside one's regular congregation. The author has also enjoyed such blessing on many occasions and has spoken at such conventions, so the following comments should not be understood as criticism of the convention movement as such.

One of the features of some conventions is the call to experience the deeper spiritual life. This too is not in itself a bad thing, but there are dangers. One danger is that it is not always clear what is meant by the deeper spiritual life. It is a fine-sounding phrase but all depends on what it is intended to mean.

One suspects that those who promoted the teaching reflected in 1 Timothy 4:3 would have felt very comfortable with 'deeper spiritual life' language, their point being that to experience a deeper spirituality you need to go further than merely accepting the simple gospel preached by people like Paul and Timothy. In their case it was through ascetic practices that you could make further progress and experience deeper spiritual satisfaction.

Such teaching is very tempting, for there is not one of us who does not need to grow in our Christian walk. But it is easy in the emotional atmosphere of a convention meeting for a speaker to sow seeds of discontent, which leaves us open to accept the solution they offer without too much critical reflection. The solution may be some form of 'second blessing' or a new method of prayer or a programme of meditation.

Paul was confronted with the same basic issue when he wrote his earlier letter to the Colossians. There he insisted that a basic faith in Christ, worked out in an appropriate moral and ethical lifestyle, is the totality of the Christian experience. There is no higher spirituality which in some sense moves beyond Christ. Christ is everything. Teaching which threatens to put Christ into a secondary position or perhaps relegate him to merely the kindergarten stage of the spiritual life calls forth the strongest reaction from Paul. Colossians 2:16-19 deals with asceticism in this context.

The call to the deeper spiritual life is fine when it is a call to know Christ more fully and to follow him with a greater commitment. Paul writes of his own passion for such growth in Philippians 3:7-16. But when it becomes a call to try some new method which is offered as the key to your sense of stagnation in the Christian life, be careful, especially if it is implied that no one in the 2,000 year history of Christianity has been clever enough to think of this before but that now at last the crucial key has been found.

The Work of Leadership in the Church

In the remaining verses of the chapter the topic seems to change, from condemnation of the false teaching to Timothy's life and work. However, these two things are not really two different subjects, but opposite sides of the same coin, which can be described as positive and negative approaches to the Christian life. He has already (4:1-5) described the negative, pointing out that the way of compulsory asceticism is no true Christian life at all but is in fact contrary to the doctrine of the goodness of creation as the work of God. (As we have observed, this does not rule out voluntary asceticism, for particular reasons and especially for limited periods.)

The remaining part of the chapter shows how believers can be encouraged to approach the Christian life positively. The leader must give proper guidance and set the example, which is why Timothy's life and work is highlighted here. We can divide the material into two sub-points: Timothy's work as a leader (in this section) and his character (in the next).

To begin with, Timothy must teach the truth. The new paragraph begins on this note (4:6), with Timothy reminded of his responsibility to instruct the other members of the church in the matters about which Paul has been writing. Paul is not writing for Timothy's benefit alone but so that he may communicate this important teaching to others. *These instructions* are literally *these things*, a phrase which occurs three times in this chapter (4:6, 11, 15), referring back to what has just been discussed or in 4:6 possibly to the teaching of all the letter to this point.[60]

---

[60] So Mounce, *Pastorals*, 248.

The focus on teaching continues to the end of the chapter. Teaching is mentioned again in 4:11, 13, 16. In 4:11, for example, Timothy is instructed to *insist on and teach these things*. So it is very clear that teaching is one of Timothy's basic tasks as leader of the church.

One of the bishop's tasks is teaching (3:2) and, as we will see later, elders (or some of them at least) have the same responsibility (5:17). We can hardly fail to see that teaching the truth is an absolutely necessary aspect of leadership in the church. It is difficult for the church to be the *pillar and bulwark of the truth* (3:15) unless the members of the church are instructed in the truth. Without regular and adequate teaching in the church, the fundamental importance of the truth can very easily be forgotten, and false teaching can fill the vacuum. That is Paul's concern here, that false teaching, no doubt dressed up in an attractive form but in reality nothing more than *profane myths and old wives' tales* (4:7), might gain a credibility which it does not deserve. Timothy is to reject such myths and tales, by not teaching them or allowing others to teach them and by not wasting his own time on them. He has better nourishment available to him.

The terms used in 4:13 alongside *teaching* are worth reflecting on. One is the *reading*. What is meant here is the *public reading of scripture* (as paraphrased in several modern translations). Further comment about this is given in one of the subsequent reflection sections. The other word in this verse is (literally) *exhortation* (NRSV *exhorting*). The translation *preaching* (NIV, TNIV) is not so helpful, for we tend to understand this word to mean the particular style of formal speaking with which we are familiar in our own church. The translation *exhortation* accurately conveys the essential idea here, that the ministry of the word is not a purely abstract or academic exercise. To exhort means to use the word of God to encourage the hearers to live the Christian life more adequately, which should always be the ultimate aim of a public speaking ministry. Whether *exhortation* and *teaching* can be sharply distinguished as two different activities is doubtful.[61] If a distinction is intended, it may be that teaching focuses on the theological content of what is said and its systematic presentation and exhortation on the personal and practical application of what is taught.

The following verse (4:14) reminds Timothy of the gift (Greek *charisma*) which was given to him. In the comments on 1:18 we have

---

[61] Towner, *Timothy-Titus* (1994), 110-111, has a helpful discussion.

already looked at some of the issues to do with Timothy's call to ministry and his being set aside (ordained, if you like) for his work; see also the comments later on 2 Timothy 1:6. What is of interest here is the call not to *neglect* the gift. We should not jump to the conclusion that Paul felt that Timothy was in danger of falling by the wayside, but it is certainly possible that this sort of thing can happen. Not every student who begins a Bible college course with great passion and enthusiasm actually continues into the hard challenges of Christian ministry, and not every minister who begins his or her work with great hopes and expectations perseveres when the going gets tough. When things do get tough, it is good to be reminded that the capacity to fulfil one's ministry depends not on one's own strength but on the gift God has given.

Another vital aspect of Timothy's responsibility as a leader is that his life must be an example (4:12). A leader's teaching work is very important. But if he is not a good example, no one will listen and his teaching will be fruitless. This is a theme of some importance in this chapter, and we look more fully at this in the section which follows.

The Character of a Church Leader

At the very beginning of this section (4:6), after reminding Timothy that he must instruct others in the matters about which he is writing, Paul makes it clear that the teaching is not just a weapon for Timothy to use on others but something to be applied to himself. He can hardly teach others unless he himself is *nourished on the words of the faith and of the sound teaching*. The truth is to be the Christian leader's nourishment, that which feeds his soul. Without the conviction which comes from a regular diet of such spiritual food a leader's ministry will lack spiritual power. In contrast to this positive nourishment is set the *profane myths and old wives' tales* which Timothy must *avoid* (4:7). We are not told what these were, but this appears to refer in a general way to the false teaching which was being promoted at Ephesus (*myths* have already been mentioned in 1:4). With what does Timothy fill his mind? This is a question of crucial importance, not only for Timothy but for all Christian leaders. It is surely not necessary to add that the purpose of such food is not only to feed the minister's intellect but to mould his or her life; see the above comment on *exhortation* in 4:13.

So, alongside the theme of teaching is the importance of the minister's own personal life. Paul's instruction is not only *teach others* but *train yourself* (4:7): *train yourself in godliness*. The noun *godliness* (as well as related verbs and adjectives) is a characteristic word in the PE, already in 2:2 and 3:16, and further examples in 1 Timothy in 4:8, 6:3, 5, 6, 11. It usually refers to the *practical expression of religion*, in terms of a life that is focused on God and aims to please him.

Godliness is set in contrast with physical training. The latter is not to be despised, for it does have benefit. Perhaps some today would want to argue that physical exercise is of very great value, especially for people whose normal daily work is of a non-physical kind. But Paul would no doubt still insist that relatively speaking physical training is only of small value compared with training in godliness. This, he says, is *valuable in every way* (4:8), for its benefits extend to the *life to come* as well as the *present life* (4:8).[62] The statement here should not be understood as promoting a doctrine of salvation by works, nor a prosperity gospel which says that doing God's will guarantees material rewards of all sorts. There is no such guarantee in the Bible, though it is right to say that that only those who live a God-pleasing life can hope to receive God's blessing, a truth which is taught throughout the Bible, New Testament as well as Old.

Characteristics of Timothy's personal life are again mentioned in 4:12. This verse begins with mention of his youthfulness. By this time Timothy had had considerable experience in ministry, accompanying Paul on many of his travels and serving as a trusted colleague. He was no mere child but may have been 30 to 35 years old. Nevertheless, to some at Ephesus this would seem quite young, and so Paul encourages Timothy not to let anyone *despise* his *youth*. This is easier said than done, but Paul immediately says how it can be done, namely by being an *example* to the *believers*. Setting a high standard in his own life is the best way for Timothy to demonstrate his Christian maturity and his suitability for leadership, and so deflect any possible criticism of his relatively young age. Here is a word of encouragement and advice to the Timothys of our own time. It is also a word to churches who have a relatively young man or woman in a significant ministry position - a word not to give them a hard time merely because they are younger than many in the congregation.

---

[62] According to most (e.g., Kelly, *Pastorals*, 101; Fee, *Timothy-Titus*, 104-105; Knight, *Pastorals*, 198; Marshall, *Pastorals*, 554; Towner, *Timothy-Titus* (2006), 308-309; Witherington, *Commentary*, 256) this statement (that is, 4:8) is the trustworthy saying referred to in 4:9, though 4:10 (or 4:10b) is also possible (Mounce, *Pastorals*, 247-248).

One might sincerely hope that there are no ministers of the gospel who adopt the attitude, 'Do as I say, not as I do.' If the gospel message and its implications are not demonstrated in the life of a Christian leader, the message loses its credibility. If there is no visible example from the leadership, one can hardly expect believers to guess what it means to live the Christian life. Nor can one expect that the rank and file of church members will live by a higher standard than their leaders.

Five words spell out the areas in which Timothy is expected to set an example. *In speech* is literally *in word*, here probably not limited to the words spoken in the context of preaching or teaching but including all that Timothy says. A preacher might be very good in the professional speaking role, showing great eloquence and rhetorical skill, but at the same time very bitter or sarcastic or angry in personal conversation. *Conduct* hardly needs any explanation, a word covering the whole of Timothy's manner of life. *In love, in faith, in purity* describe further basics of the Christian life. *Love* and *faith* have already been mentioned together in this letter (see 1:5, 2:15), and are linked in many other places (such as the well-known 1 Cor. 13:13). *Purity* should perhaps not be restricted to purity in sexual matters but it certainly includes this aspect of life, a point specifically made in 5:2 which instructs Timothy regarding his conduct towards younger women; see also 5:22.

Finally, we have a summary in 4:16: *pay attention to yourself and to your teaching.* According to this NRSV translation the last phrase implies *the teaching you do,* that is, Timothy's *ministry* of teaching. This interpretation is assumed by most commentators, and there is no doubt that the passage as a whole emphasizes the need for Timothy to teach. But in fact the word *your* is not in the Greek (which is literally *attend to the teaching*), and the meaning could equally *be attend to your study of the teaching and its application to your own life.*[63] This would fit in with the opening verse of this section (4:6, where the same word *teaching* occurs), and thus emphasize again the absolute importance of Timothy setting a good example by applying the gospel to his own life before he presumes to tell others how they should live. A further command is to *continue in these things,* a reminder of the need to persevere and not be tempted to give up when things become difficult. It is only by such attention and

---

[63] This possible interpretation is recognized by Marshall, *Pastorals*, 571; Towner, *Timothy-Titus* (2006), 327.

perseverance that Timothy can expect to experience salvation as well as to be the channel by which salvation comes to others. What Paul now says to Timothy he had already said to himself, for when writing to the Corinthians (1 Cor. 9:27) he had expressed the concern that even after preaching to others he himself might be disqualified. He was conscious of the need of a high level of personal discipline in living the Christian life.

Reflection: The Nourishment of a Leader

There is a common understanding that a Christian minister is on duty 24 hours a day every day, without exception. The author has met very few Indians involved in full-time pastoral ministry who can say that they consistently take one day off per week. This problem arises partly from congregational expectations, which often mean that, though we say that our minister should have adequate rest and refreshment, we also expect that he should always be available when we decide to call him. The other part of the problem may arise from the pastor's own psychological need to be needed and the feeling that people will think poorly of him if he is not available to meet every request, no matter how small it may be.

This passage (4:6-16) speaks of the proper nourishment of a Christian leader. There is necessary spiritual nourishment: he or she must be nourished on the words of the faith and of the sound teaching (4:6). This instruction can be applied in different ways. It surely will mean as an absolute essential that the minister takes time to grow in his or her own faith, applying the word of God to their own life. Taking time is a key phrase here. It does take time even to do simple things like reading the Bible and praying on a regular (daily) basis. But simple Bible reading is not enough, for a leader whose role is to teach and to guide the affairs of the congregation as a whole and each believer individually needs to reflect on the implications of the Bible passage in order to find appropriate ways to apply it in the present-day situation. As one listens to sermons, one wonders how much time is actually spent doing this, for many sermons consist of little more than platitudes, fine-sounding words which add up to very little meaning and hardly any challenge regarding how the listeners might respond in practical terms.

Adequate spiritual nourishment should also include regular reading. How sad that many theological graduates have hardly read 10 pages of theological literature since their graduation from seminary. Reading and study is not only for the person doing so-called higher studies, but is the only way to train oneself to think theologically about the issues of the day. Without this the preacher will hardly be capable of doing more than repeating the same tired old clichés which the congregation has heard 100 times before. If it is difficult to find good books or for an individual pastor to afford the cost of many books, groups of pastors can organize themselves to buy copies which can be distributed among themselves, or the same can be done by diocesan or regional church authorities. Whatever it takes, pastors, don't allow yourselves to become theologically brain-dead. This result will mean that you have lost your capacity to guide your congregation adequately in an ever-changing world.

A word about the internet may be appropriate. Much material is available on the internet but it needs to be used with great care. For one thing, it can hardly be a good thing if all of a pastor's sermons are taken from the internet. A pastor who does this is not preaching his or her own sermons but someone else's. Even if the material is good, it is most likely that the sermon will not come from the pastor's heart. An internet sermon may solve an occasional problem when you have had an impossibly busy and stressful week, but don't be tempted to take this short-cut too often. Another issue is that you cannot assume that everything that appears on the internet is orthodox and reliable. Material printed in a book or a reputable magazine has been examined by others, but the internet allows any individual to promote their own weird and wonderful ideas, without the benefit of an editor's wisdom. The internet is potentially a wonderfully useful resource but it needs to be used carefully.

Another aspect of a pastor's self-nourishment relates to physical well-being. Paul writes of physical training as having less value than training in godliness (4:8) but he does not say that it has no value at all. Indeed, the opposite is the case. We may make jokes about the pastor looking rather 'prosperous' these days, but it is no joke to see a pastor who does not take exercise, eats too much and is grossly overweight. Pastoral ministry causes emotional and spiritual stress in any case, and so it is absolutely essential that the pastor does not add the stress of his or her own poor physical condition. Appropriate physical exercise can play an important role in prolonging one's ministry. It may not always be easy to find a convenient time or place but it is no less important because of challenges like these. Mention has already been made of taking adequate time away from the job. Yes, it is a job, as well as a calling, and we can hardly imagine that God intended to exempt pastors when he wrote into his created order the principle of one day of rest in seven. Even Moses needed some relief from the burden of his duties (Exod. 18:18) and if Moses could take some time off God is well able to do without our labours for a few hours.

Reflection: Reading of Scripture

Our passage mentions the importance of the public reading of scripture (4:13). This is not discussed as though it is a matter of controversy but is mentioned in an incidental way, a reminder to Timothy of something which he already knew and accepted. Whether it is known and accepted in many Indian churches is a different question.

Mainline churches which follow a liturgical tradition have regular Bible reading built into their service structures. Thus, for the service of the Lord's Supper there is an OT reading and two NT readings, with the possibility of a psalm also. However, there are a number of questions which may be raised. Are the readings done well? When the reading is given to someone as they arrive for the service, there is a strong possibility that it will not be well read, especially if the person's language ability (in English or whatever the language of the service) is limited and if they do not understand the meaning of the passage (which is very likely in many cases). Is sufficient scripture covered? Some liturgical churches follow a three-year cycle of readings, after which they return to the beginning and start all over again. This means that many parts of the Bible are never read in church. Are church members able to gain a systematic knowledge of the Bible through the liturgical readings? The usual lectionary patterns are not systematic: one week the epistle reading may be from Galatians, the next week from James, and so on, and there is no opportunity to follow a book through from beginning to end. These are matters which ministers in charge of churches and the wider leadership of mainline churches could profitably look into.

Sadly, however, there are some churches where the Bible is hardly read at all. Sometimes the reading may be no more than one or two verses which are to be used as the basis of the sermon. This is likely to happen in churches which most strongly defend the inspiration and authority of the Bible, and yet their practice tells a contrary story. If the Bible is not given a central place in the Sunday service, it is hardly surprising that church members receive the message that it is not really as important as their leaders say it is.

The author's own practice in ministry (when pastor of a church in a mainline, liturgical tradition) was to include at least two substantial readings in every service, one OT and one NT. One was the passage for the sermon (but not just one or two verses), nearly always systematically working through a book of the OT or NT. The other reading was from the other Testament, again working through a book (a chapter each week, or less if it was a long chapter). In a ministry of 12 years in the one church this meant that all the NT was read (some parts many times) and much of the OT.

God our Saviour

Before we leave chapter 4 let us take a moment to look at the statement about God in 4:10. In 1:1 and 2:3, God is described as Saviour. But what is interesting here is that God is said to be the *Saviour of all people*.[64] In 2:3 it is stated that it is God's *desire* for all to be saved but not that all *will* in fact be saved. It is also unlikely that our present verse means that all will actually be saved, which would contradict the entire message of the NT that it is only through faith in Christ that a person can be saved.

The sense is probably that God's saving work is for all. No one is excluded from the possibility of benefitting from that work. Jesus *gave himself a ransom for all* (2:6). All come within the scope of the work of God in Christ. But as the last words of 4:10 indicate, there is a difference between *all people* and *those who believe*. We might put it like this: all people *can* be saved (and in that sense God is Saviour of all, providing the possibility of salvation for all) but only believers *will* be saved (because they alone have taken the necessary step of faith).[65]

The fact that salvation in the PE always refers to spiritual salvation (unless 2:15 is considered to be an exception) makes it unlikely that *Saviour* here means two different things: preserver of all in a general sense (the giver of life and so on) but the provider of spiritual salvation for those who believe.[66]

1 Timothy 5:1-16

Appropriate Behaviour Towards Different Groups

Chapter 5 begins a new section of the letter, in which Paul turns from general instructions about Timothy's personal life and his work in ministry to specific instructions for different groups in the church.

The opening two verses give quite brief instructions which virtually cover all adult members of a church: older and younger men, and older and younger women. Paul does not tell us the actual ages of *older* and *younger*, and it is not necessary for us to know. These are simply terms to describe people of all ages. Timothy can use his commonsense to decide who (for him) is older and who is younger. The main point is that though

---

[64] For the possibility (not accepted by most) that this statement is the faithful saying referred to in 4:9, see Mounce, *Pastorals*, 247-248.

[65] So Fee, *Timothy-Titus*, 106; Towner, *Timothy-Titus* (2006), 311-312.

[66] This is suggested by Barrett, *Pastorals*, 70; Guthrie, *Pastorals* (1957), 108. It is discussed and rejected by Knight, *Pastorals*, 203; Witherington, *Commentary*, 257.

it is necessary to treat all believers with honour (1 Pet. 2:17), there will be different approaches for people of different ages.

Behaviour towards an *older man* is dealt with first. The word used here (*presbyteros*) is found a few verses later (5:17), but the context makes it clear that here it has a general application to men in an older age bracket, whereas in 5:17 it has a more specific reference to those who hold the office of elder in the church. Negatively, Timothy must not *speak harshly to* (NIV *rebuke harshly*) an older man, that is, he is to show him the respect due to his age. The positive command is to *exhort him as a father*. Here NRSV has simply *speak*, but something more is meant by the word that is used: *exhort* or *encourage* or even *instruct*. Paul is speaking not merely about general conversation, but about Timothy's task of leadership. (The same verb is not repeated but is implied for all the other three groups mentioned in these two verses: Paul has in mind Timothy's duty of exhorting or instructing men and women of all age groups.)

Paul recognizes that there may be times when a hard word needs to be spoken to an older man. The phrase *exhort him as a father* combines the element of courageously dealing with the issue (not running away from what might be a difficult confrontation) with proper respect to one who is perhaps much older than Timothy. One might suggest that in a normal family a son *never* instructs his father, but in the Christian family (the church) a spiritual responsibility is given to leaders to perform such difficult tasks when necessary.

A leader who has to face such situations with older men in the congregation may be tempted to treat *younger men* with some contempt. But by using the word *brothers* Paul reminds Timothy that the church is the *household of God* (3:15), a family whose members treat each other, young and old alike, with proper respect. In a healthy family, family members do not abuse each other but are fiercely loyal and absolutely supportive, even when a word of rebuke or correction may be needed.

The second verse speaks of women, older and younger. *Older women* are to be treated as *mothers*, not only when things are going along smoothly but also when necessary instruction is to be given. Similarly, *younger women* are to be treated as *sisters*. In the case of younger women special importance is placed on the necessity for a male leader to behave with complete *purity*. Paul is realistic enough to know the temptations that might face someone of Timothy's age when he is dealing with young and attractive women.

The Duty of the Church Towards Widows

The following fourteen verses give directions about the treatment of widows (5:3-16). It has been suggested by some scholars that the passage is referring to a ministerial 'order' of widows to whom certain duties in the church were given.[67] There is evidence of such an order in the later history of the church,[68] but that is not sufficient reason to interpret this passage in such a way. There is nothing in these verses that demands this interpretation, and in fact no hint of any specific duties in the church which the widows discussed here were expected to perform.

In that day and age there was no government provision for people such as widows, and certainly no insurance or pension arrangements. Widows were entirely dependent on others for their support, unless they were young enough to remarry (which was at least a more likely option than it is for many widows in contemporary India).

This need required some action on the part of the church, such as we find in the book of Acts early in the church's history, when a perceived inequality in the distribution made to widows in the Jerusalem church led to the famous appointment of the seven (Acts 6:1).

It is this same issue which is in Paul's mind here. The passage begins (5:3) with instructions about the widows who were to be *honoured*. At first sight this might be taken to mean simply respect for widows, but there are several reasons why this is not the meaning. First, it is only *some* widows who are to receive this honour (5:3), whereas we would expect *all* widows to be treated with respect. Second, the purpose of excluding some widows is to avoid a burden on the church (5:16), a clear indication that some sort of material support is the issue. Third, we find the word *honour* used again in the next paragraph (5:17), in the section about elders, where the following verse (5:18) shows again that support of a material kind is in mind.

Since support for widows was already being undertaken very early in the church's life, we may assume that Paul is not telling Timothy to

---

[67] So Kelly, *Pastorals*, 112.
[68] See Mounce, *Pastorals*, 300-302.

begin something new at Ephesus. Rather, he is tackling problems that must have arisen in administering such a scheme.

The widows who are to receive such *honour* from the church, or in plain language financial or other material support, are described as those *who are really widows* (5:3). This does not mean that there were women who were only *pretending* to be widows, but it stands in contrast with other types of widows, who are also mentioned in the passage and will be considered in the following sections of these comments. But for now we focus on these 'real' widows and note the several qualifications that Paul mentions.

The first requirement is that she is someone *left alone* (5:5), not just without a husband but absolutely without anyone from whom she can reasonably expect assistance. In these circumstances her hope is entirely on God, to whom she turns continually to meet her daily needs (5:5). Again, this does not mean that other widows do not have a proper hope in God. In fact, all believers are expected to put their hope in God (4:10, 6:17). But the 'real' widow does so with a more desperate and immediate sense of need.

A second requirement is an age limitation (5:9): she must be at least 60 years of age. There might be two reasons for such an age. One is that she would certainly be too old at that age to remarry (as recommended in 5:14 where possible), and another that she may also be too old to support herself by her own work. Although there were cases in the ancient world of people living to an advanced age, generally speaking someone was considered to be very old at the age of 60.

A third point comes in the same verse (5:9) and can be literally translated the *wife of one husband*. NRSV says *married only once*, and if this is the sense the point may be that a widow who had been married more than once would surely have some living relative who could care for her. But perhaps NIV captures the sense better with *faithful to her husband*. In this case it becomes irrelevant how many times she had been married, as long as she had remained faithful within marriage. It is certainly clear from 5:14 that there was no prejudice against a second marriage (for a woman who had been widowed).

Fourth, we note the several activities listed in 5:10 which in modern terms might be described as items which should appear on the widow's CV. To take this as a list of duties to be performed by those enrolled in an order of widows[69] is to go beyond what the text indicates. The verse begins by saying that *she must be well attested for her good works*, which is virtually a heading for the list that follows, drawing attention not only to her good works but to the need for a good reputation or testimony. She must have *brought up children*. This could mean her own children, but in that case they must have all since died (as she has no one to care for her at present). Or it could mean the orphaned children of other parents. The widow who now seeks support from others should have shown a willingness in the past to help those in similar desperate need. She should have *shown hospitality*, a requirement also of bishops as we have seen (3:2), not meaning entertaining friends in her home but providing accommodation for travelling believers who were visiting Ephesus. This reference to hospitality may explain why the next item is that she should have *washed the saints' feet*, as this would be one of the first needs of a traveller who had been walking dusty or muddy roads. Also, she should have *helped the afflicted*, which need not be limited to the affliction of persecution but possibly also includes the general afflictions of life. The final phrase in this verse returns to a more general description, requiring that she has *devoted herself to doing good in every way*. Here, we might suggest, is the main point of the verse: she should be the sort of person who has not only done all kinds of good to others, but who has taken the initiative to find opportunities to act in this way. The preceding phrases are not to be taken legalistically; for example, it would be harsh to penalize a widow who had not raised children if she had not had the opportunity to do so. Rather, they are examples of the sort of life the deserving widow should have lived. All the examples speak of unselfish care and concern for others. That is the basic criterion which Timothy should look for.

5:9 mentions a *list* of widows. It is not necessary to draw the conclusion that this implies a formal order of widows. In fact, it need not even mean a written list at all but could simply be a list of names in the minds of the church leaders. The Greek word translated *put on the list* could also be translated as simply *selected*.[70] The point is basically the identification of those for whom the church has a responsibility to provide support. The nature of the list (if there was an actual list) is a secondary matter.

---

[69] As does Kelly, *Pastorals*, 115-116.
[70] For possible meanings, see Marshall, *Pastorals*, 591-592.

The Duty of the Family Towards Widows

It has been noted that the church does not have the responsibility of caring for *all* widows. It is only those who have no other means of support that the church must help. This means, among other things, that if there are children and grandchildren they must provide for their widowed mother or grandmother. This point is made three times in the passage (5:4, 8, 16), though each verse has its own difficulties of interpretation.

The first reference is 5:4. The phrase *they should first learn* is slightly ambiguous, because it is not specifically stated who is meant by *they*. We take it to mean the *children* and *grandchildren* just mentioned. Another ambiguity is the *parents* (which could also be translated more generally *ancestors*), most likely the ancestors of the children or grandchildren, including of course a widowed mother or grandmother. An alternate understanding is that *they* means the widows (a singular verb would have made this clearer, i.e., *she should first learn*),[71] with the *parents* the deceased ancestors of the widow.

The most likely sense is that children and grandchildren must show appropriate honour and respect by providing for the needs of their widowed mother or grandmother. There may be a hint that some families avoided this responsibility by diverting their assets in other directions; in Mark 7:10-12 we find Jesus' criticism of a similar attitude. The alternate interpretation is that widows must show gratitude for the care they had received from their parents (and grandparents) by caring for their own offspring. However, this would involve a change of theme; Paul's concern in this passage is how widows should be cared for, and so the first suggestion is to be preferred.

Again there are complications in the second reference (5:8). First, who is meant by *whoever* (NIV *anyone*)? In line with our preferred understanding of 5:4, it probably means anyone in the category of children or grandchildren, though it could mean *any widow*, in line with the alternate interpretation of that verse. Also, the meaning of the words translated *relatives* and *family members* is not as clear as we might wish. The second certainly means *members of one's household*, but to whom then does the first refer? The word itself means simply *one's own* (as in NASB

---

[71] This is the view of some earlier scholars. A singular verb is in fact the reading of at least one very late Greek manuscript though not at all likely to be the original text. See Towner, *Timothy-Titus* (2006), 339 note 35.

his own), which most translations interpret to mean *relatives* (presumably intended to refer to the extended family).

The person who does not provide for their own family is said to have *denied the faith*. We may wonder why this particular act (or failure to act) should be regarded so seriously. Some scholars consider it not to be so serious, and so claim that "it cannot refer to apostasy".[72] Yet a similar comment is made about the Cretans who deny God by their actions (Tit. 1:16), so that there is a consistency in the PE in condemning behaviour which is deliberately disobedient to what is known to be God's will. It *is* equivalent to apostasy.[73] Perhaps the issue here is a blatant rejection of the command to honour one's parents (Exod. 20:12, Deut. 5:16). Again, in regard to the last words of the verse, we may ask why such a believer should be *worse than an unbeliever*. The *same* as an unbeliever might seem harsh enough, but why *worse*? Perhaps it is because unbelievers do not treat their needy parents in this way. But even if they do, what makes the believer worse is that he or she is rejecting the known will of God (whereas an unbeliever might be excused on the grounds of ignorance).

Finally we come to 5:16. The general point seems to be the same as in the other two passages, but here again there are some details which provoke questions. First, it is the *believing woman* who is given the responsibility. It is interesting to note that some NT manuscripts have the masculine form *believer* (which according to Greek usage could refer to either a male or a female believer), while others have *male or female believer*, expanding the phrase to include both a masculine and a feminine form. There is little probability that these variations represent the original text (which is the one translated in NRSV, NIV and others), but they do reveal the discomfort which some ancient interpreters felt at this point. But before we accuse Paul of having a sexist attitude, perhaps there is nothing more here than recognizing the practical reality that the burden of care for a widowed relative would normally fall on a woman. A second detail is the plural *widows*, which suggests that a believing woman might have more than one widowed relative to care for. This could include a widowed mother-in-law in addition to the woman's own widowed

---

[72] Mounce, *Pastorals*, 285.
[73] So Towner, *Timothy-Titus* (2006), 344-345.

mother, or her widowed grandmother or sister. We can only guess what circumstances Paul had in mind.

Despite some uncertainty in the details, the general point is clear enough: *let her assist them*. And the reason (or at least one of the reasons) for doing so is equally clear: *let the church not be burdened*. No church has unlimited resources, and it seems that the church at Ephesus was no exception. Whatever resources a church does have must be used for genuine need, in this context *so that it can assist those who are real widows*. Those who can be supported in other ways should be so supported. Those who have genuine need and no other resources should not be deprived of assistance because of the greed or selfishness of those who do not strictly need to be helped or because of careless management by church leaders.

Real Widows and Other Kinds of Widows

Three times in this passage we find the phrase *real widow(s)* (5:3, 5, 16). We have already noted that this does *not* mean that some widows were frauds, pretending to be widowed when in fact they were not. What it does mean is shown by contrast with three other types of widows.

First, the *real widow* is in contrast to one who has others to help and provide for her. If a widow is not *left alone* (5:5) she is not a real widow, for the purpose of church assistance.

Another contrast is presented in 5:6 where Paul talks about the woman *who lives for pleasure*. (The word *widow* is not in the text. It is likely, as most translations assume, that this is implied. But even as a general statement about a certain type of woman, it would include any widow that fitted the description.) This woman is a seeker of pleasure, who enjoys and focuses on the luxuries of life, not necessarily in ways that are immoral but certainly in ways that are not appropriate for a believer. It must be assumed that she is a woman with resources, which would be enough reason not to include her among the widows who are to be helped by the church. But that is not the main point of this verse.

We have here (as in 5:8 on which we have commented already) a very severe condemnation. Though such a woman is alive she is already dead. This can only mean that she is *spiritually* dead; whatever may be her outward profession and church affiliation, she is not a true believer.

What does Paul mean? In the light of positive comments about receiving the good things of God's creation with thanksgiving (4:3-5) it can hardly mean that a person who enjoys some of the luxuries of life is disqualified from being a believer. Yet there is no condemnation of this sort of woman other than that she *lives for pleasure*. It would appear that her life is so focused on pleasure-seeking that God is virtually forgotten. She stands in stark contrast to the real widow of the previous verse who *has set her hope on God*. It does not necessarily follow that a person with some resources to be enjoyed cannot have a genuine hope in God, but this verse is a reminder of the extra challenge that comes to the wealthy and how easy it is for material resources to become our master rather than our servant, and for our rightful Master to be ignored. Jesus, of course, had some strong words to say on this very subject (e.g., Mt. 6:24, Mk 10:23).

The third contrast is found in 5:11-15, where instructions are given about *younger widows*. The basic guideline is that these are not to be considered eligible for help from the church (5:11a). In support of this Paul mentions (a) problems that arise when these widows are given support (5:11b-13, 15), and (b) the alternative that is available to them (5:14).

Several problems are mentioned. First are *their sensual desires* because of which they *want to marry* (5:11). It is not at all likely that Paul is condemning sexual urges as such, which he knows are part of normal sexuality (e.g., 1 Cor. 7:3). He certainly does not disapprove of marriage, which he firmly recommends in 5:14 (see also 4:3, as well as passages in several of his earlier letters). The problem in this present case is that their urges *alienate them from Christ*.

The reason why this is so is that to marry is to break a *pledge* that they have made (5:12). We can only speculate about what precisely was happening in the church at Ephesus, but the following is a reasonable reconstruction. The assumption may have been that widows seeking the church's support were acknowledging that they had no other option and as part of the arrangement they pledged themselves to Christ in an absolute way, including the commitment not to remarry. This was the *first pledge*. If, however, circumstances changed and the widow did remarry, that involved a second pledge (to her new husband), thus breaking the first and being alienated from Christ. The problem with which Paul is dealing is that younger widows were very likely to want to remarry, and the way to avoid the problem was to prevent them making the first pledge.

The very serious nature of all this is further stressed in 5:15, where we read that *some have already turned away to follow Satan*. The fear expressed in 5:11 has already become a reality in some cases. This is probably not a conscious and deliberate following of Satan, but even if not a deliberate choice that is the effect of their breaking their oath to give themselves completely to Christ. To break an oath of that sort is to hand oneself over to Satan. Again, Paul would say, better not to make such a pledge in the first place.

There are other ways of understanding the phrase translated *first pledge*. The word translated *pledge* is the usual word for *faith*, leading to the suggestion that Paul is referring to marriage to an unbeliever, which would therefore involve "abandoning their former faith, the Christian faith they had before they remarried".[74] The phrase is difficult, as on the one hand to translate the word as *pledge* involves giving this common Greek word a meaning unusual in the NT,[75] whereas on the other hand 5:11 says that the problem is simply the desire to marry, not the desire to marry an unbeliever.

Another practical problem of including younger widows in the list for the church's support is identified in 5:13. To provide support gives them time to spare, and because they are younger they also have energy which needs to be used in some way. Unfortunately, their time and energy are used wrongly. *They learn to be idle* (or perhaps a better translation might be *unproductive*, failing to produce anything useful). Instead of engaging in useful activity they interfere in other people's lives, *gadding about from house to house*, and causing problems by being *gossips and busybodies*. These problems are not necessarily limited to younger women, but in this context it is perhaps assumed that the older widow on the list who has lived the sort of life described in 5:9-10 has the maturity to avoid this sort of behaviour.

Unlike a widow of over 60 years of age, younger widows have an alternative, which is given in 5:14. That is simply that they should *marry, bear children and manage their households*, and thus automatically have plenty of productive activity to fill their life. This will prevent

---

[74] Mounce, *Pastorals*, 291. See also Towner, *Timothy-Titus* (1994), 121; Marshall, *Pastorals*, 599-601.

[75] For the meaning *pledge*, see Kelly, *Pastorals*, 117 (though he explains the pledge in the context of an order of widows).

criticism by hostile observers, by avoiding the sort of activity described in the previous verse and by fulfilling the role expected by the society of that time.

As we have suggested previously (e.g., in the comments on 5:10), we need not interpret all this legalistically. For instance, it is not hard to imagine a situation where a younger widow was unable to remarry, and compassion would demand that the church should meet her need. These are general guidelines, revealing a very practical response to the realities of the prevailing circumstances. Paul is not merely an abstract theologian. He is above all a pastor, as seen here and revealed throughout his letters. But his pastoral response is based on sound principles and is not merely a spur of the moment reaction to an unexpected situation.

We might also add that the cultural differences should be considered when seeking to apply a passage like this to our own situation. It is assumed in that situation, for example, that widows would remarry if young enough, but it may not be so simple as that in an Indian cultural context. Such realities must be fully taken into account.

Reflection: Caring for Widows and Others

Throughout its history the Christian church has been known for its acts of compassion, not only for the benefit of its own members but also for others, including opponents and persecutors of the church and members of other faith communities, especially in times of crisis. This has made a very positive contribution to the church's witness in the world.

In this chapter Paul's focus is on widows who are within the Christian community. As already noted, there were no government or private pension schemes through which support could be provided for a widow who had no family to care for her, and so such widows were an obvious group for whom the church needed to make some arrangements.

The details of Paul's instructions may not be totally relevant in our Indian cultural context. On the one hand there are many widows who are provided for through pension schemes, so that even if they have no living relative they may nevertheless be able to live without financial difficulty. On the other hand Paul's refusal to accept younger widows as eligible for the church's help on the grounds that they should remarry may be difficult to apply in India where in many places there are prejudices against remarriage of a widow. In these circumstances even younger widows may need help from the church. Such examples show that statements of the Bible cannot be merely taken out of their ancient context and simplistically applied in today's situation. When that is done, the result may often be not faithfulness to scripture but possibly the opposite of what Paul intended.

We need to avoid the mistake of applying scripture in a simplistic manner, but we should also avoid the opposite mistake of thinking that the Bible is from a different age and therefore irrelevant. There are at least two principles in 5:1-16 which can be applied in today's context. One is that where there are needy within the ranks of the church, appropriate assistance should be given. These situations will require wise consideration. Just as Paul needed to give careful guidelines about which widows really needed help, so we will have to do the same. Help should not be given to everyone who holds out their hand, or simply to someone who has contacts in high places (friends on the church committee or such like). The question to be asked is who really is in need. No doubt much church money has been wasted on people who do not need it, and that may make us extremely hesitant in providing assistance to anyone. But though it is difficult to put our hand near the fire after our fingers have been burnt, this response should be resisted and the church needs to err on the side of generosity (even if some funds end up going to the wrong people). The principle discussed here is the same as expressed in Galatians 6:10, "Whenever we have an opportunity, let us work for the good of all, and especially for those of the family of faith."

Help need not only be in the form of material assistance. In the case of a younger widow who wishes to remarry but faces prejudice, there may be a place for the church to arrange a suitable marriage. The view that a widow is cursed is a non-Christian idea and the church should give positive teaching to overcome this wrong attitude.

A second principle is the opposite side of the same coin, namely that the church is not an endless source of funds. Paul recognizes this when he says that wherever possible support should be provided in other ways for those in need (such as their own family members), so that no unnecessary burden may fall on the church. Whatever may be seen as the church's duty, the fact remains that fulfilment of duty is totally dependent on available funds. If there are no funds, nothing can be done.

What sometimes happens, unfortunately, is that pressure is put on the pastor to provide money from his own pocket. Reports are heard of churches which take no responsibility for the ministry of social assistance but fully expect that when someone comes to the church in time of need the pastor should help them. Of course it is difficult for a pastor who has a sensitive conscience to resist such appeals. But usually a pastor's salary is hardly sufficient to meet his own and his family's needs, and so this sort of demand can cause great stress. Where the church has funds which can be used for such purposes, an amount should be allocated in the church budget. If the church does not have funds, then some other way must to be found to respond to situations of need in order to avoid causing distress to a faithful pastor.

One area where the church should definitely not be burdened is in the case of church members who have abandoned the care of elderly relatives. Traditionally Indian culture has been admired for its strong emphasis on the extended family, including providing for elderly parents and others who can no longer support themselves. Unfortunately one hears of cases where elderly parents have become a nuisance to the plans and ambitions of the younger generation and have been put away, without proper provision. In such cases the church may be forced to give assistance, though this should be a matter of great shame to Christians who profess to follow Christ who was such a wonderful example of sacrificial compassion.

1 Timothy 5:17-25

The Work and Payment of Church Elders

The subject now seems to change completely, but the reference to *double honour* (5:17) may be the clue why issues concerning *elders* are dealt with here. The previous section began with the instructions regarding the widows who were to receive *honour* (5:3). So the theme of who should receive support from the church continues. However, in practical terms we do have a new topic here, as Paul deals with several issues to do with elders in the church.

The first verse of this chapter has already mentioned older men, using the Greek word *presbyteros*. The same word is used here (5:17) but the context makes it clear that Paul is not talking about older men in general. Rather it is a group of leaders in the church, people who, according to Titus 1:5, have been appointed to this position. Presumably these leaders were in fact older men (otherwise the use of this Greek word is meaningless), but not all the older men were necessarily elders in the more limited sense.

This verse distinguishes between different types of elders. When we read of *elders who rule well*, it is implied that there are other elders who do not rule well. This could be taken as an indirect criticism of the quality of the work of some of the elders, but it is unlikely that Paul would cause unnecessary resentment and ill-feeling in this way. It is equally unlikely that he is asking Timothy to cause trouble for himself by dividing the elders into good and not so good. It is possible that Paul is making a negative comment if it can be assumed that some elders were among those who were promoting the false teaching which concerns Paul.[76] But if not a judgement on the relative value of the work of the elders, it is perhaps simply a reference to work load: it was plain for all to see that some elders were able to give more time to the task than others, and these are the ones Paul describes as the *elders who rule well.*[77] The suggestion that it refers to those performing a wider range of work, including *preaching and teaching,*[78] is not very much different.

The word translated *rule* (NRSV) or more fully *direct the affairs of the church* (NIV) does not indicate authoritarian control but means to *give the lead*, as much by setting an example as by issuing instructions. The use of the same word in the context of *giving a lead in good works* (Tit. 3:8, 14) is instructive.

Such elders are to be *considered worthy of double honour*. The following verse makes it clear that this is some sort of payment, but whether a regular salary or an occasional payment, or even whether money or some other form of recompense we cannot say. *Double* probably means twice as much as other elders,[79] as a recognition of the time and effort they give to the task, which of course limits their ability to earn income in other ways. If translated *twofold* the sense would be two kinds of honour: respect and payment.[80]

Among those who lead well and are to be considered worthy of double honour are *those who labour in preaching and teaching*. These need not be considered a separate group of elders but are simply those who are *especially* in Paul's mind as he writes. The translation *preaching and teaching* might suggest a distinction between evangelism (of unbelievers) and teaching (in the church to believers), or between public addresses to larger groups and instruction to small groups or on a one-to-one basis. It is not clear that the Greek words imply any of these distinctions. Literally

---

[76] So Towner, who sees the focus here as being on "proficiency and, given the context of heresy, faithfulness in service" (Towner, *Timothy-Titus* (2006), 362).

[77] So Kelly, *Pastorals*, 124.

[78] So Marshall, *Pastorals*, 611-612.

[79] So Kelly, *Pastorals*, 124-125.

[80] So Fee, *Timothy-Titus*, 129; Knight, *Pastorals*, 232; Towner, *Timothy-Titus* (1994), 124; Mounce, *Pastorals*, 309-310.

the phrase is *word and teaching*, which may not be intended to distinguish two different types of work but is possibly just a general description of the ministry of the spoken word (in technical terms a *hendiadys*, in which two words are used to express a single concept).

5:18 has also been briefly mentioned as showing that some form of payment of elders is intended. Thus, *honour* in this context is not merely *respect* (important though that also is). The word *scripture* stirs our curiosity, for it appears that it is applied not only to the first quotation (from Deuteronomy 25:4) but also to the second, which is known to us from Luke 10:7 and Matthew 10:10. These Gospels may not even have been written when Paul wrote to Timothy and in any case were not generally accepted as having the status of scripture until the second century AD and later. It is likely that Paul knew this saying from a pre-Gospel collection of sayings. Some interpreters[81] regard the word *scripture* as applying only to the first quotation here and not to the second, but even if so, our present passage is evidence that the sayings of Jesus were treated as authoritative from the beginning (which is what we might have expected anyway), and indeed as having the same authority as the words of the OT.

Complaints against Elders

Most of us have experienced situations in our church in which complaints are expressed about elders (or whatever label we give to our leaders). Perhaps this is inevitable in any human society. Here it is recognized that this also happens in the church, and in 5:19-21 Paul gives guidelines for dealing with this matter. One of the problems (not only in church but in other groups and indeed in society in general) is that false information is easily spread and people are only too ready to believe whatever gossip they hear. Paul says that no accusation is to be given a hearing unless there are at least two witnesses. This is an OT principle (Deut. 17:6, 19:15) which remains valid. Of course even this principle does not prevent the deliberate creation of malicious rumour but it may be a safeguard against the accidental spread of false information. Here is at least a guideline which provides some protection for an innocent elder who might be the target of jealous gossip and rumour.

[81] E.g., Kelly, *Pastorals*, 126; Mounce, *Pastorals*, 311; Towner, *Timothy-Titus* (2006), 364.

On the other hand, elders are not perfect and they can fall into sin, and this possibility is considered in 5:20. *Those who sin* (NIV) may mean *those who persist in sin* (NRSV), indicating not simply one slip but a sinful habit that the elder has not dealt with. Timothy must *rebuke* these *in the presence of all* (NIV *publicly*). This may seem a light penalty in comparison with the severe words addressed to others who do not hold such high office in the church (5:8, 11, 15). Perhaps it is assumed that the elders have been well-chosen (see the comments on the following verses in the next section) and that a public rebuke will cause sufficient shame to bring them to repentance and change.

5:21 affirms the solemn importance of this matter and warns Timothy to be on his guard against *prejudice* and *partiality*. It is almost inevitable that he will be predisposed to favour one side or the other, according to the strength of his relationships with the different parties in the dispute. But he must not allow his personal preferences to influence the way he handles an accusation.

Choosing Elders

Another matter is how to choose elders. Paul gives the command not to *ordain anyone hastily* (5:22). He uses the language of *laying on of hands* (NIV), which was a common way of recognizing God's call and gifts and of commissioning someone for a particular ministry. Timothy himself had received the laying on of hands (4:14).

The fundamental rule is not to be in a rush, thus allowing time to evaluate a person's suitability for the role. It is perhaps a different way of expressing the requirement that a bishop must not be a *recent convert* (3:6).

The second part of the verse warns Timothy *not* to *participate in the sins of others*. This of course is a good rule in all circumstances. But in this specific context the implication is that to be involved in ordaining someone who proves to be unsuitable is to share the responsibility for the sins they commit. Better to delay ordination and first see whether there are sinful habits which need to be corrected. Similarly, the instruction to *keep yourself pure* is applicable to the whole of one's life (as previously in 4:12, 5:2), but here it particularly applies to avoiding becoming contaminated by involvement in other people's sins.

As we move beyond 5:22 the chapter seems to wander off into different and unrelated topics. This is reflected in our translations, most of which treat 5:23 and 5:24-25 as separate paragraphs. However, it might be better to identify 5:22-25 as a single paragraph, with 5:23 a digression within this paragraph.

If we do this, we can see a link between the reference to people's sins in 5:22 and the observations about the same topic in 5:24. There are some people whose *sins are conspicuous*, plain for all to see. For those responsible for deciding a person's suitability for a leadership position in the church, these cases are easy to deal with. But there are others who are able to keep their sins secret. It is in this sense that their *sins follow* them, hiding in their shadow, we might say. They will eventually become known but are not immediately seen.[82] Such a reality reinforces the point about not rushing into decisions regarding ordination.

5:25 is the opposite side of the same coin with its observations about *good works*. Generally speaking these are *conspicuous* (as Jesus said in the Sermon on the Mount, Matt. 5:14). Sometimes they may not be, as in the case of the person who takes seriously Jesus' command not to publicize one's good deeds (in the same sermon, Matt. 6:1). But even these *cannot be hidden*: eventually they become known, thus revealing a person's suitability for an office of leadership and responsibility.

Some understand the references to the sins that follow (5:24) and the good works that cannot be hidden (5:25) as references to the final judgement when all things, good and bad, will be revealed.[83] This is reflected in NRSV's addition of the word *there* (that is, to the place of judgement, 5:24), which is not in the original. But while this is no doubt theologically correct, reference to such a future revelation does not seem very relevant to Timothy's present duty to select appropriate people to serve as elders.

Reflection: The Ministry of Teaching

The PE contain many instructions related to leaders and leadership in the church. Paul speaks about his own ministry, he gives direction to his trusted colleagues Timothy and Titus, and he provides guidelines about the character and the work of those who perform different functions in the church. Also his

---

[82] So Knight, *Pastorals*, 241; Towner, *Timothy-Titus* (1994), 130; Johnson, *Timothy*, 282.

[83] For this interpretation see Kelly, *Pastorals*, 129-130; Marshall, *Pastorals*, 625-626; Towner, *Timothy-Titus* (2006), 377.

negative comments about opponents and false teachers provide further insights into his understanding of the nature of true Christian ministry.

One element of true leadership which is consistently seen is the task of teaching. Paul describes his own ministry primarily in terms of his responsibility to speak: he was appointed a herald and an apostle and a teacher of the Gentiles (2:7). Timothy must attend to the public reading of scripture, to exhorting, to teaching (4:13), and it is clear that one of his main tasks is to give instruction in one way or another (1:3, 4:6, 11, 13). A bishop is required to be an apt teacher (3:2), and one of the roles of some of the elders is preaching and teaching (5:17).

Of course it is not simply that teaching must be done. It is not good enough for simply anything to be taught, but it is absolutely essential that what is accepted and taught by leaders be correct theology. Timothy needs to be nourished on the words of the faith and of the sound teaching (4:6). False teachers are those who teach doctrine different from biblical truth (1:3) and whose activity is contrary to the sound teaching that conforms to the glorious gospel (1:10-11). Even those who may not actually be involved in the work of teaching, such as deacons, are required to hold fast to the mystery of the faith with a clear conscience (3:9), which shows that there is no room in church leadership for anyone who does not believe the basics of the faith with full commitment and a clear conscience.

We may ask whether leadership which places a primary emphasis on teaching is valued very highly in the churches of India. When a seminary student says that he or she hopes to go into a teaching ministry, the reference is never to a church context; they are only thinking of lecturing in a classroom. On the contrary when the NT refers to the ministry of teaching, the context is never the classroom. The only possible context was the instruction of ordinary believers either on an individual basis or when they met as a church.

But what is today's situation? Our bishops seem to fill their time attending functions or chairing committees or raising funds or administering their diocese. Is there more than a handful of bishops who are known for their teaching role, or to put it in different terms, for their focus in maintaining the truth of the gospel and expounding it for their people in relevant contemporary ways? Similar things might be said about many pastors, who become so involved in a variety of activities, usually because that is what their church members expect, that there is little or no time to devote to teaching the truth of the gospel, by which we mean not only the basic message of salvation but also the implications of the gospel which the pages of scripture are concerned about.

A teaching ministry requires a deep commitment, for it does not happen accidentally. It is more than fulfilling the duty of saying a few words from the pulpit each Sunday. It requires a commitment to prepare conscientiously, which involves a commitment of time during the week (not just a few minutes on Saturday night). It requires advance planning because a teaching ministry which is fresh (not just repeating the notes obtained from seminary) involves an ongoing programme of reading (biblical commentaries, other works of theology, and not least books and articles which comment on events in contemporary society).

In India where are the churches that look for leaders with this sort of focus? Or where are the seminaries which focus on training for this sort of ministry?

Reflection: Dealings with Complaints

One does not need to be associated with church life for long before you realize that churches are far from being examples of heaven on earth. Churches are mixed communities. Even if every church member is a committed believer (an almost impossible situation to ensure) or even if a church consists of people entirely from the same ethnic group or the same caste background, there will still be differences. Within any group of people there are different perspectives and points of emphasis, and the possibilities for misunderstanding are endless. Even in India where conformity is highly valued and where to stand out as different is so difficult, it is impossible to avoid conflict. Human beings are simply not all the same, even within an essentially homogeneous group. It is realities like these which make life interesting, for how boring it would be if we were all identical.

This means that complaints will arise in the church, and in this passage Paul recognizes the possibility of complaints against elders (5:19). The guidelines he gives for responding to these circumstances are particularly relevant to today's Indian context. He warns against unsubstantiated accusations, which are so easily spread and almost impossible to deny. To guard against these there need to be two or three witnesses to support an accusation. One might suggest that Paul would have just as strongly condemned the unsigned letter, which is a cowardly way of causing trouble, but which sadly is often treated seriously instead of being thrown in the garbage where it belongs. But just as he warns against assuming guilt, he equally warns against assuming that an elder could never be guilty of a serious offence. It is important to accept this, knowing that elders (or church leaders with any other titles) are human beings like the rest of us and are certainly capable of committing sin. He also warns against prejudice and partiality on the part of people like Timothy who must deal with charges that are brought. To know the right people and have the right connections is of the greatest importance in India, but this can easily lead to an unjust and biased decision in a matter of church discipline. *Conversely it is also true that a person who does not know the right people is in danger of being treated unfairly.*

There are many ways in which common justice can be denied, and common justice is the very least which should be expected in the church, where we claim to worship a God of justice and righteousness.

A Little Wine

We have suggested that 5:23 can be considered a parenthesis within the paragraph that continues to the end of the chapter. The advice to Timothy to *take a little wine* seems to be quite unconnected with what has preceded. It certainly has little or nothing to do with the subject of choosing elders, but perhaps there is a link with the instruction about purity (5:22).[84]

It appears that Timothy had made a deliberate choice not to drink wine but to restrict himself to water. This letter has made it clear that those in leadership positions must not be addicted to alcohol (3:3, 8) and Timothy may have felt that the simplest way of ensuring that he had no problem in this area was to avoid wine altogether.

If that was Timothy's decision, Paul does not criticize it. His advice here is for practical reasons only, as a means of improving Timothy's health, *for the sake of your stomach and your frequent ailments* (whatever these may have been). If Timothy felt that this might compromise his purity (5:22), Paul assures him that this need not be so.

Reflection: Partaking of Alcohol

The word of encouragement to Timothy to take a little wine (5:23) has often provoked interest. Christians today tend to have strong opinions about whether it is right or wrong to partake of alcoholic drinks (wine, toddy, arrack or whatever other descriptions we use). The Bible itself offers no clear-cut rule. A positive attitude is seen in a story such as Jesus changing the water into wine (Jn 2:1-11) and there is little reason to think that Jesus himself would not have joined in the celebrations by drinking some of the wine himself. The OT contains positive statements about the enjoyment of wine (Gen. 43:34, Ps. 104:14-15, Eccl. 10:19). But there are equally strong warnings against the misuse of alcohol (Prov. 20:1, 23:29-32) and drunkenness is strongly condemned (Eph. 5:18), not least in the PE (3:3, 8, Tit. 1:7, 2:2).

---

[84] So Marshall, *Pastorals*, 624; Mounce, *Pastorals*, 318.

This passage gives no approval to either side in that debate. On the one hand alcohol is not condemned absolutely. On the other it is not recommended for pleasure but only for medicinal purposes. These words are sometimes used to support the claim that a little alcohol taken regularly helps to maintain good health. In fact nothing is said here about maintaining health but only about dealing with an existing health problem. One might suggest that in modern India we know of better medications for most physical problems.

Even if the Bible does not lay down an absolute rule, the social context in India is a factor which needs to be taken very seriously. It is the poor who are most likely to suffer from alcohol abuse. In this context it may be considered that the wisest advice is to avoid alcohol altogether. For the poor who struggle to survive, alcohol is of absolutely no value except to help them drown their sorrows. Unfortunately it may drown other things as well, such as their ability to work or their ability to pay for the necessities of life for self or family. In the West there are church leaders who think it sophisticated to drink alcohol in moderate amounts and who do not hesitate to encourage others to do the same. In India such an attitude and such advice may be seen as irresponsible, not because drinking alcohol is itself a sin but because of the damage alcohol can and very often does cause. It cannot be claimed that there is a black and white biblical rule, but where the Christian community has created its own rule of absolute abstinence, there are good practical reasons for this.

1 Timothy 6:1-2a

Instructions for Slaves

A new chapter is not very appropriate at this point, since this short paragraph really continues the general theme of the previous chapter. In chapter 5 Timothy has been given instructions about different groups of people in the church: older and younger men and women (5:1-2), widows (5:3-16) and elders (5:17-25). Here we have instructions for slaves. We may wonder why there are no instructions for masters, for it is clear from 6:2 that there were Christian slave-owners. Perhaps at Ephesus problems in this area arose from the attitudes and behaviour of slaves (rather than masters).

As elsewhere in the NT there is no attempt here to discuss the rights and wrongs of slavery as such. It is not condemned (which some may feel is a weakness of NT social ethics), but neither is there any attempt to justify it as right and proper. It is simply accepted as a fact of life of that time, as indeed it was. The only detail of interest here is the phrase *under the yoke* (6:1). This could be understood to imply the harshness of the slave's lot, but in reality there was great variation in the conditions experienced by slaves in the Graeco-Roman world. It can never be suggested that slavery was a good thing, for at the very least it always involved dislocation in the slave's life, including removal from their own natural environment, and perhaps the death of other members of their family and the destruction of home and property. But many slaves became trusted and respected members of their new household and even when freed would normally take the name of the family (becoming known as a *freedman of so and so*) which gave them a recognized place on the social scale.

However, while they remained slaves they were expected to behave appropriately. It does not require much imagination to realize that a Christian slave who had discovered a new status in Christ, indeed a new freedom and acceptance in the fellowship of the church, might feel that he or she should express that freedom in ways that may not have been acceptable in the social context of that time. This tension would be increased if some of the slaves were also elders in the church. Some scholars[85] have in fact interpreted 6:1 in this way. The verse begins (literally) *as many as are slaves*, which could mean *as many elders as are slaves*, with a close link with the end of chapter 5. It is perhaps more likely that 6:1-2 is addressed to Christian slaves in general, not only to those who were also elders, though if some were elders it would have a special relevance to them.

6:2 clearly refers to slaves who have believing masters, and it is tempting to see 6:1 as referring to slaves with unbelieving masters.[86] However, the first verse is more probably addressed to all slaves. They are instructed to *regard their masters as worthy of all honour*. Here honour is clearly not financial payment (as in 5:3, 17) but rather *respect* (NIV). However, it does have a material dimension, in the form of the *service* (5:2) which a Christian slave should perform.

It is easy to be critical of the fact that the NT does not explicitly condemn slavery. However, the social implications of the gospel were already revolutionary. When Paul says that in Christ there is neither slave nor free (Gal. 3:28), the Christian slave even though not released

---

[85] E.g., Barrett, *Pastorals*, 82.
[86] So Knight, *Pastorals*, 243-244; Towner, *Timothy-Titus* (1994), 132-133.

from his or her slavery is given a new status within the body of Christ. A slave could easily misinterpret the significance of this, and with the zeal of the new convert could begin to act as if the master-slave relationship was already abolished at an earthly level. It is this matter that 6:1 seeks to address, reminding Christian slaves that they were still slaves and should treat their masters with appropriate respect.

Concern is expressed about the reputation of the Christian faith (at the end of 6:1). Slaves need to realize that inappropriate behaviour will bring their faith, and their God, into disrepute. This would certainly happen if the master was an unbeliever, who would see for himself his slave's behaviour and draw negative conclusions. But even in a situation where both master and slave were believers, others (unbelievers) outside the household would hear reports of the slave's behaviour and also react negatively. Such a negative response would be understandable, but just the same it would be *slander* (NIV, better than NRSV *blaspheme*), for the slave's wrong behaviour would not be a true reflection of what was being taught in the church. To avoid such slander every believer (slave or otherwise) must live in a way that brings honour to God and the gospel.

The second verse clearly identifies a situation where a Christian slave has a master who was also a believer. Slaves must take care not to *despise* such masters, that is, to treat them with less than proper respect. On the contrary, they must *serve them all the more*. The verb here is rather stronger than *serve*. It has the sense *do the work of a slave* and is a reminder that the slave is still a slave, though now a believer.

The instruction not to despise is linked with the fact that *they are brothers* (NIV) but the logical connection is uncertain. It could describe the excuse used by a slave for being disrespectful (I do not need to treat my master as my superior because we are Christian brothers and therefore equals;[87] NRSV and NIV reflect this interpretation). Or it could provide the reason why a slave should *not* be disrespectful (a slave should show his master respect because both are Christian brothers).[88] A further reason for slaves to serve well is that *those who benefit by their service* (their masters) are members of the same Christian community. The relationship that exists between a Christian master

---

[87] So Kelly, *Pastorals*, 130; Knight, *Pastorals*, 246; Marshall, *Pastorals*, 630-631; Johnson, *Timothy*, 284; Towner, *Timothy-Titus* (2006), 384; Witherington, *Commentary*, 279.

[88] So Fee, *Timothy-Titus*, 138-139; Mounce, *Pastorals*, 328.

and a Christian slave should be a positive motivation for a slave's good service, not an excuse for being a bad slave. Again it is possible to find here a general principle of Christian behaviour (applicable to all believers, not only Christian slaves), namely that one must show appropriate care, honour and love to all other believers, no matter what their station in life may be.

Reflection: Equality in the Family of God

The chapter begins with instructions to Christian slaves. As we have noted, Paul makes no attempt to challenge the institution of slavery itself, for the very good reason that to have done so would have been a major challenge to the structure of the society of that time. The challenge would have been bitterly resisted and would probably have led to the extermination of the church very quickly. If we are tempted to criticize Paul (or any other leader of the NT church), we should first see that our own house is in order. Where bonded labour continues in India and indeed where household servants are little better than slaves, we need to be careful not to draw attention to the splinter in someone else's eye while ignoring the log in our own.

To approach the matter more realistically, there are social inequalities in any culture. At a practical level not all people are equal. There are differences of education, professional rank and status, wealth and language. To take the last of these as an example, it is natural that in a situation where good English language skills are valuable, a person with those skills will be given higher responsibility than one with less ability. This is inequality, but it is unavoidable and natural. We might say that it is 'objective' inequality, based on indisputable fact. Differences of skin colour are also visible for all to see, though in this matter it is hard to find an objective reason why fairer skin should be seen as preferable to darker skin. Caste background is another matter of fact (unfortunate as it may be) which even in the church can determine one's status.

In these verses Paul speaks of both slaves and masters as members of the church (6:2). He is concerned that slaves do not take advantage of this in a wrong way, but he does not deny the fact of slavery. The point is the same as in the well-known Galatians 3:28, that in Christ there is no longer slave or free. Yes, there were still slaves and free people in the church, but those social distinctions were irrelevant as far as belonging to the body of Christ is concerned. Similarly today there are distinctions of different types. A large urban cosmopolitan English-speaking congregation may contain people of vastly different educational levels, but the fact that a person is a college professor with a PhD does not make him or her a better Christian than a young person who needs several attempts to pass their first year BA exams. Someone with fairer skin should not be considered a more desirable member to elect to a church committee, nor should someone else simply because they belong to the dominant ethnic group in that church. So while people are not equal, it is not the inequality as such which is the problem but the prejudice and injustice which often follows from it.

It has often been observed that though the NT does not directly attack slavery as such, it sows the seeds which eventually led to the abolition of slavery at a legal level in many parts of the world. One such seed may be observed in our present passage, where Paul speaks of masters as "those who benefit by their [the slaves'] service" (6:2). The common attitude at that time was that, because the master was in the socially superior position, it was he who benefitted the slave by providing the necessities of life. Here however Paul speaks of the master as the beneficiary and the slave as the one who provides the benefit. In an indirect and subtle way, Paul reverses the social order. Such is the effect of a true Christian understanding of our equality in Christ. The things that divide us in the normal social order are irrelevant in the family of God - or at least should be irrelevant. In India there are no doubt many opportunities for those who may normally be regarded as higher on the social scale to give way to those of lower rank, and to encourage and recognize their contributions to the life of the church.

Reflection: Blaspheming the Name of God

Biblical ethics are seldom a matter of simple rules: 'this is right and this is wrong' or 'do this but don't do that'. That is sometimes what happens in the church, where (for example) the way we dress is decided by the decree of the pastor or our particular traditions, though no one can really explain the reasons. When the Bible speaks about the way believers should behave, there is always a reason. One of these is that we are called to reflect the character of God himself, as in 1 Peter 1:15, "As he who called you is holy, be holy yourselves in all your conduct."

Another reason is highlighted in the present passage. Slaves are to behave in such a way that the name of God and the teaching may not be blasphemed (6:1). The underlying concern is the effect of our behaviour on a watching world. This theme is strongly entrenched in the OT. On the positive side there is the picture of Israel as a light attracting the nations to God (Isa. 2:2-4, 60:1-3). Of course for God's people to be a light they must first walk in the light (Isa. 2:5). These verses speak of the future fulfilment of what had been God's purpose for Israel from the beginning, that the nation was to be a kingdom of priests (Exod. 19:6), in the role of mediator between

God and the other nations. On the negative side the failure of God's people to walk in the light and thus to be a light to the other nations meant that God was dishonoured. When Judah's sin led to judgement and exile, God was greatly dishonoured (Ezek. 36:20-21). This is precisely the point Paul makes in Romans 2:24 (referring to Isaiah 52:5): Israel has failed in its God-given task.

Following Israel's failure the church is given not only the privilege of being the renewed people of God but also the responsibility of fulfilling the same role in relation to the world. God does not call us simply for our own personal blessing. He calls us too to be the light of the world (Mt. 5:14). That is our mission. We may not call ourselves missionaries as traditionally defined, but we all have a role within God's mission.

This is a major theme within the PE, as the observant reader may have already noticed. Only one who is well thought of by outsiders (3:7) is a suitable candidate for the work of being an overseer. The rules about widows are framed with an eye on the adversary, who must be given no occasion to revile us (5:14). The same is implied in the reference to the person whose behaviour reveals them to be worse than an unbeliever (5:8); Paul is very conscious of the wider context in which the church must live out its faith. The world is watching, and what they see will give either a positive or a negative impression.

In many of our churches we may be regularly encouraged to share our faith, to witness in word to our relationship with God through Jesus Christ, perhaps to be involved in tract distribution or similar activities. But the old cliché is true: actions speak louder than words. Words are important, indeed essential, to explain our faith. But when our actions contradict our words, no one will listen. In India what do people see when they observe the life of the church? Do they see a group of people living by God's standards, people of diverse backgrounds worshipping and functioning together in harmony? Or do they see behaviour which causes the name of God to be blasphemed?

1 Timothy 6:2b-10

True and False Teaching

Timothy is reminded to *teach and urge these duties* (literally *these things* as NIV). *These things* refers to what has already been written, perhaps the instructions relating to different groups within the church (i.e., from 5:1 onwards), or if it is considered that Paul is here beginning to draw his letter to a conclusion *these things* could mean the whole of the letter till now.

An instruction similar to 6:2b was given in 4:11 (not quite the same words), and in fact right from the beginning of the letter (as in 1:3) teaching what is true and right is emphasized as a basic element of Timothy's responsibilities. This now leads to further warning about those whose teaching is of a different kind. That is why the last part of 6:2 is in many translations (including NRSV and TNIV, but not NIV) placed with the following verses as the beginning of a new paragraph.

So at the beginning of 6:3 Paul speaks of those who *teach different things* (a rough translation of the verb used here, the same word which comes in 1:3 but nowhere else in the NT). Timothy has been told what he must teach, and so *different things* means teaching contrary to the authorized apostolic teaching which Paul has given. They are *false doctrines* (as NIV translates).

The false teachers do *not agree with the sound words of our Lord Jesus Christ and the teaching that is in accordance with godliness*. Here are two characteristics of true teaching: it must be according to the word of the Lord Jesus, and consistent with godliness. The words of Jesus may be actual sayings of Jesus which have been handed on in the church (his parables and other teachings).[89] This is the simplest understanding of this phrase. But it is possible that the phrase means teachings which focus on Jesus, in contrast to the controversial and speculative ideas which the false teachers were promoting.[90] True teaching is also according to godliness: it must promote a changed life which is pleasing to God. This reminds us of what was said in 1:5-6, where also Paul condemned false teachings which have no practical aim but are just meaningless talk.

6:4-5 provide a description of the false teachers and the results of their activity. It is not a flattering description: they are *conceited* (or the word could mean blinded), ignorant (*understanding nothing*) and sick (with a *morbid craving*). Their diseased mind and spirit is revealed in their obsession with mere disputation (*controversy* and *disputes*). The unhappy results are things like jealousy, disagreement, doubts and quarrels, which

---

[89] So Knight, *Pastorals*, 250; Witherington, *Commentary*, 283.
[90] So Fee, *Timothy-Titus*, 141; Kelly, *Pastorals*, 133-134; Mounce, *Pastorals*, 337; Towner, *Timothy-Titus* (2006), 394.

stand in stark contrast to the godliness which should be the product of teaching in the church. Such teaching should present the truth of God but these people have no grasp of the truth.

Godliness and Contentment

At the end of 6:5 one symptom of the diseased and corrupted mind of the false teachers is mentioned: they think that *godliness is a means of gain.* Godliness here can hardly refer to true godliness, for a person who is truly godly does not think like this. There is an outward form of godliness which is not genuine godliness at all (2 Tim. 3:5). That seems to apply to the false teachers Paul is describing here: they have heard the word godliness, they have realized that in Christian circles godliness is highly approved, and so they have learned how to appear to be godly. They see this as having personal benefit: it is a *means of gain.* They have seen that elders receive financial remuneration for their work (5:17) - some of them even double honour. Why not get in on that party, they think, and so they pretend to be something which they are not. There is nothing wrong in receiving payment for work performed, but if receiving payment is one's main motivation there is something seriously wrong, and especially if one pretends to be something one is not in order to achieve this outcome.

Paul uses this situation as an opportunity to speak about the true benefit of true godliness (6:6-8). He uses the same words *gain* and *godliness* but with different meanings. Godliness here is not the pretended godliness of the false teachers but true godliness which is characterized by *contentment.* Clearly the *gain* which comes from such godliness is not financial or material but something which is inward and spiritual.

Contentment is an interesting word. It is literally *self-sufficiency,* and it is used in Greek philosophy (e.g., by Plato) to describe the "state of one who supports himself without aid fr[om] others" (BDAG). In this sense it is considered by the Stoics, the Epicureans and the Cynics to be an essential virtue. But in the NT it certainly does not mean *self-*sufficiency, except in the sense that a Christian knows not to depend on external circumstances and external objects for meaning in life. But if it is a matter of inner resources, 6:7 makes it clear that we have no resources that we can claim as our own, and the believer's sufficiency is not from himself or herself but from God. So we might more satisfactorily define the word as meaning *God-*sufficiency. Paul is saying here that gain is to found in a godliness which accepts what God provides as adequate and appropriate. This is the same point which he makes in Philippians 4:11-12 (the other main passage dealing with contentment).[91]

The theme continues in 6:7-8, beginning with the well-known statement about not bringing anything into the world and not taking anything out of it. Expressed in those words, this is a clear statement of fact. But there are some difficulties about the logical connections. The first word in the translations is *for*, suggesting that the verse provides a reason for contentment and for refusing to consider the acquisition of possessions an important goal in life. It is not entirely clear why this is so, since starting with nothing and leaving with nothing does not mean that nothing is needed during the course of our life. The point must be that the way our life begins and ends shows that material possessions are *relatively* unimportant; we should certainly not (as many unfortunately do) make the acquisition of wealth and possessions our priority in life. A second difficulty occurs in the middle of the statement, where there is a word translated *so that* in NRSV. It is highly doubtful whether the Greek word *hoti* can have this sense. Scholars have offered many suggestions about the meaning here, with the most likely being *because* (a common meaning found in many passages). With this meaning one scholar provides this paraphrase: "There was no point bringing anything into the world with us, *because* we shall not be able to take anything out."[92] NIV avoids the problem by simply translating as *and*, which is without any justification at all.

6:8 is much more straightforward, defining contentment as being satisfied with *food and clothing*. This need not be taken absolutely literally (as if we never need anything more than this), but it focuses on being satisfied with the necessities of life. Many of us have very much more than the necessities and yet we may be continually dissatisfied and always be looking for ways to obtain more.

Money

In contrast to contentment are those who *want to be rich* (6:9). Such people cause themselves great trouble. There are three things into which they *fall*.

---

[91] For a helpful survey of the Greek word *autarkeia*, see Marshall, *Pastorals*, 644-645.

[92] Barrett, *Pastorals*, 84.

The first is *temptation*. No specific temptation is mentioned, but the desire for wealth makes a person vulnerable to temptation. For example, the temptation to engage in corrupt practices is far greater for such a person than for someone who is content with whatever God provides. The second is a *snare* (NIV *trap*), for money and an unbalanced focus on acquiring it is something which entraps and enslaves. The third is *desires*, which are both *many* in number and *senseless and harmful* in nature. The wisdom of the world is that one should acquire as much wealth and as many possessions as possible for one's benefit, but here we are reminded that this is not wisdom but folly and that the result is not benefit but harm. The final words of the verse explain why overpowering *desires* to gain wealth are *senseless and harmful*. It is because they *plunge people into ruin and destruction*. This disastrous result certainly includes an eternal and spiritual dimension (as the next verse reveals), but the single-minded pursuit of wealth can also lead to disaster here and now, in the form (for example) of marriage breakdown or imprisonment for fraudulent or other illegal activity.

According to a common misinterpretation of 6:10, the Bible says that money is the root of all evil. Of course it is not *money* as such but the *love of money* which is the root of evil. Consistent with this is the beginning of the previous verse, where the problem is not people who *are* rich but people who *want to be* rich, that is, those who make the acquisition of wealth a deliberate goal and priority in their life. (On this point see further on 6:17-19 below.)

The love of money is a *root* or cause *of all evils*. This does not mean that every single sin can be linked with the love of money, for sin can arise from other causes as well (pride or lust, for example). However, love of money can lead to sins of many kinds; it is a problem with potentially very wide-ranging effects. One possible effect is financial ruin, perhaps through gambling or unnecessarily risky investment decisions (in the pursuit of quick returns). But the most serious effect is mentioned in the second half of the verse, namely the possibility of falling away from the faith. For Paul this is no mere hypothetical possibility but already a reality, for *some have wandered away from the faith*. Such people have also *pierced themselves with many pains*. This phrase has been interpreted to mean the pain of "unfulfilled desires for wealth",[93] but it is possibly

---

[93] Marshall, *Pastorals*, 653. Towner includes this as one of several possible meanings (Towner, *Timothy-Titus* (2006), 405).

something much deeper than that. The pain caused by the accusations of one's conscience is another possible understanding, but even worse than that is the pain of losing one's peace with God.[94] A trap (6:9) is something which catches someone by surprise, and the sense may be that a foolish believer, unaware of the dangers of chasing money, can suddenly and unexpectedly and very painfully discover that he or she has gained the whole world but lost their soul. Jesus' warnings about the difficulty of the rich entering the kingdom of God (Mk 10:23) or the impossibility of serving God and wealth (Mt. 6:24) provide a sobering commentary. The proper Christian attitude is godliness with contentment (6:6).

1 Timothy 6:11-21

Priorities in the Christian Life

Paul addresses Timothy as *man of God* (6:11). There is only one other NT example of this phrase (2 Tim. 3:17), which in the OT often describes those who are leaders of God's people or prophets.[95] Timothy is certainly a good example of such a person, and so this passage teaches the sort of behaviour appropriate for a church leader. At the same time there is not much in this passage which relates exclusively to leaders, and it is therefore proper to see these instructions as applying to all believers.

There are negatives and positives which Timothy must deal with. He is to *shun* (NIV *flee from*) the negatives and *pursue* the positives. These verbs are quite strong and suggest a clear-cut and decisive response. Perhaps we could say *run away from* and *run after*.

First, Timothy must abandon *these things*, perhaps especially wrong attitudes and practices regarding money but possibly also the false teaching mentioned earlier in the previous paragraph. (Instead of the literal *these things*, NRSV and NIV have *all this*, curiously adding the word *all* for which there is no equivalent in the Greek.)

Moving from the negative to the positive, Paul lists some Christian virtues necessary for growth. *Righteousness* and *godliness* speak of a life

---

[94] Johnson suggests a similar understanding, commenting that "a life driven by such constant craving is a form of self-torture" (Johnson, *Timothy*, 296).

[95] References are provided in Fee, *Timothy-Titus*, 149, and Marshall, *Pastorals*, 656 note 65.

of piety put into practice. *Faith* and *love* are fundamental marks of the Christian life: we must put complete trust in God and we must love God and one another. And in all our behaviour but perhaps especially towards opponents and in other difficult circumstances we must show *endurance* and *gentleness*. Other lists of characteristics of the Christian life are found in 2 Timothy 2:22 and 3:10-11. None of the lists is identical although there is some overlap (especially in 2 Timothy 2:22 where the first three are righteousness, faith and love). It is impossible to give an exact reason for the choice of the six words we find here, but they paint a vivid picture of a wide range of basic characteristics which should be seen in every believer as she or he grows in Christian maturity.

The instructions continue (6:12-14) with further commands which reveal that the Christian life is no half-hearted matter but a strong and enthusiastic response to God's call. Timothy is to *fight the good fight of the faith*. God's call, while full of many blessings, is not a call to sit back, relax and be comfortable, but to *fight* (the Greek word is *agonizo*, from which the English word *agonize* is derived). It is a *good* fight, for this is the only way to stay on the road that leads to life (Mt. 7:14). If we ask why there should be a fight at all, it is because God's way is not understood by most of his rebellious creatures; those who choose to enter by the narrow gate will be seen as a challenge and a threat to those who see no need to do so. In 2 Timothy 4:7 Paul claims to have fought the good fight, but of course the supreme example of this is Jesus himself (as we will see in 6:13).

The next command is to *take hold of eternal life*, with another strong verb which means to *take hold in order to make one's own*. Although we might usually think of *eternal life* as an experience of the future, the age to come, here it is something which Timothy is urged to grasp now (as in 6:19 where the same verb is used). Even in the present age a believer enters into the experience of the life of the age to come. Timothy is already a Christian leader and so it is clear that Paul is not appealing to him to *become* a Christian. But he is to take a firm grasp on the life that he already has and make sure his grip does not slip.[96]

Paul reminds Timothy that he was *called* to this life (by God) and reminds him too of the *confession* he once made, a public confession (*in the presence of many witnesses*), presumably made at the time of his

---

[96] Knight's suggested sense *struggle now and at the end lay hold of eternal life* is not convincing (Knight, *Pastorals*, 263).

conversion and baptism.[97] Others suggest that the confession was made at the time of his ordination[98] or when on trial before hostile authorities.[99] It is a *good* confession (just as the fight is good), no doubt the basic Christian confession that Jesus is Lord. This is what he is now being urged to keep a firm grip on, for his own personal benefit and also for the sake of remaining fit to exercise a credible ministry of leadership at Ephesus.

A further command, expressed as a solemn *charge* (literally *command*, 6:13) and invoking *God* and *Christ* as witnesses, relates to Timothy's responsibility to *keep the commandment* (6:14). It is not clear which commandment is meant. (NIV adds the word *this*, presumably intended to refer to the previous commandment in this passage, but the Greek words are simply *the commandment*.) It seems that the phrase is intentionally general, thus possibly including the command to respond to the gospel and live the Christian life, as well (in Timothy's case) as the command to serve, that is, his commission to ministry. NEB's paraphrase *obey your orders* adopts this general understanding.

He is to *keep the commandment without spot or blame*. The last four words here refer to the commandment, and yet they are strange words to use to describe a commandment and are more naturally applied as moral qualities of a person. The phrase may be best understood as an abbreviated form of expression, meaning keep *yourself* without spot or blame as you keep the commandment. This responsibility remains valid *until the manifestation of our Lord Jesus Christ*. Timothy cannot take a year's leave of absence. He must fulfil this solemn responsibility until the Lord comes or at least till the end of his own earthly life. The suggestion that the instruction focuses on preserving the purity of the commandment[100] rather than Timothy's personal obedience to it is not likely.

---

[97] So Fee, *Timothy-Titus*, 150; Johnson, *Timothy*, 307; Towner, *Timothy-Titus* (2006), 412.

[98] So Knight, *Pastorals*, 264-265; Towner, *Timothy-Titus* (1994), 143; Witherington, *Commentary*, 294.

[99] See Mounce, *Pastorals*, 356-357, for discussion of the options.

[100] So Kelly, *Pastorals*, 144-145; Johnson, *Timothy*, 308. The possibility of this interpretation arises from the fact that the two adjectives (*without spot* and *without blame*) could be either masculine (agreeing with *you*) or feminine (agreeing with *the commandment*).

The Greatness of God and of Christ

There are several statements in these verses about God and Christ which deserve separate attention (as well as comment on their meaning within the context).

The first relevant verse in this passage is 6:13, where God is described as the one *who gives life to all things*. This is a basic biblical theme, another way of stating that God is the creator from whom (and from whom alone) all life comes. In a significant sense Jesus is *the life* (Jn 6:35, 11:25, 14:6) and the source of life for others (Jn 1:4). Other NT writers attribute to Jesus a role alongside or under God in the work of creation (1 Cor. 8:6, Col. 1:16-17, Heb. 1:2-3), and so (at least by implication) as the source of life. But even in the Fourth Gospel where this theme is so prominent, the life which Jesus is said to have in himself is the gift of the Father (Jn 5:26).

The opening words of 6:15 speak of God's control over the time of Christ's return. Though the world seems to go on in its own way, according to the decisions of powerful nations and powerful people (as it appears), the course of history is actually within God's control; Christ will be revealed in glory when God decides. The translation *in his own time* (NIV) is better than *at the right time* (NRSV). Both are correct but NIV tells us more precisely what makes the time right: it is the time which God decides (as also in 2:6). The thought is similar to the statements of Mark 13:32 and 1 Thessalonians 5:2.

The remainder of 6:15-16 contains seven further descriptions of the greatness and majesty of God, leading to a doxology at the end of 6:16. (a) *The blessed and only Sovereign*. God has already been described as the *blessed* one in 1:11. The word translated *Sovereign* is used to describe the Ethiopian eunuch (Acts 8:27) as a ruler (NRSV has *court official*). So from one point of view there are other rulers. But God exercises a unique rule. Whatever other rulers there may be, God is greater than all of them, and in that sense the *only* one. (b) *The King of kings*. This phrase and the next express clearly the point just made, that though there may be others who bear the same title (whether *ruler* or *king* or *lord*), God is greater than them all. He is King of kings because he is the greatest king and therefore king over all other kings. In 1:17 he is called *the King of the ages*. (c) *The Lord of lords*. The same comment applies here. The title *Lord* is more usually applied to Christ (in this chapter in 6:3, 14), and in Revelation 17:14, 19:16 it is Christ (not God) who is described as *Lord of lords* (as well as *King of kings*). These observations raise profound questions about the relation of Father and Son which the NT itself does not attempt to answer and which are also beyond the scope of the present book. But when all has been said about the exalted position of Christ, we remember that ultimately he too will be in submission to the Father (1 Cor. 15:24, 28). Truly, God is *Lord of lords*, even the Lord of the Lord Jesus Christ.

Four more descriptions are given in 6:16. (d) *It is he alone who has immortality.* In him alone is life which cannot be destroyed, which by implication makes him the only reliable source of life. Here alone in the NT is God specifically described as having the condition of immortality, but a very similar thought is found in 1:17 and Romans 1:23. In those two passages NRSV and NIV actually have the translation *immortal*, though in fact a different Greek word is used (literally meaning *imperishable, indestructible*). (e) *And dwells in unapproachable light.* God himself is the light, pure light, in whom is no darkness (1 Jn 1:5), as also is Christ, the light of the world (Jn 8:12). Yet in those passages it is not an overwhelming light, for we too are expected to walk in the light (1 Jn 1:7, Jn 8:12). Here it is light of an unimaginable brightness, comparable to the brightness of the sun at which the human eye cannot look without risk of loss of sight, and hence *unapproachable*. (f) *Whom no one has ever seen or can see.* This is a natural result of the previous description. The same point is expressed in the single word *invisible* (1:17). Perhaps we can suggest biblical examples of people who *did* see God in his heavenly splendour. Isaiah may come to mind, but despite the words *I saw the Lord* (Isa. 6:1), it is clear that he did not have a direct, unmediated vision of God. In fact the passage records that *the hem of his robe filled the temple*; in reality that was as much as Isaiah actually saw, though that was enough to cause great distress and despair (Isa. 6:9).

Not surprisingly, this passage comes to a climax with the acknowledgment that (g) *honour and eternal dominion* belong to God. There is no Greek verb here, and so it is the interpreter's task to decide whether the best word is *be* (expressing a wish that these things might be so, as in NRSV and NIV, and most commentators) or *are* (expressing an already existing fact). The second seems more likely in the light of all that has been said about God in these verses.[101]

---

[101] This is acknowledged by Marshall, *Pastorals*, 668, when he says, "Two characteristic attributes are credited to God."

A further statement about God comes in 6:17, that he *richly provides us with everything for our enjoyment*. This is almost an anticlimax after the exalted descriptions of the preceding verses, in the sense that it brings the transcendent God down to the level of a real interest in human life in the world he has created. But that too is part of the greatness of God, that he who rules the world takes thought for the well-being of his creatures, even to the extent of providing for their pleasure.

We may consider more briefly the references here to Christ. The comment in 6:13 places Jesus in an earthly context, when he was on trial before the Roman governor Pilate, which in this letter may be intended to remind Timothy that he also may be called on to give a faithful testimony before hostile secular rulers. This verse may seem to give Jesus little significance in comparison to God (God is the life-giver; Jesus is merely the faithful witness). But the very fact that Paul appeals to God and Jesus *together* shows the real position that Jesus holds: he is in a very real sense equal with God (as we see also, for example, in 1:1, 2).

The greatness of Jesus is more directly referred to in 6:14, with mention of the *manifestation of our Lord Jesus Christ*. The word *manifestation* is characteristic of the PE. It focuses attention on bringing to light what may not otherwise be generally seen or known. It especially describes Jesus' *future* manifestation, what is usually called his second coming (as here and also 2 Tim. 4:1, 8), and once his previous earthly life (2 Tim. 1:10). In our present verse what will be brought to light is (at least) the fact that Jesus is the *Lord Jesus Christ*, a fact well accepted by believers but unknown or ignored by the rest of creation.

The Uncertainty of Riches

Paul returns now to the theme of wealth (6:17-19). He has already written clearly about the goodness of God's creation (4:4), and the same point comes out at the end of 6:17. However, there is a negative side to the subject and warnings to be given, and that too is seen here.

Earlier in this chapter he has given very strong warnings to *those who want to be rich* (6:9). There is a small but important difference here, inasmuch as he now addresses *those who are rich* already. They are described as rich *in the present age* (NIV *in this present world*), which is a subtle reminder that whatever wealth one has now cannot be transferred to the age to come, a point already made very plainly in 6:7.

The rich are given two negative commands. (a) *Not to be haughty* (NIV *arrogant*). Those who are rich are aware of the power of wealth, including the power to give orders to others and expect to be obeyed. This power can be misused, not least in promoting the self-deception that they are better and superior people than those with fewer resources. Christians who have been blessed with wealth must be aware of this danger and resist it. (b) *Not to set their hopes on the uncertainty of riches*. Logic tells us how foolish it is to put one's hopes on what is uncertain. But this again is a danger that the rich can easily fall into, refusing to recognize that today's wealth can easily be gone tomorrow and certainly will be gone one day.

The first of the positive instructions in this paragraph is in contrast to this second negative command. Our hope must be placed on God. Wealth is uncertain, but God is not. He is the provider of all things. A Christian must surely give greater honour to the Giver than to the gift, for to do otherwise is idolatry, replacing God with something very much more inferior. We must not misunderstand the statement that God *richly provides us with everything for our enjoyment*. It should not be claimed as a promise that God will give us whatever we think we need in order to enjoy life. It is, rather, a *general* description of God's nature as giver and provider. All good things do in fact come from him (Jas 1:17). Out of this supply an individual human is given *some* of those good things, but no one can expect to have *all* the possible good things of God's creation. What God has given is *for our enjoyment*, and we should enjoy without any sense of guilt. But let us not expect or demand more than God chooses to give.

Further positive instructions follow in 6:18 and require little explanation. One must use the blessings received for the benefit of others and not solely for one's own enjoyment. Enjoyment is one aspect but not the only one, and we should not become so absorbed in our own pleasure that we forget our duty to act responsibly to help others also. To act in this way brings the unexpected advantage of *storing up for themselves the treasure of a good foundation for the future* (6:19). To give to others is to make a deposit in an unseen bank, to store up treasure in heaven (Mt. 6:19-20).

A further possible misunderstanding lurks in the final words of 6:19 which describe the purpose of storing up this good foundation.

Taken out of context, this might be thought to teach a sort of salvation by works: be generous and you will be saved. But the PE (as the rest of the NT) show that salvation is through the work of Christ and is an act of God's grace (see 1:15, for example). The words *take hold of* more likely refer to the present *experience* of life, as in the similar phrase in 6:12. Many no doubt think that true life is experienced in the acquisition and selfish use of material possessions. Here the opposite is said: true life is experienced in the generous sharing of our possessions. We grasp the life that really is life by acting in tune with the character and will of God. To be truly alive is to be like God; as he generously provides humans with all things for their enjoyment (6:17), so we are most truly alive when we act in the same way.

Reflection: The Root of All Evils

1 Timothy 6:10 is one of the best-known texts of the whole Bible, as well as being one of the most misquoted (as pointed out in the comments above). Its misquoted form offers an even stronger warning on the subject of money and material possessions.

Indeed it is not money but the love of money which is the subject of Paul's concern. Yet this should not lull us into a false sense of security, for in practice there may not be much difference between money as such and the love of it. Those who have it can very easily find themselves loving it, as implied in Jesus' words: "How hard it will be for those who have wealth to enter the kingdom of God" (Mk 10:23).

Warnings are given to two different groups in this chapter. The first is those who want to be rich (6:9). There is a common idea that India is a very spiritual country and that we are more interested in spiritual things than material things. Whatever truth there may be in that statement, it is certainly not the whole truth. One only has to observe the constant advertising on television, in newspapers and magazines, and on roadside billboards, to realize that India is a huge and fast-growing market place, where we are constantly being encouraged to think that we need more than we already have. Businesses do not advertise unless they think there is a good chance of making a sale.

One does not have to be rich to be materialistic. If materialism is the craving for more and making the acquisition of more our focus in life and being dependent on what we possess, then it is possible for even the poorest peasant in India to be much more materialistic than the richest man in America. Such a statement is not intended to belittle the peasant, for it needs to be recognized that the poor peasant in India is often in a desperate situation and those who have an (apparently) assured supply of life's necessities should be careful before they pass judgement on the 'materialism' of the very poor. Within the Christian family we need to take steps to help those among us who are desperately poor, while also encouraging them to look to God in faith and to thank God when needs are met.

The positive message of this passage to believers who may be tempted to believe the advertising propaganda and to put a misplaced focus on possessions is 'Be content'. True gain is not in acquiring more but in godliness combined with contentment, and in this way learning that God is able to provide the needs of those who trust him.

The second group to whom warnings are directed is those who in the present age are rich (6:17). They are not told to give away all their money and possessions, as if these things are evil in themselves. Indeed the opposite is true, for what God provides is for our enjoyment. But there are special temptations for people in this category, including the danger of thinking they are somehow superior because of their wealth and entitled to give orders to others (hence the instruction not to be haughty) and the danger to make their possessions the object of their hope (hence the instruction not to set their hopes on uncertain wealth).

There are several positive messages to these people. One is 'Set your hope on God', who after all is the source of every blessing. Another is 'Use your possessions for the benefit of others', through good works and generosity. It may be difficult for the rich to enter the kingdom, but it is not impossible, as long as they learn to put their possessions in the proper place and not in the place of God.

In recent times the world's economy has experienced a significant downturn, a reminder of the uncertainty of riches. This may be a very good test for some readers. For those for whom life is already a daily struggle simply to find work and to provide food and clothing for the family, the value of shares on the world market may make little practical difference, although even for such people the recent financial crisis may have meant loss of employment or fewer employment options and opportunities. For others who have attempted to safeguard their future by investing in the share market or in pension funds, recent circumstances may have been a severe test of faith. We may be concerned that our savings have been significantly reduced and we may wonder how we will be able to finance our future needs (in our retirement years perhaps). In this context what does it mean to be content and to be generous? For that is God's call to his people in all circumstances.

Guarding the Truth

Paul's closing exhortation to Timothy (6:20-21) returns to one of the basic themes of the whole letter, a concern for the truth and for Timothy to fulfil his leadership duty to safeguard the truth. The command is literally *guard the deposit*. This deposit is probably the sum total of Christian truth which Timothy has received, and just as a bank has the duty to safeguard what is entrusted to its care by the depositor, so Timothy's primary responsibility is the same with the truth of the gospel. He may need to think creatively how to apply aspects of that truth to his own specific circumstances, but it is not his task to create the Christian message. The same is true of every leader of the church from that day till now.

Part of this command is a right attitude to what is false. At Ephesus a *falsely called knowledge* is being peddled. No specific description of the content of this knowledge is given, but only of its results, which are *profane* (NIV *godless*) *chatter and contradictions*. We recall Paul's similar warning at the beginning of the letter (1:4-5), where the false teaching is said to focus on *myths and endless genealogies* in contrast to positive outcomes such as *faith* and *love*. The problem with the false teaching is not simply that it deals with abstract debates and arguments but also that it leads to spiritual disaster. Attachment to it has produced the result that *some have missed the mark as regards the faith* (or as NIV says in more straightforward language *have wandered from the faith*). The quality of teaching in the church can always be measured by the sort of spiritual fruit it produces, or lack of fruit as the case may be.

The final words of the letter are the simple greeting *grace be with you*. Grace is recognized as a characteristic feature of the Christian faith in the first chapter of the letter (1:2, 14), and so it is fitting that this should be the heart of Paul's wish as he brings the letter to an end. It is also important to note that the word *you* is plural. On the surface the letter has been addressed to Timothy (as specifically in 1:2, 18, 3:14, 4:6, 5:23, 6:11, 20). But it has been easy to guess that others were intended to hear and respond to the teaching of the letter. Here the plural *you* specifically reveals that there are hearers or readers other than Timothy. It is a letter for the church, a reminder to the whole congregation of how ministry should be exercised, what sort of teaching is to be admitted in the church, and what sort of behaviour is expected of Christian people. Timothy (and other leaders) have a primary responsibility to exercise leadership according to these standards, but the congregation must also accept their part in fulfilling God's calling to his church to bear witness to the truth of the gospel and to bring honour to the name of God himself.

Titus

Titus 1:1-4

Greeting

The letter begins in a familiar way, similar to all of Paul's letters, with identification of the writer, identification of the recipient, and a word of greeting. Comparison with 1 and 2 Timothy will quickly reveal the general similarity of pattern. The actual greeting is very familiar, *grace and peace*, though it is different from 1 and 2 Timothy where the word *mercy* is also added. As elsewhere the source of the *grace and peace* which Paul desires for Titus and all his Christian friends is *God and Christ*, who are thus placed on an equal level.

The introduction of the letter to Titus is noticeably longer than the two to Timothy (four verses compared with two). We will look now at some of the details from the first two parts of this introduction to the letter.

Paul and His Ministry

Most of the additional length of the introduction is occupied with a fuller description of Paul himself and his ministry (1:1-3).

Describing himself he says that he is *a servant of God and an apostle of Jesus Christ*. The second phrase is familiar from many other letters (including 1 and 2 Timothy, though with *Jesus Christ* here instead of *Christ Jesus*, a change of order which has no obvious significance). Elsewhere but not often, Paul describes himself as a *servant*, or literally *slave* (twice in the introductions to his letters, in Rom. 1:1 and Phil. 1:1, and once elsewhere, Gal. 1:10; a different Greek word, also translated *servant* in NRSV and NIV, is used in 1 Cor. 4:1). Not only is this description relatively uncommon but *slave of God* is unique to this passage (in the other passages mentioned it is *slave of Christ*).

So he describes himself in relation both to God and to Christ. The phrases make several important points as he begins the letter. (a) As *God's slave* he is not his own master. The agenda he is following is not his own but God's. (b) As *Christ's apostle* he comes with a significant measure of authority, though again it is not his own authority but Christ's. As one who occupies both these positions, he can expect to be taken seriously. When he gives instructions for the life of the church, these are not just his own personal opinions which we have a right to reject if we choose. No, Paul's words come with the authority of God and Christ, whose interests he represents.

Paul's work as slave and apostle is further defined by a series of other phrases and clauses which continue to the end of 1:3. First, it is *for the sake of the faith of God's elect* (literally *according to the faith ...*). He cannot simply do what he pleases, according to his own view of what is appropriate. His work is to be done within the context of building up the faith of God's people.

Second (within the same phrase introduced by *according to*), it is to perform the task of promoting *the knowledge of the truth* among God's people. This phrase comes in several other places in the PE (1 Tim. 2:4, 2 Tim. 2:25, 3:7), usually in the context of unbelievers coming to a knowledge of the truth, or we might say being converted. Here, however, it is more in the context of the apostle's continuing ministry to believers, to bring them to a growing and fuller grasp and application of the truth.

A third detail comes in the words *in accordance with godliness* which is a description of *the truth*. We know that many different claims can be made about what is the truth. How can we assess what is true and what is not? This phrase does not give a complete answer, but it tells us a necessary part of the story. What is true will be consistent with godliness of life; it will produce godliness in those who accept it. If what is taught in the church does not have this result, we may doubt that it is the truth.

Fourth (in 1:2) is the phrase *in the hope of eternal life*. The word *in* is literally *on the basis of*, and the phrase describes the foundation of Paul's work. There are eternal issues at stake, and the Christian gospel says that the believer's eternal destiny is *eternal life* in relation with God. Take this away and the gospel loses its meaning and power. Take this away and the ministry of Paul (and any other minister of the gospel) becomes an exercise in futility. But with this hope there is a solid foundation which makes the gospel the pearl of great value (Mt. 13:46), worth any cost to find and worth any cost to proclaim to others.

Fifth is an assurance that this hope of eternal life is not just wishful thinking. It is life *that God, who never lies, promised*. To say that God never lies is to say that he is completely trustworthy (an adjective applied to Christ in 2 Tim. 2:13). Furthermore it is not a recent thought on God's part but a promise made *before the ages began*. Even before mankind was created, it was God's intention that his human creatures should enjoy the life of eternity.

Sixth, if the promise was God's commitment so long ago, it is now in Paul's generation that the gospel has made known how eternal life can be received. That is what Paul speaks about in 1:3. God *has revealed his word*, this word being the content of the gospel, and has done so *at his appointed season* (NIV, which makes clear that God is the one who has decided the time, and so is better than NRSV *in due time*). He has chosen to do so *through the proclamation*, which emphasizes the fact that the message has been given to human agents to announce. One of those agents (though certainly not the only one) is Paul himself. He sees his work of proclaiming the gospel as a *trust* given to him by *command of God*. From Paul's perspective the work he does is not his own decision but a compulsion laid on him by God himself. From the perspective of those who hear what Paul proclaims, this gives the message an authority it may not otherwise have, for it is not a human decision to spread a man-made philosophy but a word originating from God and proclaimed at God's command.

Titus

Like Timothy, Titus was a much-valued colleague of Paul's and one to whom Paul entrusted several important tasks. Titus is relatively unknown, for whereas Timothy is mentioned many times in the book of Acts, Titus is never mentioned in that book. It is only in Paul's letters that we read about Titus.

We do not know anything about Titus' background, except that he was a Gentile believer with a Latin name and described as a Greek in Galatians 2:3. He is referred to here as a *loyal child* (NIV *true son*) in the faith, which may mean that it was through Paul's ministry that he was converted, but we cannot be certain of this.

He travelled with Paul to Jerusalem on the visit mentioned in Galatians 2, and his uncircumcised condition became a test case to show that circumcision was not necessary for a Gentile convert (Gal.

2:1-3). Later he acted on Paul's behalf when Paul's relationship with the Corinthian church deteriorated, and in that context he is mentioned in eight references in 2 Corinthians.

Titus is now working on the island of Crete (on which see the comments below on Tit. 2:5-9) where he has been given significant responsibility (1:5). Paul urges him to join him at Nicopolis on the west coast of the Greek mainland (3:12), where Paul planned to spend the winter. The final reference is in 2 Timothy 4:10 where Paul reports that Titus has gone to Dalmatia. This is an area further north along the same coastline (moving beyond the border of modern-day Greece and into Albania), which suggests that Titus did in fact go to Nicopolis as requested and from there to Dalmatia some time later.

God, Christ and Salvation

We have already noticed in 1 Timothy how God the Father and Jesus Christ are mentioned together in equal partnership (we might say), as in 1 Timothy 1:1-2. The same point can be observed here, especially in 1:4 where God the Father and Jesus are seen equally as the source of grace and peace (not a direct claim that Jesus is divine but a very significant pointer in that direction). Not quite so obvious but also important is 1:1, where Paul attributes his authority as a Christian minister to both God and Jesus.

Also of interest in this regard are the references to both as Saviour, God the Father in 1:3 and Jesus in 1:4. This is not a contradiction, for both have a role in the salvation of mankind. In fact, it is worth observing that in each chapter of this letter we have a reference to God as Saviour (1:3, 2:10, 3:4), followed soon after by a reference to Jesus as Saviour (1:4, 2:13, 3:6). It is almost as if Paul wants to emphasize that it is not one or the other who should be thought of as our Saviour, but both in equal measure (though of course in different ways).

More broadly on the subject of salvation, we see here that it was something *promised before the ages began* (1:2), the focus of God's intention from "before time began".[102] Those who benefit from this promise of God are called *God's elect* (1:1). A description like this always raises the issue of predestination (in contrast to human freewill) and the justice

---

[102] Marshall, *Pastorals*, 126.

of choosing some but not others. This is an impossible issue to solve according to human logic. In fact the Bible never attempts to provide a logical solution to satisfy our curiosity. Nor does the Bible see this as an attack on God's justice, which is assumed throughout the Bible. If the justice issue is a problem to *us*, that probably simply shows that we cannot see the full picture from our limited human perspective. The Bible's purpose in calling believers the elect seems to be intended mainly as an encouragement and assurance to us, a reminder that our place in God's family is God's doing. We are not encouraged to speculate why others do not (as far as we know) enjoy the same privilege; in reality we do not know who are God's elect, but we can be sure that God will bring his purposes to completion, and with justice.

The other element about salvation which these verses mention is that salvation consists of *eternal life* (1:2). This is something which we no doubt have begun to enjoy in the present life, but the emphasis here is on the *future* aspect of eternal life. It is our *hope* (1:2) and therefore something which provides a focus and direction for our present existence. Life now gains purpose from the fact that we know where we are going, the knowledge that our eternal destiny is assured.

Reflection: The Basis of Ministry

In the comments on the opening two verses of this letter we have noted a series of phrases which constitute a comprehensive definition of the nature and scope of Paul's ministry. The phrases cover such things as the origin and authority of his ministry (he is God's slave and Christ's apostle), its basic immediate purposes (to strengthen the faith and knowledge of God's people), a criterion for assessing its quality (it should produce godliness of life), its broader framework (it looks ahead to the eternal life which is offered as our hope), and its sure foundation (it comes from the promise of an absolutely trustworthy God).

It is very easy to skip quickly over verses like these, seeing them as a necessary but not very interesting part of the formal greeting of a NT letter. But when we pause and reflect, we realize that there is a tremendous depth of meaning in these phrases from which we can learn much today.

To begin with, they offer a convenient summary of several fundamentals of the gospel. It is not the whole message (no summary can hope to capture every significant point), since (for example) there is no mention of the death and resurrection of Christ (though if we continue into verses 3 and 4 we find the description Saviour applied both to God and to Jesus).

But Paul's more immediate purpose is to draw attention to some of the crucial aspects of his own ministry. For those of us who are involved in full-time ministry today, this should encourage us to ask questions about our own ministry. The most obvious question is whether we are able to give simple answers (in the equivalent of two verses) which convey an accurate picture of what our work is all about. We are not apostles and so we are different from Paul, and our answers may not be exactly the same as his. Nevertheless it should be possible to state simply and clearly what we think we are aiming to do in our ministry.

The practical reality of the life of the average minister or pastor in India is that we become involved in a multitude of different activities. Each day is busy, sometimes with planned programmes (such as meetings that have been scheduled or, on Sundays, the regular services), but sometimes with much that is unplanned (such as a call to visit someone in need or time spent with people calling at our office or home or the need to respond to an unexpected situation like a sudden death). The unplanned activities often crowd in on us, demanding our immediate attention, and it is very easy to come to the end of a day and wonder what it is all about. We can list the activities, but what do they all mean?

They may mean a very great deal. But the problem is that it may seem to be nothing but a big jumble of activities. All pastors (and indeed others involved in any other form of Christian ministry) need to take time to ask what it is all about. We all believe that God has called us to ministry. But to what exactly? Ministry can be a very vague term, which sounds good and pious but perhaps has no clearly defined content. What exactly do you believe God has called you to do? Can you say what are the basic features of the ministry to which you have been called, as Paul was able to say? To be able to answer a question like that may help to give meaning to your daily frenzy. It may also help you to discern what things you should be doing (or doing more) and what things are less important and perhaps could be set aside altogether. It may help you to see that there are less public activities (prayer and Bible study, for example) which are being pushed aside in favour of responding to today's requests, which may come to you as urgent but are perhaps not so important in the bigger picture. What can you do to ensure that you focus on the really important elements of your ministry?

Titus 1:5-9

Crete

Crete (1:5) is a large island in the Mediterranean Sea south of Greece. It is part of the modern nation of Greece. It is not clear how the gospel came to Crete. The book of Acts contains no record of Paul preaching the gospel on Crete. There is one reference to Paul visiting Crete, but he was a prisoner travelling on a ship to Rome; during that journey his ship came to a harbour in Crete called Fair Havens but it did not remain there long (Acts 27:8, 12). There is no hint that Paul left the ship to preach or that any locals came on board where they might have heard the gospel.

One other NT reference to Crete is in Acts 2:11, in which those who heard Peter on the day of Pentecost included residents of Crete (Jews or Gentile converts to Judaism). It is definitely possible that some of these may have accepted the gospel and established churches in Crete on their return. But it is more likely that Paul himself established the churches on Crete after being released from prison in Rome, as there are reasons for believing that the churches mentioned in this letter had been established fairly recently.[103] All we do know for certain is that at the time of this letter there were churches in Crete and that Paul considered Crete part of his apostolic responsibility and care, whether or not he had directly founded those churches.

Getting Things Right in the Church

The first item on Paul's agenda as he comes to the real business of this letter is the issue of sorting out the church. We readily think of Paul as an itinerant evangelist but may not realize that his role as an apostle involved pastoral care for the groups of believers which came into existence under his ministry. Evangelism and conversion are just the first steps along the path to maturity in Christ, which Paul tells us is the goal of his ministry (Col. 1:28). Once we come to this fuller understanding of his ministry, we are not surprised that getting things right in the church comes high on his list of priorities, for the church is a believer's new family and it is in the church that he or she is nurtured in the faith. If the church is not right, God's plan for his people is affected in a major way.

Paul has left Titus in Crete (1:5). This seems to mean that Paul had been involved in ministry in Crete with Titus and that he left Titus behind to continue the work when he departed. It was at the time of his departure

---

[103] See Mounce, *Pastorals*, 386, for explanation of this point.

that he gave Titus instructions, including the instruction to appoint elders. It is less likely that the word *left* here has the sense *assigned*, which Paul could have done even without being in Crete himself.[104]

Titus' task is first described in general terms. It is that he should *put in order what remained to be done* (1:5). Perhaps the translation *put in order* is not quite strong enough. This could be taken to mean simply to bring a little more order into the church's disorganized administration. But in fact it means something like *set right* or *correct*. Paul's concern is not just a small amount of disorganization but things that were actually *wrong* that needed to be corrected. NIV's *straighten out* is closer to the point. In other respects, the scenario is perhaps similar to the description of Paul's first missionary journey, described in Acts 13-14. There, churches were established, but only after some time were elders appointed (Acts 14:23). So too in Crete, the initial task of establishing churches had been undertaken, but the next step of appointing leaders had not yet been done. If this is a correct reconstruction of the circumstances, it is not surprising that there were things that *remained to be done* in order to *set things right*. Of course, there are always matters in which a church can and should be improved, but in the early stages especially every effort needs to be made to set a church on the right foundation.

Elders and Bishops

Within the context explained in the previous section, the matter of good leadership is of crucial importance. Paul reminds Titus of the instruction to *appoint elders in every town* (1:5). This tells us that there were churches in several places in Crete, though we cannot say whether many or few (*every town* means every town where there is a church rather than every town on Crete);[105] that elders were important for the leadership of the church; that Titus had the authority (under Paul) to appoint elders. No details are provided about how these appointments were to be made, how much consultation, for example, was expected, or whether there was a democratic vote (which is unlikely). But it was Titus' responsibility to see that it happened.

---

[104] This understanding is preferred by Towner, *Timothy-Titus* (2006), 678. For discussion of the meaning of the Greek verb, see Marshall, *Pastorals*, 150.

[105] So Knight, *Pastorals*, 288; Marshall, *Pastorals*, 152.

Necessary qualities of elders are listed in 1:6. Several of the characteristics mentioned in this verse (and in 1:7-8) are similar or identical to those listed in 1 Timothy 3:2-3 and where that is the case little or no further comment will be necessary. (a) *Blameless*. This is a very general word and is virtually a summary of the whole list. The same word is used in 1 Timothy 3:10 to describe the character of deacons. In 1 Timothy 3:2 a different word (translated *above reproach*) is used in the list of the bishop's qualities but with virtually the same function as a summarizing term at the beginning of the list. (b) *Married only once* is the same phrase as in 1 Timothy 3:2. In the comment on that passage it was suggested that this is not a good translation. The focus is on faithfulness in marriage (if indeed the man was married, which was not necessarily the case). (c) *Whose children are believers* (again, *if* the man was married). Requirements regarding children are also expressed in 1 Timothy 3:4 (though in different terms). Here it is expected that the elder's children should share the faith of their father. Though such a thing cannot be guaranteed, it is assumed that in most situations genuine and credible faith in the life of the parents will lead to a positive acceptance of the same by the children.[106] The following phrases in 1:6, *not accused of debauchery and not rebellious*, also refer to the elder's children (not the elder himself); this point is made clear in NIV, though NRSV is ambiguous.[107] The first of these two phrases describes the children's moral life in general and the second their acceptance of their parents' rightful authority.

At the beginning of 1:7 the word *for* (NIV *since*) links the following statement with the preceding requirements, meaning that 1:7 provides the reason for 1:6. This connection makes sense only if the *elder* (1:6) and the *bishop* (NIV *overseer*) (1:7) are one and the same person. In our own churches bishop and presbyter (elder) belong to different orders of ministry, but in the NT context there is no reason why the two terms

---

[106] Kelly, *Pastorals*, 231, Marshall, *Pastorals*, 157-158, and Towner, *Timothy-Titus* (2006), 682-683, prefer this interpretation, as does Mounce, *Pastorals*, 388-389, with hesitation, but others prefer the other possible translation *faithful* or *trustworthy* in a more general sense (Knight, *Pastorals*, 290; Towner, *Timothy-Titus* (1994), 225).

[107] Mounce's comments are confused at this point, for he mentions "qualities that an overseer must not have" (*Pastorals*, 389), though later he contradicts this when he refers back to this verse as "Paul's description of what overseers' children should not be" (*Pastorals*, 396).

could not have been used to describe the same person and the same office. *Elder* describes the person from the viewpoint of age and status. He was literally an older person, for the respect which came from age was regarded as a necessary requirement for one to hold a position of leadership. *Overseer* is equally a leadership term but describes the person from the viewpoint of function, his role being to exercise supervision over the affairs of the congregation. As far as translation is concerned *overseer* and *elder* are probably better than *bishop* and *presbyter*, for the latter have too many ecclesiastical associations and we may wrongly read into the meaning of the words what we understand by bishops and presbyters in our own day.

There seems no doubt at all that overseer and elder were one and the same thing in the situation in Crete, as addressed in this letter. Whether this was the case in other NT contexts is not so easy to say. The closest parallel is 1 Timothy, where overseers (3:1-7) and elders (5:17-22) are both mentioned. Are these merely different descriptions of the same person? This is possible, for both are involved in leadership through teaching and management. But this cannot be asserted dogmatically, for the two terms come in different chapters and with no direct link between them. Or we may think of other passages, such as Philippians 1:1 where Paul greets the *bishops and deacons*. Why not elders? Possibly because there were no separate elders, if bishop/overseer and elder were merely different descriptions of the same person. The opposite reasoning might apply to Acts 14:23, where *elders* were appointed. Why not bishops? Perhaps simply because there was no concept of bishop as a separate office and function. Another significant Acts reference is Paul's meeting with the leaders of the church of Ephesus; in that passage they are described both as *elders* (20:17) and as *overseers* (20:28). A similar point is revealed in 1 Peter 5:1-2 where Peter speaks of the elders as exercising oversight. These arguments do not all carry the same weight, but they tend to point to the conclusion that overseers and elders were the same.

On the other hand, in other passages where ministry is discussed (especially 1 Cor. 12 and Eph. 4), there is no mention of either overseers or elders. Nor are any specific office-bearers identified in Paul's letters to the churches in Thessalonica, Colossae or Rome. That is not proof that there were no duly appointed office-bearers. But consideration of all these passages should make us suspicious of any claim that the NT churches had a uniform pattern of ministry with standard titles consistently used.[108]

After this change of label in 1:7, from *elder* to *overseer*, which may have come as a surprise to us but which for Paul may have been very natural and perhaps even subconscious, we return to the list of qualities. (a) *Blameless* is repeated from 1:6. The fact that he is *God's steward* (NIV *entrusted with God's work*) provides a fundamental reason for this requirement. It is God's household that he is managing, which means that it is God's property that he is caring for and God's reputation that is at stake. Naturally therefore he must be *blameless*, which does not mean morally perfect but that he is not liable to be charged with any offence. (b) *Not arrogant*. In colloquial English we might say that an arrogant person is 'full of himself'. That is the opposite of what a leader in the church should be. He should not be so focused on his own interests and pleasure that he fails to recognize the feelings and interests of others. (c) *Not quick-tempered*. He should not be easily overcome by anger. (d) *Not addicted to wine*. This requirement is expressed in exactly the same words in 1 Timothy 3:3 (and in similar expressions applying to deacons in 1 Tim. 3:8 and older women in Tit. 2:3). (e) *Not violent*, again as in 1 Timothy 3:3. (f) *Not greedy for gain* is exactly the same phrase as in 1 Timothy 3:8 (in reference to deacons). The same idea is expressed as *not a lover of money* in 1 Timothy 3:3.

Following the list of negatives that are to be avoided (1:7), we find in 1:8 a list of positive characteristics. (g) *Hospitable*, as in 1 Timothy 3:2. (h) *Lover of goodness*, a word used here only in the NT, and a very general description of a character which takes pleasure in good things and good people, with no attraction to anything that is of doubtful moral quality. (i) *Prudent*, another word used in 1 Timothy 3:2, though there translated *sensible* in NRSV (in both places NIV has *self-controlled*). (j) *Upright*. This adjective (literally *righteous*) does not occur in any of the other lists of virtues in the PE, but *righteousness* (the related noun) is mentioned as something to be desired (1 Tim. 6:11, 2 Tim. 2:22, 3:16); the same thought is expressed by a different (but also related) word in 2:12 (*upright* in NRSV and NIV). Though one is not saved by *works*

---

[108] For discussion of terminology and other relevant issues, see Knight, *Pastorals*, 175-177; Marshall, *Pastorals*, 170-181; Mounce, *Pastorals*, 153-167, 306-309.

of righteousness (3:5), a believer and especially a Christian leader is expected to live a life of righteousness. (k) *Devout*. This word can also be translated *holy* (NIV) or *pious*, though it should not be understood to refer only to religious activities in a narrow sense. Such a person is God-pleasing, inwardly and outwardly. In its only other NT occurrence (1 Tim. 2:8), this adjective describes the hands of those who pray, where the reference is to inner character and not merely ritual purity. (l) *Self-controlled*. This is the same translation which NIV used instead of *prudent* a few words previously, whereas here NIV has *disciplined*, which shows the similarity in meaning between the two words. The Greek word is not used elsewhere in the NT.

The positive characteristics of an overseer continue in 1:9, not in a single word or short phrase but in a longer description of one of his most necessary qualities: *he must have a firm grasp of the word*. This *word* is further described as *trustworthy in accordance with the teaching*. NRSV (reproduced here) is more literal than NIV, but it is all rather awkwardly expressed. In particular, one may ask what difference is intended between the *word* and the *teaching*. Possibly *word* means the message which the elder proclaims, and *teaching* is the apostolic tradition which alone is the proper source for what is proclaimed.[109] In this case the translation *have a firm grasp of* is not so suitable (as it suggests more of a theological understanding at an intellectual level); an alternative is *be devoted to*, meaning devotion to the task of proclaiming.

Apart from these problems of detail, the overall sense is clear enough. The overseer is to engage in a ministry of proclamation, the message not being his own clever thoughts but the gospel as passed on in the Christian tradition. Just as the message to be proclaimed was entrusted to Paul by God's command (1:3), so the elders or overseers to be appointed for the churches of Crete must proclaim the same.

This ministry has a twofold purpose, as expressed in the second part of 1:9. The first purpose is that devotion to this task will enable him to give the necessary encouragement (NIV *encourage* is more accurate than NRSV *preach*) to God's people. And in case the point was not already clear, the phrase *with sound doctrine* makes sure that the scope of the proclamation is defined. The elder's task is not to invent the message

---

[109] So Kelly, *Pastorals*, 232-233. Mounce, *Pastorals*, 391, suggests that *word* means the gospel and *teaching* "the doctrinal exposition of the gospel".

he proclaims but to provide encouragement from within the framework of the inherited Christian tradition.

The second purpose at first sight seems more negative, namely the prevention of false teaching. The verb *refute* could also be translated *rebuke*, which in effect means to stifle the false teaching and prevent these people speaking. But the translation *refute* suggests something more positive, namely convincing the false teachers of the error of their ways and bringing them to an acceptance of the truth. The same verb is used in 1:13 where the hope of such a positive outcome is specifically expressed. Certainly the false teaching is to be stopped at all costs, but if the false teachers can be persuaded to accept the truth, so much the better.

It is worth noticing the parallel quality in the 1 Timothy list. There it is said that the overseer must be *an apt teacher* (3:2). That phrase is expressed by a single word in Greek, in contrast to the 21 Greek words of Titus 1:9 (36 English words in NRSV). Despite this difference, both passages express the same concern, that a major responsibility of the leader (overseer or elder) is the propagation of the truth, for the building up of believers and the refutation of heresy.

Reflection: Patterns of Ministry

We have noted that the terms overseer (or bishop) and elder (or presbyter) refer to the same office in the situation which Paul addresses in Crete. If we belong to a church which uses these words to describe orders of ministry, almost certainly bishop and presbyter do not refer to the same office. When we read about matters like this in the NT, we may be tempted to interpret the text in the light of our own modern practices. One reason for this is our desire to justify our contemporary practices as biblical. But this is hardly a satisfactory way to interpret the meaning of the NT.

Matters like this tend to become fixed and unchangeable as time goes by, but in the early days patterns of ministry were not strictly defined. In the beginning leadership was naturally in the hands of the apostles, and other forms of ministry developed according to need. Thus, in Acts 6 we read of the seven who were appointed to attend to tasks which the apostles did not have the time to do. These are often seen as the first deacons (though in fact the word deacon is not used to describe them). Then at the end of Paul's first missionary journey we read of elders being appointed in each church (Acts 14:23), an obvious necessity since Paul and his team would not be with them to provide leadership. Of course, the churches had a large measure of independence. Although there was a deep sense of partnership with believers in other places, there was no centralized structure (such as a modern diocese) and no imposed pattern of ministry. Unlike the Jerusalem Conference (Acts 15), called to discuss the basis on which Gentiles could be admitted to the church, there was no conference to agree to a standard pattern of ministry.

In this context ministries developed in response to local needs, no doubt using terms and descriptions familiar from other contexts (perhaps from the Jewish synagogue or from the Graeco-Roman world). The interchangeable use of overseer and elder in Titus shows that we have a fairly primitive stage in the development of forms of ministry, as in the rest of the NT. Some of the relevant passages have been noted in the commentary above.

Today we have highly formalized patterns of ministry with fixed titles for different sorts of ministers and ministries. We easily become dogmatic about the patterns followed in our own particular church and can be quite aggressive in defending these as the NT pattern. But it is difficult to paint a uniform picture of 'ministry in the NT churches'. No church can claim a monopoly on correct forms of ministry. In particular the episcopal churches might speak of the apostolic succession and look condescendingly at the younger churches which seem to have sprung up recently out of nowhere. But the only true apostolic succession is faithfulness to the apostolic gospel. That is the truly significant legacy left to us by the apostles, not a specific pattern of ministry, and churches of all backgrounds need to monitor themselves regularly to see that they are faithful to Jesus and the gospel above all else.

Titus 1:10-16

Problems in the Church

Paul has already indicated that there are problems in the churches in Crete by mentioning Titus' commission to set things right (1:5). The most specific response to this situation must be to appoint elders or overseers, and these must not just be any who happen to be available but people who fulfil the necessary requirements as listed in 1:6-9.

A more specific reason for Paul's concern now becomes clear as we move to the final part of this chapter (1:10-16). The word *for* (1:10) indicates that the following statement provides the reason why the appointment of the right type of leaders was so important. It is because of the presence in the church of *many rebellious people, idle talkers and deceivers* (1:10). They are *rebellious* in the sense that they will not accept the authority of rightful leaders and the central place of apostolic teaching. (It is amusing to note that the same word *rebellious* has been used in relation to children in 1:6, which may suggest that these people who pretend to be leaders and authorities are no better than badly behaved children.) Their rebellion has led to them being *idle talkers*, saying many things but with little substance. In fact it is worse than that, for it is not only a waste of time to listen to them but actually harmful, since they are also *deceivers*. If such people are allowed to peddle their doctrines, they will lead believers astray.

Many of these false teachers are *of the circumcision*, meaning that they are from a Jewish background. Presumably they claim to be Christians, converts from a Jewish background (otherwise they are not likely to have had access to the churches). Some undesirable aspects of their Jewish past have remained with them, for in their teaching they emphasize *Jewish myths* (1:14) and they engage in *quarrels about the law* (3:9) which Paul obviously considers to be a distraction from more important matters. We have seen something similar in 1 Timothy where Paul is concerned about people who claim to be *teachers of the law* (1:7), who similarly have an unhealthy interest in *myths and endless genealogies* (1:4). We know from 1:12-13 that the teachers referred to in Titus were from Crete itself, though it is possible that these same people were also active in Ephesus. But even if there were two different groups, they certainly had similar ideas and came from similar backgrounds.

Titus is given the responsibility to deal firmly with them: *they must be silenced* (1:11). There are times when a 'softly, softly' approach is appropriate, but this is not such a time. The danger is great and must be confronted head on. Of course, if they can be persuaded to abandon their error and accept the truth (as seen as a possibility in 1:13), that would be a wonderful result, but the immediate need and first priority is to stop them from spreading their ruinous teaching.

Paul is not just imagining what might happen. He is speaking of things that are already happening. By teaching *what it is not right to teach* these deceivers are *upsetting* believers. *Upset* means more than a slight psychological disturbance. The word is more literally *overturn* (NIV *ruin* captures the sense well). It is spiritual disaster, and on a broad scale for it is *whole households* that are being affected. Their motive is identified as financial *gain*. Such gain is *sordid* (literally *disgraceful*), not only because financial profit is always an unworthy motive for Christian ministry but also because in this case the gain is from what causes harm. There are plenty of modern examples of false teachers (especially members of cult groups) calling on homes and offering to sell literature which is in fact heretical. Paul seems to be describing a similar situation, except that the deceivers in his context must have gained some credibility within the church, for it is apparently within Titus' power to silence them.

The warning about these false teachers continues with an interesting quotation in 1:12, in which the character of Cretans in general is described. Paul does not tell us the source of the quotation, but it is usually considered to come from one Epimenides, himself a Cretan but who according to the philosopher Plato lived and worked for a time in Athens many centuries earlier. Plato describes him as a *prophet*, as Paul does here.

Epimenides' description of his own countrymen is not flattering. They are *liars*, he says. This was a proverbial accusation, based on the false claim made by the Cretans that Crete was the burial place of Zeus (the chief of the Greek gods). They are *vicious brutes*, wild animals, characterized by inhumane behaviour, and *lazy gluttons* (literally *idle bellies*) with an interest only in fulfilling their bodily pleasures and desires.

Scholars have observed that if Cretans are liars, Epimenides' own testimony cannot be accepted. This may be true from the viewpoint of logic, but Paul is not engaging in logical quibbles here. The force of the quotation lies in the very fact that it comes from *one of them*, implying that it has greater credibility than, say, the opinion of a hostile outsider.[110]

Whatever one may think about the credibility of a Cretan prophet who comes from a nation of liars, Paul goes on to assert that *that testimony is true* (1:13). It can hardly be imagined that Paul is trying to condemn all Cretans, including the Cretan members of the churches for which Titus is responsible. His focus is on the false teachers and he is merely saying that they fit the stereotypical picture of a Cretan. His message to Titus and the believers in Crete is that because they

---

[110] For comment on the source and meaning of the quotation, including the 'liar's paradox', see Marshall, *Pastorals*, 198-203; Mounce, *Pastorals*, 397-399; Towner, *Timothy-Titus* (2006), 699-703.

are *liars,* you should not believe their message. Because they are *vicious brutes,* you should realize that they have no concern for your well-being. Because they are *lazy gluttons,* you should expect that they are only interested in their own benefit. You should have the same suspicions about these teachers as you might have about other unbelieving Cretans.

The instruction to *rebuke them sharply* (1:13) is virtually a repetition of the previous command to silence them (1:11). After all these hard words, it may come as a surprise to read the possible positive result expressed by the following purpose clause (*so that* …). This clause runs to the end of 1:14, and includes the hope that *they may become sound in the faith* (soundness or healthiness in Christian truth is an important theme in the PE, as we have just seen in 1:9, and also in 2:1, 2, 8, 1 Tim. 1:13, 4:3). Such spiritual health will be seen when they reject *Jewish myths* (1:14), the sorts of stories that are also mentioned in 1 Timothy 1:4 where they are condemned because they produce speculations and arguments rather than a genuine Christian character; and also when they reject *commandments* which are merely human, such as appear in many churches in the form of legalistic rules which again do not produce a genuine Christian character but only add a miserable burden to the life of a believer.

Paul continues: *To the pure all things are pure* (1:15). This must not be twisted to mean that a Christian can do absolutely anything he or she wishes, because there are moral absolutes which the Christian must observe and evil actions which must be avoided (as mentioned in this letter in several places, such as 1:7, 2:12, 3:3 and elsewhere). Paul's words here are clearly intended as a contrast with the commands of the false teachers. We can imagine rules of the type 'don't do this' and 'don't do that', based on the assumption that you will become defiled if you do certain things or eat certain foods. As in 1 Timothy 4:3, this verse indicates that asceticism was part of the false teaching.

The *pure* are those who have been cleansed within by the work of Christ (2:14) and they are not defiled by mere externals. Jesus taught the same (Mk 7:19) and in 1 Timothy 4:3-5 Paul asserts the goodness of God's creation. It is only the *corrupt and unbelieving* who are afraid of ritual pollution; to them *nothing is pure.* Their defilement is an inner problem of *mind* and *conscience.* Their understanding and attitudes are wrong and this produces unnecessary rules which only appear to deal with the problem of impurity. Again we think of Jesus' criticisms of the scribes and Pharisees (Mt. 23:25-26).

The final damning comment is that they do not truly know God (1:16). They may have even claimed that their rules and regulations gave them a superior spirituality and a higher or more intimate knowledge of God. But though *they profess to know God*, there is clear evidence that they do not. *Their actions* are an eloquent denial of their claim. The particular action suggested by the context is their rejection of what God has pronounced to be good, but the last words of the verse (see comment below) may suggest that Paul is thinking of other actions also.

The false teachers are described by three further words or phrases. First, they are *detestable*, no doubt primarily to God because they reject what God approves. It is implied that they should be detestable to those who share God's values. Second, they are *disobedient*, again mainly to God whose instruction they have rejected but perhaps also to the authorized leadership of the church (such as Paul and other apostles). Third, they are *unfit for any good work*. This translation (similar in NIV) means that they are unfit to do any good work, but a more satisfactory translation is *rejected in respect to every good work*, which means that when measured by the standard of the good works that God expects they are seen to have failed the test.[111] This then is virtually a repetition of *they deny him by their actions*, applied in a more general way to *every good work* which may be used as a standard.

Good works are a significant theme in the PE and in Titus especially. Though works are not the way of salvation (3:5), they are considered to be of great importance in the Christian life (2:7, 14, 3:1, 8, 14). Not least they are a measuring stick of true faith, for as Paul indicates here ungodly actions effectively deny the claim that a person knows God. In 1 Timothy 5:8 similarly, a person who does not act in an appropriate way is *worse than an unbeliever*.

Reflection: Faith and Works

It is the letter of James which most naturally comes to mind when the topic of faith and works is mentioned. In much popular thinking James is understood

---

[111] So Mounce, *Pastorals*, 403; Towner, *Timothy-Titus* (2006), 711.

to be in conflict with Paul on this matter. James, it is said, teaches the necessity of works, whereas Paul teaches that faith is the only thing that counts. This statement is a serious misunderstanding of both James and Paul. We cannot look into the subject properly in this brief reflection, but Paul's statement at the end of Titus 1 is a good place to begin to ask whether the popular understanding of Paul's attitude to works is accurate.

We have noted Paul's evaluation of the false teachers that despite their claim to know God they deny him by their actions. It is hard to imagine a stronger way of emphasizing the absolute importance of actions or good works in the life of the believer. The problem in the sort of popular misunderstanding mentioned above is that it tends to put the question in terms of faith or works, as if the two things are mutually incompatible. But in fact the NT puts them firmly together. You cannot have one without the other, a point on which James and Paul agree.

This truth has already been observed in 1 Timothy 5:8 where failure in the ethical realm amounts to denying the faith and making the person worse than an unbeliever. As we continue in Titus we will see the same emphasis on the necessity of good works many times in the remaining two chapters (2:7, 14, 3:1, 8, 14). Worth noting especially is 2:14, in which one of the purposes of Christ's work for us is that we will be a people of his own who are zealous for good deeds. A changed life is not an optional extra but is seen to be at the very heart of God's intention for those called to belong to him.

For the benefit of the reader who may suspect that Paul is not the author of the PE, we may add some references from elsewhere in Paul's writings where the same point is clearly demonstrated. In Galatians 5:6 he says that the only thing that counts is "faith working through love", which clearly links faith and works. Similarly, we find in Romans the phrase the "obedience of faith" as a shorthand description of the purpose of his ministry in the Gentile world (1:5, 16:26). He labours to bring about the response of faith which in turn will lead to a life of obedience. The same focus on obedience as the outcome is seen in Romans 15:18. In fact we would have to read Paul's letters with one eye closed to overlook the strong emphasis on an obedient life as an assumed result of the work of God in our life.

Of course works are not the way of salvation. Later in Titus Paul quite explicitly denies that it is possible to be saved by our works of righteousness (3:5). So we can hardly imagine that he gives works this significance in 1:16. The point is that true faith and true knowledge of God will inevitably lead to the right sorts of actions. Yes, salvation is available only through our response of faith to God's acts of mercy in Christ, but the only evidence of true faith is our works. Without good works, faith is nothing more than an empty claim. In a slightly different context Jesus made the same point: "you will know them by their fruits" (Mt. 7:16, 20).

Titus 2:1-10

The Importance of the Task of Teaching

At the beginning of chapter 2 Paul addresses Titus directly, with instructions about his own ministry. In 1:5 he has reminded Titus of instructions previously given, about setting right what was lacking in the churches and especially appointing elders. In expressing concern about the false teachers he has said that they must be silenced (1:11), by implication a responsibility that would fall on Titus' shoulders. But this now is the first time that Titus is given a direct instruction.

It is interesting, therefore, to observe that it is an instruction about what he should *say* (2:1). We are often told that actions speak louder than words. No doubt that is true, but like many proverbs it is only part of the truth. What one says is also of great importance, as Jesus himself assures us (Mt. 12:36-37). The context in this letter is ministry in the church, and already we have been left in no doubt about the importance of the spoken word: the proclamation entrusted to Paul (1:3), the role of the bishop in encouraging and rebuking (1:9), and on the negative side the threat from false teaching (1:11).

So it is hardly surprising that the first direct instruction given to Titus has to do with his words. He must *teach* (2:1). (The Greek word is actually *speak*, though in this context it is clear that it is not his speech in general conversation but his official speaking that Paul has in mind.) What he teaches must be *consistent with sound doctrine*. This also is not surprising, as *sound doctrine* has already been mentioned in 1:9 as the basis for what the bishop is to say in his speaking ministry. Paul makes the same point in other ways, when he speaks of the *proclamation with which I have been entrusted* (1:3), indicating that it is not his own message but God's. Conversely, the false teachers are condemned as *idle talkers* (1:10), who focus on *Jewish myths* and *commandments* which do not come from God but from godless men (1:14).

This remains a firm principle for any who would exercise a speaking ministry in the church. If we do not have a message from God we should remain silent. And if we cannot demonstrate (from scripture) that our message is from God, our audience has a right to be suspicious of what they hear. On the other hand, if we have a scriptural message which we know is from God, we have a freedom to speak with his authority and without apology.

Titus' role in giving instruction will be seen in later passages also (2:15, 3:1-2, 3:8-9), and the importance of good speech in general is also mentioned (2:8).

In stressing the speaking role of the minister, we must not minimize the importance of actions also. This is emphasized throughout the letter. Already we have read about people who *deny God by their actions* (1:16), and in contrast God's people should be *zealous for good deeds* (2:14). It is not a choice of one thing or another, but both at the same time. Right theology and right behaviour are both essential aspects of the Christian life, especially for one who has been given responsibility in leadership in the church.

Reflection: God's Word or Ours?

The comments above have once again drawn our attention to the spoken word as a central part of the ministry of those who give leadership to the church. One of the points observed in the passage is that Titus must teach what is consistent with sound doctrine. What would Titus have understood as sound doctrine? The only source of sound doctrine was the apostles who had been entrusted with the message of the gospel. Paul claimed to be one of those apostles to whom this proclamation had been entrusted (1:1-3) and he has been accepted as such by the church through the ages.

The twofold authority behind the apostolic proclamation was their experience of Christ (they were witnesses in a sense which is not true of other believers then or later) and the Bible, meaning of course the books of our Old Testament but now freshly understood from a Christ-centred perspective. The work of Christ was God's plan all along, though only now has this 'mystery' (as it is sometimes called) been revealed.

Writing to Titus, Paul speaks of this sound doctrine (1:9, 2:1, 10) or the word of God (1:3, 2:5) or the truth (1:1) without ever precisely defining it. He did not need to do so because Titus already knew what it was. Paul also speaks of the opposite, what it is not right to teach (1:11), assuming that Titus was able to identify that as well. There was a clear distinction between right and wrong teaching, depending on whether it was the apostolic teaching or not.

How can we discern today what is sound doctrine? Circumstances have changed but the principles have not. We no longer have the apostles with us, but we do have the books of the NT, the written record of the apostolic witness. One important difference is that whereas people like Titus were very much aware of the apostolic presence (looking over his shoulder, we might say), we probably do not have the same consciousness today. The apostolic witness and presence is the Bible, which can easily be perceived as a book belonging to the past and not so interesting or relevant to us today.

Many of our churches have a strong theoretical adherence to the Bible. When the preacher is introduced, we are told that he or she will bring us 'the word of God'. The preacher quite likely will carry a Bible into the pulpit. But the Bible may merely be a convenient place to keep the sermon notes, and when one listens carefully to what is announced as 'the word of God' one often finds that the message makes little or no reference to the Bible. Even if a passage has been read, too many times it is only a starting point and otherwise it is virtually ignored in the message.

The alternative may be a personal testimony or a reflection on some contemporary issue, things which are quite appropriate as an occasional variation in the Sunday preaching programme but if they are the normal Sunday sermon diet it can no longer be claimed that the congregation is hearing the word of God. These alternatives may be justified on different grounds. A common one is a sense of not being competent to explain a Bible passage clearly and relevantly, and so instead of that 'I will just share my experience'. One appreciates the honesty of such a speaker, which again is not a problem as long as this type of message is not what the congregation hears every week. A more disturbing excuse goes something like this: 'the Bible scholars can tell us what the text means but I believe that the Bible is relevant to us today and so I just want to talk about the subject in today's context.' This sort of statement (which the author has heard in India) seems to assume that there are two different and separate things: academic study of the Bible (which comes into the area of ancient history and so is optional and probably irrelevant) and living the Christian life today. It may also assume that there is a difference in principle between preaching and teaching. Both of these assumptions are exactly the opposite of what we read about in the PE. The first assumption is challenged by the vital and necessary link in the PE between the historic gospel (yes, about things that happened in the past) and the life of the believer, and the second by the observation that teaching is the normal description in the PE of what happens in a normal church on a regular basis.

The heading for this reflection is "God's Word or Ours?", with the implication that what we hear in our churches may not necessarily be the word of God. The fact that a statement comes from the mouth of a respected Christian does not make that statement the word of God. There is only one way we can be sure that what we hear is the word of God, and that is to insist that our preachers use the Bible, explain the meaning of the words of the Bible, and in order to be *sure that it is the word of God for us today to insist that they show how those Bible words are relevant and applicable to our modern situations. Then and then only can we claim that our church is truly a Bible-believing church.*

Practical Christian Living

Paul has spoken about teaching which is *consistent with sound doctrine* (2:1). This does not mean teaching Christian doctrine only (although this is definitely part of what should be taught), for the following instructions (2:2-10) which Titus is to give to others are very practical. There needs to be clear application of doctrine to the practical realities of daily life. Conversely practical instruction needs to be consistent with sound doctrine, not just the minister's personal ideas of what is right or wrong and not just affirming the practices of the local culture, but a way of living which flows out of the gospel truths which we have accepted.

The passage continues with instructions for five groups of believers: old men (2:2), old women (2:3), young women (2:4-5), young men (2:6) and slaves (2:9-10). For each group appropriate instructions are given. We will look briefly at each group.

Older men. For the old men (2:2) the first instruction is to be *temperate* or sober, a word we have seen in 1 Timothy as a necessary characteristic of a bishop (3:2) and a deacon (3:11). It can mean (literally) not addicted to alcohol or (metaphorically) restrained and clear-headed, and perhaps both senses are appropriate here. *Serious* (NIV *worthy of respect*) has also appeared in the 1 Timothy lists, referring to the deacons (3:8) and the women (3:11). *Prudent* (NIV *self-controlled*) has already been used in this letter in relation to the bishop (1:8), as also in 1 Timothy 3:2.

The fourth item is *sound* or healthy, with three areas of good health specified. This word is a favourite of the author of the PE (which contain most of the NT examples). It is used especially in the phrases *sound doctrine* (1:9, 2:1; 1 Tim. 1:10, 2 Tim. 4:3) and *sound words* (1 Tim. 6:3, 2 Tim. 1:13). But it is not only the doctrine that must be sound but the people also, as in this verse and in 1:13 where Paul has expressed the hope that the false teachers *may become sound in the faith*. We might suggest that it is by accepting *what* is sound (the sound teaching) that a *person* becomes sound. Here the focus is on the old men, and they are to be sound *in faith, in love, and in endurance*. It is worth noticing the high standard expected of the elderly. We live in a culture that gives outward respect to the elderly, but perhaps with the unspoken feeling that you cannot really expect very much of them; after all, they are only old people and we must make allowance for the idiosyncrasies of their age. That is quite the opposite of what this passage (including the next verse) says.

Older women. The requirements for *older women* are given in 2:3-5. Within the paragraph the responsibility of these women for *younger women* is also mentioned (2:4-5) and so in fact it is really only 2:3 which speaks specifically about the older women. First, they must be *reverent in behaviour*, which in simple language means they must behave in a way that is appropriate for Christian women. They must not be *slanderers*, a potential danger arising from a situation where they have time to sit and gossip about people (also identified as an issue for younger widows in 1 Tim. 5:13). Nor must they be *slaves to drink*. The danger of alcohol abuse is raised several times in the PE. It is mentioned in the lists of required characteristics of leaders (of an overseer in 1:7, 1 Tim. 3:3; of a deacon in 1 Tim. 3:8), and of ordinary Christian people here (note also the word *temperate* in the previous verse). This suggests a significant problem in society, and evidence has been produced by scholars that it was a particular problem in Crete.[112] A sad aspect of alcohol abuse is that the person concerned usually feels that the matter is under control ('I can stop whenever I wish'), but the word *enslaved* that is used here suggests the opposite (as ministers and counsellors who deal with such people know very well).

Following the two negative commands Paul returns to the positive. The older women are to *teach what is good*, not in the context of a public teaching role in the church, but as the following verse reveals in their instruction of the younger women. Again, as with the older men, Paul does not imagine the older women as being fit only to be sent to an eventide home or kept isolated in their own room. On the contrary they have a positive contribution to make to their own household and perhaps to other households within the Christian community.

Younger women. The contribution of the older women is described more fully in 2:4-5, a passage with a double focus. Though it begins with the older women as the subject and speaks of their role and responsibility,

---

[112] Witherington, *Commentary*, 137.

the focus soon turns to the *younger women* who need to be encouraged, and it is the characteristics that are desirable in the younger women which dominate the passage. The verb translated *encourage* is not the normal word that is thus translated. Its meaning is *bring to one's senses* and suggests that there was a need to recall the younger women to proper behaviour within marriage against a background of moral laxity in Cretan society.[113]

Seven characteristics are mentioned. The first two can be considered together: they must *love their husbands* and *love their children*. This is more than simply telling the younger women that they should do this, which they surely knew already. More likely, the intention is that the older women will show *how* they can do this in practical ways, giving detailed advice and showing from their own experience what is important for a successful marriage and happy family life. From all this we can see that it is assumed that the younger women are married, as would certainly have been the case under normal circumstances in that society. This means that these verses (2:2-6) lack any advice for single women (young or old).

The next two characteristics desirable for the younger women (2:5) are that they be *self-controlled* and *chaste* (NIV *pure*). The concept of self-control has already been applied to the older men in 2:2, and will occur again in 2:6 in reference to the younger men. It can be claimed that the same was expected of the older women also, as suggested by 2:3 even though the phrase self-control does not appear in that verse. Clearly this was a very significant Christian virtue, perhaps made even more important by the characteristic behaviour of Cretans in general (as we have seen in 1:12). In a context of lack of self-control among the members of society, the Christian community has the opportunity to demonstrate the power of the gospel through a different and better standard of personal behaviour. The next item refers especially to moral purity, rather than cultic or religious purity. It is one aspect of self-control, and an obvious requirement especially in a society where moral standards may have been lax and where there may have been occasions for sexual temptation. Christians in general need to be reminded of this, and especially younger believers (male as well as female, it should be added).

The next word in the list is *managers of the household*. NRSV adds the adjective *good*, a word that is not in the text but is no doubt implied,

---

[113] For discussion of the Greek verb, see Towner, *Timothy-Titus* (2006), 725-726.

inasmuch as the expectation is not simply that the younger women will perform the task but that they will do it well. The first two items in this list have already given the impression that the life of a younger woman is mainly centred on home and family, and this word now reinforces that impression. But it should not be assumed that they were not much better than household servants, for to manage the household is a significant responsibility. Following this is *kind*, which would apply especially to her treatment of those over whom she may have responsibility in the household, though it need not be limited to those.[114]

The list began with the instruction to love their husbands and now finishes with *being submissive to their husbands*. Several observations are appropriate here. (a) The Greek phrase is stronger than the translations indicate, literally *their own husbands*, which emphasizes the point that a woman is not asked to be submissive to men in general but only to her own husband. (b) The instruction is directed to the woman. It is her duty to show proper submission but not the husband's role or right to demand it. Though this may seem a minor distinction, it can have important practical consequences.

The list of duties concludes with a statement which draws attention to the wider influence of the way that these women conduct themselves. The purpose of living according to the standards that have been mentioned is *so that the word of God may not be discredited* (2:5). There are similar statements at the end of 2:8 and 2:10, and we will consider these together in the following section.

Younger men. In contrast to the much longer list of expectations of the younger women in the preceding verses, there is only one demand made of the younger men (2:6): they are *to be self-controlled*. It is highly unlikely that this means that a lower standard was expected of younger men. Self-control has been a constant feature of this whole chapter till now, appearing in the lists for the older men (2:1, where NRSV has *prudent*) and the younger women (2:5). We have also suggested that self-control is a suitable summary of some of the characteristics of the older women in 2:3. So its further appearance here may be considered a way of saying that the younger

---

[114] The word translated *kind* can also be translated *good*. NRSV appears to have (accidentally?) translated the Greek word twice, as a separate characteristic *kind* and by adding *good* before *managers of the household*.

men are to strive for the same sort of Christian character as others in the congregation.

In the following two verses Paul sets out his expectations of Titus himself. The three verses (2:6-8) belong to the same sentence in Greek, suggesting that Titus is included within the category of younger men. Titus is told to be *a model of good works*, an example no doubt to all members of the congregation but in particular, it is surely implied, to his own age group.

This raises the question of who is a young man. What age group does Paul refer to? In 1 Timothy 4:12 Timothy's youthfulness is mentioned, and yet we know that Timothy had had significant experience in Christian ministry by that time. He was from the city of Lystra (Acts 16:1), almost certainly converted during Paul's earlier visits to that city (Acts 14). We can only guess his age at conversion, but even if he was as young as 15 at that time, he would have been at least 30 when 1 Timothy was written, relatively young but certainly not a child. Titus also had been a colleague of Paul's for some time, in fact a senior colleague and not merely a junior apprentice, and now is in a position of significant responsibility in Crete, and so he could hardly have been younger than Timothy.

All this means that when this chapter speaks of younger men (and of course younger women also), Paul does not mean teenagers, but young adults in their 20s and 30s. They can be fully expected to exercise self-control and other similar virtues, even when the surrounding culture does not value such characteristics (as seems to have been the case in Crete).

Titus. As we have seen already, Titus is instructed to be a good example, *a model of good works* (2:7). Though Titus may well be included as one of the younger men, he is of course more than that. As Paul's representative, he is not much different from an apostle himself, and his manner of life is of the utmost importance. Believers and unbelievers alike can reasonably conclude that what they see in Titus is the normal pattern of Christian living. He dare not lower his standards. The same is true of any Christian leader, even though leaders today cannot claim the direct authorization of an apostle.

The following phrases (2:7-8) mention three further areas of Titus' life and ministry. NRSV and NIV treat all the three items *integrity, gravity* and *sound speech* as aspects of Titus' activity of *teaching*: in his teaching he is to show these things. That is a possible understanding, but there are other possibilities. One alternative is to see these as three separate items, with only the first related to teaching (integrity in teaching), the second describing a serious life (that is, not frivolous), and the third referring to sound speech in general.[115]

The comments just made show that we cannot be certain of the exact intention of the author in these two verses, but this does not make much difference to the bigger picture. It is clear that Titus is expected to live a life of good works, to take his teaching ministry seriously, to be serious-minded, and to be careful in his speech. Whether the last two refer to his life in general or to his teaching in particular, in reality both are implied, for a person who is serious-minded about his or her teaching and sound in speech in the teaching context will also most likely be the same in their life in general, and vice versa.

The instructions to Titus conclude at the end of 2:8 with a reminder of the wider effects of his life (as similarly in 2:5). We will return to this in the next section.

Slaves. This is the final group for whom instructions about appropriate Christian behaviour are given. They are different from the others inasmuch as they are not defined by age or sex but by social class. As in 1 Timothy 6:1-2, slavery is recognized as part of the social fabric of that time, though that is not the same as regarding it as something good or desirable. Though no NT writer challenges the institution of slavery, the effect of masters and slaves belonging to the same body of Christ is to challenge slavery in an indirect and subtle way and ultimately to undermine it. This present passage raises the status of slaves in a significant way by speaking of the positive effect of their appropriate behaviour (at the end of 2:10).

Similar to 1 Timothy 6:1-2 and perhaps for the same reasons, only slaves are addressed and not masters, probably because it was the Christian slaves who misunderstood teaching about Christian liberty and were causing problems (see the comments on that passage).

Five separate instructions are given for slaves (2:9-10), but in effect they can be summed up very simply: they are to be good slaves. They no doubt have their own thoughts and feelings about being slaves, but the fact is that at present that is what they are, and legally so within the laws

---

[115] For a helpful discussion of all this, see Knight, *Pastorals*, 312-313.

of the time. It will do no good to them and it will do no credit to God or the church or the gospel if they do not act in ways that are appropriate.

The details require little explanation. They are *to be submissive* (as also the younger women to their husbands in 2:5). This is required only in relation to *their own masters* (with emphasis on *their own*) not to society in general; they are not a lesser breed of humanity but simply in a particular social position at present. They are also *to give satisfaction* (or *to try to please them* as in NIV). *In every respect* (NRSV) or *in everything* (NIV) can be taken with either the first instruction (NIV, *subject to their masters in everything*) or the second (NRSV, *give satisfaction in every respect*).[116] They are *not to answer back*, a simple expectation that they should show proper respect; *not to pilfer* (NIV *steal*); and *to show perfect and complete fidelity.*

As in 2:5 and 8, there is again a reminder in conclusion (2:10) of the wider effects of the believer's behaviour, which will be the focus of the section "For the Sake of the Gospel" a little later.

Reflection: Applying New Testament Ethics

Among the instructions given for the guidance of the younger women is that they should be "managers of the household" (2:5) or "busy at home" (NIV) or literally simply "working at home". What does one do with an instruction like this in modern India?

Some will say: It is in the Bible and therefore it is a clear command to be obeyed. A woman's place is in the home. Let her stay there and find her purpose in life by fulfilling her domestic responsibilities. The opposite type of response may be that this is written for a particular cultural situation and is not binding on the Indian woman of the twenty-first century.

There are problems in both of these understandings. The first fails to take account of significant differences between the cultural contexts of the Bible and today. Even within the Bible different situations call for different instructions. For example, in 1 Corinthians 7:8 Paul recommends that the unmarried remain that way, whereas in 1 Timothy 5:14 he recommends that younger widows should marry. To take a command and say simply that 'the Bible tells me so' is to ignore the context. Furthermore, if we do take this approach we cannot choose what to accept and what to ignore. In our present passage the assumption is that every younger woman is married and has more than one child, and so any

---

[116] Marshall, *Pastorals*, 259, argues strongly for the interpretation reflected in NIV. So also Towner, *Timothy-Titus* (2006), 736 note 95.

young woman in a different situation would have to be regarded as living an 'unbiblical' lifestyle.

The second type of response mentioned above suffers from the problem that the Bible quickly becomes totally irrelevant if we draw the conclusion that because an instruction was given in a particular context it is irrelevant today. That applies to the whole of the Bible. Even the command not to murder was given in a particular context.

On the other hand, both these understandings have their strengths. To recognize the context is absolutely important. That is the solution to the problem raised by the two apparently contradictory pieces of advice about marriage mentioned above. They were given to different people in different situations. Or to put it differently, an instruction needs to be understood in its own context. At the same time we do need to take the Bible seriously. It is the word of God and it comes to us with a message that God intends us to respond to, not just as a book to read and ignore. The challenge is how to put together the positive insights of the two views we have identified.

Returning to the instruction for the younger women, we may begin with the cultural observation that it is very likely that Paul has in mind an actual problem in Crete (either that in Cretan society in general home and family life was given a low priority or that Christian women were responding wrongly to their 'freedom' in Christ and neglecting duties which were important). This will mean that the things he says (in 2:4-5) focus on the problem area and do not provide a complete picture. A complete picture would recognize that not all younger women were in fact married, and that even if they were they did not necessarily have children. A complete picture would recognize that a married woman in that society was not restricted to a life of domestic duties. A complete picture might add the observation that in the PE men also have household responsibilities (1 Tim. 3:4-5, 12). Comments such as these have the effect of relativizing the instruction. It ceases to be a 'Bible tells me so' type of command but requires thoughtfulness to interpret in its original context and to ask what it may mean for us today.

But taking the Bible seriously will mean recognizing that there are always matters of principle contained in a biblical command, even if it needs to be applied in a different way. One principle here is the importance of home and family life - and thus in modern India where it often happens that the careers of husband and wife mean prolonged family separation, it is important that we stop and assess what effect this has on the family and not simply accept that this is the way things are. Another principle is the witness of our home life (and our lives in general) in the wider society, a point that Paul specifically mentions in our passage (2:5).

For the Sake of the Gospel

In another letter Paul wrote, "I do all things for the sake of the gospel" (1 Cor. 9:23). Here he applies this principle to all other believers as well, for, as we have noticed, on three separate occasions he concludes his instructions to particular groups with a comment that draws attention to the wider effect of their behaviour, in the form of a purpose clause (*so that* ... , 2:5, 8, 10); NRSV spoils this parallelism by replacing *so that* with *then* in 2:8. Considered together these clauses provide a powerful additional motivation for Christians to act in the right way, with an awareness that their conduct is a witness for good or evil.

In 2:5 the instructions which the older women are to give to the younger women conclude with the words *so that the word of God may not be discredited*. Most of the requirements in the preceding list relate to her role in the home and her household relationships (with husband, children and others, possibly including slaves). It is known that there were tendencies on Crete during this period of history towards loose standards of sexual morality and lax attitudes towards fulfilling traditional roles in the home. Young married women who were believers must be recalled to better ways, not only better in terms of traditional cultural expectations but also better in terms of being consistent with their Christian profession. To do otherwise will result in the *word of God* (the gospel, the Christian faith) being *discredited*. The same point can be expressed positively: if these wives act in the right way their behaviour will bring credit to the gospel and so serve as a positive witness to the wider society.

It is possible that some of the women addressed here may have had non-Christian husbands. In that case the matter becomes even more urgent. But even with Christian husbands, inappropriate behaviour in the home would sooner or later become known outside the home and lead to a negative view of the Christian faith.

Titus must not only give instructions to others but in 2:8 is reminded of the effect of his own behaviour. In his case the purpose clause is *so that those who oppose you may be ashamed because they have nothing bad to say about us* (NIV). In one respect this translation may be misleading. Instead of *those who oppose you*, NRSV has *any opponent*. The point is that the word *you* does not occur in the Greek. The opponent is not just an opponent of Titus, but an opponent of Christians generally, as the word *us* at the end of the verse clearly shows. While it is true that the behaviour of each and every Christian is a witness to a watching world, this is especially true of a Christian leader. There are always opponents of the faith who gleefully grasp every opportunity to point out the failures of Christian leaders, as proof (so they think) that Christianity is a second-rate religion. The importance of a Christian leader being well-regarded by the wider community is mentioned in 1 Timothy 3:7, and the concern to remove opportunities for opponents to criticize is also seen in 1 Timothy 5:14 in the instructions regarding widows.

We may think that Paul is optimistic in his suggestion that Titus' good behaviour will stop opponents speaking evil of us. Some opponents do not need any evidence of a leader's wrong behaviour in order to speak evil of the faith. They are very happy to spread false rumours with no basis at all. Of course, Paul knew this very well, for he had experienced such misrepresentation in his own ministry (e.g., Rom. 3:8). But here his point is very simple: do not provide ammunition for opponents. Those with malicious intent will no doubt create their own ammunition, but opponents who are fair-minded may be willing to be convinced by the positive example of the Christian leader, and of course other Christians as well.

Finally, the effect of the behaviour of slaves is mentioned at the end of 2:10: *so that in everything they may be an ornament to the doctrine of God our Saviour.* Slaves may be low on the social scale with little or no influence on others under normal circumstances, but this statement shows that they can have a potentially great influence, far beyond what their social status may lead one to expect. Furthermore, these words express the matter positively. Whereas 2:5 and 2:8 speak of preventing negative results, this verse unfolds the possibility of a very positive consequence flowing from the good behaviour of the slave: a slave's right behaviour will adorn the *doctrine of God our Saviour,* that is the Christian faith. Just as a woman's jewellery enhances her natural beauty, so the gospel which already has its own beauty will be further adorned by the believer whose life shows the fruit of the gospel.

We may note that 1 Timothy 6:1 also speaks of the potential influence of the behaviour of a Christian slave, although there the matter is expressed from a negative point of view. It is possible, Paul says, that inappropriate behaviour will cause the Christian faith (there *the name of God and the teaching*) to be *discredited*. The same word *discredited* is used in 2:5 in the instructions for the younger women.

All these verses add up to an important general principle. A believer can never say: it is my life and I will live it the way I choose. He or she is a representative of the God whom we claim to serve. We must remember that our behaviour is inevitably either a positive or a negative witness to others. This should be seen as a solemn warning against un-Christian behaviour. But it is also an encouragement, a reminder that whether we are great or small in the eyes of the world, even our silent witness can have a great influence and bring honour to God.[117]

Titus 2:11-15

The Role of Grace

At first glance we might think that the remainder of the chapter moves from the practical to the theoretical. In 2:1-10 we have seen the instructions given to different groups of believers, and now we come to a statement which can be described as a summary of God's work of salvation. However, we will see that this statement is equally concerned with the practical matter of living the Christian life and it fits well in the context established by the preceding verses.

The first word of the paragraph (in the Greek word order) is the verb *appeared*. The closest English equivalent is found in the word *epiphany*. (This is still used in some Christian traditions as a description of one of the seasons of the Christian calendar, the main story of the Epiphany season being the coming of the wise men to see the recently-born Jesus, otherwise known as the *revelation* of Christ to the Gentiles.) 'Epiphany' language is relatively common in the PE (in both noun and verb forms). Here it is grace which has appeared; in 3:4 it is God's goodness and loving-kindness; in 2 Timothy 1:10 it is Jesus himself. These passages all

---

[117] For a balanced discussion of the teaching of this section of the letter (2:1-10) against the social background of the time and Paul's attitude to existing social structures (the family and the institution of slavery), see Witherington, *Commentary*, 129-133.

refer to *past* revelation at the time of Jesus' earthly ministry. But there are other references to revelation in the *future*: in this same paragraph the *appearance* (NRSV *manifestation*) of Jesus' glory (2:13) and also the appearance of Jesus himself (1 Tim. 6:14, 2 Tim. 4:1, 8). These passages refer to what we describe as the second coming. In other words, this 'epiphany' language covers both major aspects of God's saving work: the ministry of Christ in his incarnate state and the climax of history at the second coming.

In 2:11 what has appeared, we are told, is *the grace of God*. We would not have been surprised if Paul had written *Christ* appeared. That is, of course, what he is referring to, but *the grace of God* is a very adequate alternative way of saying the same thing. Paul was very conscious of the crucial role of God's grace in his own life (1 Tim. 1:14; also Tit. 3:7, 2 Tim. 1:9), and he naturally slips into this way of describing what God has done.

There are two main aspects of the role of grace according to these verses. The first is that it saves (2:11): God's grace appeared *bringing salvation to all*. *Bringing salvation* translates a single Greek word (occurring here only in the NT) which may be simply translated as *saving*. It is God's saving grace. This is a very familiar concept, especially from passages like Ephesians 2:5, 8 where grace and salvation are closely linked. We see the same link in the PE (2 Tim. 1:9), and in this letter grace is also presented as the basis of our justification (3:7). Here in 2:11 Paul simply states the fact, without further explanation and with little elaboration.

The only extra detail are the words *to all*, indicating the potential scope of God's salvation (as also in 1 Tim. 2:4, 4:10). This does not mean that all actually receive salvation, for that depends on our response of faith, but that all (however good or bad, from whatever background, race, socio-economic group and so on) come within the scope of God's saving work. Apparently NIV perceives a theological problem here, which has been solved by placing the words *to all men* after the verb *appeared*. This is unnecessary, and it is not the most natural understanding of the Greek text. The more recent TNIV helpfully expresses it as *the grace ... that offers salvation to all people*.

The second role of grace is introduced in 2:12. If the first role is totally expected, the second role may take us by surprise. Here Paul says that grace has a *training* role. NIV has *teaches*, but the word is stronger than that and could even be translated as *discipline*. Discipline is not just punishment but direction, and that is the role of grace.

This may also have been a less familiar aspect to the believers in Crete, for here much more detail is given. There are negative and positive aspects to the training which grace brings. Negatively, there are things which we must *renounce* (NIV vividly translates as *say "No"*), including *impiety and worldly passions*. Positively, grace will lead the believer to a life which is *self-controlled, upright and godly*.

The final words of the verse are *in the present age*, which are a further reminder of the main point being made here. When we emphasize salvation by grace, we may then mistakenly think that grace is only relevant to receiving Christ and the gift of salvation. Once we have done that, we can pack grace away and forget it, for it has done its job; it is relevant to get us to heaven but that is all. But not so, for here we see that grace is relevant in the *present age* also, and has a crucial part to play throughout the believer's life.

We may wonder why this training role is attributed to *grace* (rather than, say, the Holy Spirit in our life). How does grace train or discipline the believer? As we have observed it is not discipline in the sense of punishment or threat (as when a parent threatens to punish a child if he or she will not do as the parent wishes). It is much more positive than that and is an encouragement to do what is right. Grace continually reminds us of how merciful and kind God has been to us, and so we are encouraged to respond not just by *saying* thank you but by living lives that honour and please him, thus *expressing* our thanks in visible ways. The ability to do this is also a matter of God's grace, for only in the power of the indwelling Holy Spirit (God's gracious gift) can we live a God-pleasing life.

The appropriateness of this aspect of the work of grace is expressed in 2:13, which reminds us of things that lie ahead in the future. This life is not all there is. We have a *blessed hope* for the future also, elsewhere described as the hope of eternal life (1:2, 3:7). The believer therefore does *not* live life now with the attitude, "Let us eat and drink, for tomorrow we die" (Isa. 22:13, 1 Cor. 15:32). This life is (from one perspective) preparation for the future. Another future event is *the manifestation of the glory of our great God and Saviour, Jesus Christ*. The moment of his revealing will also be the moment of our revealing (Col. 3:4), and it is the earnest desire of the true believer not to be ashamed before him at his coming (1 Jn 2:28). All these provide further motivations to live the right sort of life now, a life that is self-controlled, upright and godly (2:12).

The Divinity of Christ

The statement about God's grace finishes in 2:13 with reference to *the manifestation of the glory of our great God and Saviour, Jesus Christ*. We have here what seems to be a clear statement that Jesus is God. The reader who has been working carefully through this commentary will not be surprised at this, for in a number of ways we have observed how God the Father and Jesus are linked on equal terms - in this letter, for example, as equally the source of grace and peace (1:4) and both as Saviour (1:3-4).

Such a direct statement that Jesus is God has not been allowed to pass without objection. Some scholars have doubted that this is the correct understanding, partly because the NT is normally quite reluctant to identify Jesus as God in a specific and unambiguous way. In the Pauline epistles, only Romans 9:5 offers a similar identification. In both passages it is possible to translate differently and avoid the conclusion that Jesus is God, and these alternatives are seen in the footnotes of NRSV. In our present passage the NRSV footnote has *of our great God and our Saviour Jesus Christ*, where the effect of repeating the word *our* is to see God and Jesus as separate persons. It must be said that such an alternative translation is possible.

The arguments are quite complex and technical, occupying five or more pages in the larger commentaries. One of the simplest and strongest arguments is the fact that there is only one Greek definite article (the word usually translated *the*) before the two nouns *God* and *Saviour*, whereas if these nouns were intended to refer to two separate persons one might expect the article to have been repeated. It is also difficult to know what the (single) appearance of both God and Jesus might mean.

A survey of some of the well-known translations is instructive. The identification of God and Jesus as two separate figures is followed by J. Moffatt and J.B. Phillips; one wonders how much these translations are influenced by theological assumptions, which are certainly a factor in the whole debate. But the majority of familiar translations prefer the version given in NRSV. The alternate translation is given in a footnote in RSV, NEB and NRSV. But NASB, NIV, TNIV and NKJV do not even bother to give the alternate version at all. These support the understanding which identifies Jesus as both our great God and our Saviour. Many of the substantial recent commentaries also prefer this interpretation.[118]

The Work of Christ

For convenience we treat 2:14-15 under a new heading, though in Greek the same sentence continues; in fact all of 2:11-14 is one sentence. The mention of Jesus in 2:13 leads into this wonderful statement of the significance of his earthly ministry.

It is said that he *gave himself for us*, almost identical wording to what we read in 1 Timothy 2:6, a reference to Jesus' death on the cross and a reminder that this had nothing to do with any misdeeds or faults of his own but was completely on behalf of others. It is a summary statement of the substitutionary nature of his death.

The purpose of this self-giving has both a negative and a positive aspect. The negative aspect is to *redeem us from all iniquity*. Here is indicated the problem of the human race, namely that our sin (here expressed by the word *iniquity* [NIV *wickedness*] which refers to our sinful actions) has produced the disastrous result of alienating us from God and putting us under the power of Satan and making us subject to judgement. From this we need deliverance and that is what the death of Christ achieves. In this explanation of Jesus' death as a means of redemption we see another similarity with 1 Timothy 2:6; in that passage NRSV and NIV use the word *ransom* (rather than *redeem*), but the Greek words in both passages express the same basic concept.

The positive purpose is expressed in the words *purify for himself a people of his own*. In the first place this purification is an inner cleansing, a spiritual purification, removing the guilt and penalty for our sin. In this aspect it is an intensely personal matter as the individual is enabled to move from alienation and fear of God to a relationship of positive harmony and fellowship with God.

---

[118] These include Fee, *Timothy-Titus*, 196; Knight, *Pastorals*, 322-326; Towner, *Timothy-Titus* (1994), 247-248; Marshall, *Pastorals*, 276-282; Mounce, *Pastorals*, 426-431; and Witherington, *Commentary*, 144-146. The opposite conclusion is reached by Kelly, *Pastorals*, 246-247. But Towner, *Timothy-Titus* (2006), 752, points out that the translation *the glory of our great God and Saviour, Jesus Christ* (e.g., NRSV, TNIV) allows for the view (which he prefers) that Jesus is not identified as *God* but as *the glory of God*.

However, it would be a mistake to limit purification to these things. It is not only spiritual and not only personal. First, we observe that the passage speaks of the purification of a *people*. Jesus' work certainly has enormous benefit for the individual who responds to it positively, but in many places the NT makes it clear that God's work is to create a new people, a people defined not by ethnic origin (that is, Jews rather than Gentiles) but by acceptance of Jesus as the necessary and only way by which our sin can be dealt with. Those who so respond to Jesus are brought into the people of God. This is not an optional extra (as some believers who do not treat church seriously seem to think) but an automatic result of accepting God's work in Christ. It is also a great privilege, for this is a people *of his own*. NIV helpfully adds a little emphasis, *his very own*, the word indicating a very special status.

We also note that this is a people *zealous for good deeds*. With this phrase we are reminded of the practical orientation of the whole passage. The words suggest that the redemption which the verse speaks of is not simply redemption from the guilt and penalty of sin but also release from bondage to sin. The word *zealous* should be given its full meaning. For a believer, doing good works is not something we do grudgingly but something to which we are fully committed; this is what we want to do, with the same enthusiasm with which Paul was zealous in persecuting the church (as he describes himself in Gal. 1:14, Acts 22:3). A similar phrase occurs in 1 Peter 3:13.

Thus the work of Christ has the double purpose of creating a new people of God and of making this people a different people.

The chapter finishes in a similar way to how it began, with an exhortation to Titus regarding his teaching ministry. The first verb is the same as in 2:1, in NRSV *declare* (though in 2:1 *teach*, which is the NIV translation in both verses). The second verb is *exhort* (NIV *encourage*), as previously in 1:9 and 2:6, and the third *reprove* (NIV *rebuke*). This is to be done *with all authority*, an authority which springs not from his own eloquence or personality or importance but from the fact that his message and ministry are given by God. Finally comes the command *let no one look down on* (NIV *despise*) *you*. In 1 Timothy 4:12 a similar instruction to Timothy is that no one should despise his *youth*, which may also be the reason for this command to Titus (though we cannot be sure of Titus' age). But whatever the precise reason for this instruction, Titus can avoid being looked down on by carrying out his ministry in a way that will command respect, by acting with integrity, fulfilling his duties conscientiously and with his personal Christian character consistent with the direction he desires to see in the lives of others.

Titus 3:1-7

A Changed Life

The subject of the believer's practical life continues at the beginning of the new chapter. In spite of the apparent doctrinal digression of 2:11-14, practical Christian living has been the constant theme since the beginning of chapter 2, for we have seen that even 2:11-15 has a very practical concern, namely to show that the work of God's grace is intended to change the life of the believer and especially to produce a new community of God's people who are zealous for good deeds.

Titus is told to *remind them* (3:1), which tells us that this is not a new subject but one with which the believers in Crete were already familiar. But, as we all know, it takes more than one lesson to learn a subject well, and, especially when it comes to the way we live our life, it may take many reminders before a good habit is well established. Paul is no longer addressing the specific context of a particular group within the church, but the word *them* refers to all believers. The instructions of 3:1-2 may be grouped in different ways, but here we follow Marshall's classification.[119]

First, there is subjection to authorities, expressed in the words *to be subject to rulers and authorities, to be obedient*. Paul encourages a right attitude to the governing authorities in Romans 13:1-7 also. It is not immediately obvious why he should do so here. He has already spoken of the need of submission in the younger women (2:5) and the slaves (2:9), and it is possible that there was a general problem in the congregation, perhaps arising from a misunderstanding of the new life of Christian freedom into which they had entered. Also Cretans had not always had

[119] See Marshall, *Pastorals*, 300-304.

a good relation with their rulers.[120] But this instruction in 3:1 may simply be another way of encouraging the sort of behaviour which would commend the gospel to unbelievers, following the earlier references to the potential influence of the behaviour of Christians on non-Christian society (2:5, 8, 10). Certainly the next verse suggests that a broad range of relationships is in Paul's mind as he writes.

Second is a readiness for good works. We have noticed the strong emphasis on the theme of good works, most recently in 2:14 but also in 2:7. We will not be allowed to forget the point, for it comes again in 3:8 and 3:14. It is possible to draw the conclusion from the context that it is the works of a good citizen that Paul is thinking of (noting that Rom. 13:3 also speaks of good conduct in the context of the instruction to be subject to rightful government).[121] On the other hand the instruction here is expressed in very general terms, and there is no reason to limit it to one's role as a citizen. There are many other contexts in which a believer should demonstrate a life of good works, as the other references (given above) suggest; the same point is confirmed by similar phrases in 2 Timothy 2:21 and 3:17.

Third come several points which speak of non-aggression (3:2): *to speak evil of no one, to avoid quarrelling, to be gentle*. The first of these three points is a verb which in other contexts means *blaspheme*, but here in the context of the way we relate to other humans the translation *speak evil* (NIV *slander*) is appropriate. The other two requirements also appear in the list of qualities to be sought in an overseer (1 Tim. 3:3, which is the only other NT passage where these words occur). The translation *avoid quarrelling* (NRSV) limits the reference to verbal interaction, which is no doubt an important part of the meaning, but *peaceable* (NIV) is broader and perhaps a more satisfactory understanding of a word which literally means *not fighting*. It is not only in our speech that we should cultivate peaceableness in our relations to other people. The final word in this group is *gentle*, which without further explanation seems to suggest a meek and mild manner and an insipid and dull personality. One definition of this word is "not insisting on every right of letter of law or custom" (BDAG), for which other translations are possible, such as *yielding* or (as in NIV) *considerate*. Expressed in these terms, it is a word

---

[120] Kelly, *Pastorals*, 249; Witherington, *Commentary*, 155.
[121] So Kelly, *Pastorals*, 249, and more cautiously Marshall, *Pastorals*, 301.

which brings a strong challenge to the attitude which insists on one's own rights, and rather than indicating weakness of character suggests a considerable strength to be able to resist what comes so naturally to most of us.

Fourth, there is patience:[122] *show every courtesy to everyone*. The key word here can be translated in ways similar to the preceding (e.g., *gentleness, courtesy, considerateness*). So it is uncertain whether this is really a fourth area. The suggestion that this is an active taking of the initiative whereas the preceding are more passive qualities[123] is a doubtful distinction.

An important observation in these instructions is the point already noticed: Paul has a wide range of relationships in mind. This is seen at the start in the expectation of submission to the state, but in a more personal way it comes out in the command to speak evil of *no one* and to show courtesy to *everyone* (3:2). We note too *every* good work (3:1). God looks for right behaviour in the believer not just in a limited range of relationships (such as home and family only or church only), but in all areas of life. It is a high expectation indeed.

If that is what it must be like now for the Christian, it has not always been so. This sad truth is vividly expressed in 3:3. The word *once* recalls Ephesians 2:3, where the same word is used in a similar context describing the Christian's earlier life as an unbeliever. Again, it will be convenient to follow Marshall's threefold classification of the seven points here.[124]

First, we were wandering in ignorance: *foolish, disobedient, led astray*. The unbeliever often considers him or herself very wise and clever (and this may be true in terms of expertise in some area of learning, such as their professional competence). However, they are foolish in the matter of what life is all about, and specifically in their failure (whether conscious and deliberate or otherwise) to give God his proper place. The fact that they do not obey God points to their lack of true wisdom. Thus, they can be said to be *led astray*, a translation which suggests that someone is leading them astray, though the verb can equally be translated *wander about aimlessly*, and this may be preferable here.

---

[122] Following Marshall's classification (Marshall, *Pastorals*, 304).
[123] So Marshall, *Pastorals*, 304.
[124] See Marshall, *Pastorals*, 309-311.

Second, we were slaves to pleasure: *slaves to various passions and pleasures*. The word *passions* has the basic sense of *desires*, in themselves neither good nor bad, though often used in the NT in a negative sense (as in the phrase *worldly passions* in 2:12). Similarly the word *pleasures* does not necessarily mean something wrong. It is not a sin to find something pleasurable or enjoyable. What makes it sinful is to be *slaves* to these things. It is very often true that people are enslaved to things which are not at all bad in themselves but which by coming to dominate a person's life push God to the side or out of the picture altogether.

Third, we were guilty of anti-social behaviour: *passing our days in malice and envy, despicable, hating one another*. This is not an attractive picture of a human life; expressed this way it is totally undesirable. Yet it may be true much more often than we prefer to think. Naturally it will be dressed up to look more attractive than the picture presented by these blunt words, but sadly many people boost their own self-esteem by pulling others down.

The phrases used in this verse may have been chosen particularly with weaknesses of the Cretan character in mind. But we note that Paul says *we* (not *you*), and, even if specially relevant to the Cretans, his words are to be understood as intended to be a general description of sinful humanity.

Reflection: Teaching with Relevance

In several previous reflection sections we have noticed the central place which teaching should have in the ministry of those who lead the church. We have observed, among other things, the common misunderstanding that 'teaching' is essentially theoretical and abstract and belongs only in the seminary classroom. As a result there is considered to be no place for teaching in the ongoing life of a local church.

This is in such contrast with the picture of church life in the PE that it should give us a shock and make us ask where the modern church in India has gone wrong. Or to express the point in another way, what is so different about our churches today that they no longer need what was considered by Paul to be absolutely essential?

We need to start with some basic questions. What is teaching? What needs to be taught (not just in the seminary but to the regular members of our congregation who gather Sunday by Sunday)? There is definitely a theological component, and church members need regular reminders of the basics of Christian belief: the truth about God, Jesus, and the Holy Spirit; humankind and sin; the gospel of salvation; God's grand design to establish his kingdom. Truths such as these (which are not a complete list by any means) are foundational, and no doubt were at least part of what Paul had in mind when he spoke of the bishop who must be able to preach with sound doctrine (1:9).

But if there is one thing which the PE make perfectly clear, it is that one way to evaluate whether the teaching is correct or not is its effect in the life of the believer. Paul sees his ministry as promoting the knowledge of the truth that is in accordance with godliness (1:1). True teaching is never simply to communicate theological information, but is intended to lead to a changed life.

Growth in godliness does not imply preaching which encourages greater piety at a purely personal and spiritual level, nor a greater religiosity. Godliness is essentially a God-pleasing life, which covers every aspect of life, in family, workplace, and community, as well as church. This is seen very plainly in the last two chapters of Titus, where Titus' teaching deals with personal moral characteristics, proper behaviour and good relations in the home and the church, and right responses to the secular authorities, with a special focus on the effect of our life on unbelievers who observe us. These are different aspects of what Paul means when he speaks of being "zealous for good deeds" (2:14) and "ready for every good work" (3:1).

What is delivered from the pulpit each Sunday should fit the description 'teaching'. It is not just telling stories. It is not just sharing testimonies. It is not just seeking to create an emotional atmosphere in which people are tricked into making decisions which turn out to be meaningless as soon as they have left behind the emotions of the meeting. It should not be just devotional, encouraging greater religious piety which is unrelated to real life.

On the other hand, it should not just be communicating theological or biblical facts and information. The preacher who thinks that his or her task is to explain the meaning of every Greek word gives biblical preaching a bad name. That sort of preaching is not at all what Paul intended when he gave instructions such as we find in Titus. But despite this caution, proper preaching must have a theological and doctrinal basis. Teach what is consistent with sound doctrine (2:1). Yes, the message must have a practical application, showing what action is an appropriate response to what the passage says. But the application needs a base, and the theological foundations must be solidly laid if the Christian community is to live in a God-pleasing way, for what we think and believe always determines how we behave.

Where can these foundations be laid, and how can the practical relevance of theological truth be explained? In most churches, the only practical context is the Sunday morning (or evening) service. That is when believers gather. If there are other meetings (such as home fellowships and prayer meetings), well and good. But the Sunday service is the heart of congregational life in most churches, and that opportunity must be well utilized for the sort of teaching which Paul shows is vital for the health of the congregation.

God's Initiative to Save

The portraits of the character of the believer (3:1-2) and the unbeliever (3:3) could hardly provide a greater contrast. But what can produce such a change? The answer is given in one long sentence in 3:4-7.[125] These verses contain the second major description in this letter of God's saving work, the other being in 2:11-14. In such a short letter it is noteworthy that there are two significant statements of this kind, which helps to correct a possible false impression that the letter to Titus is mainly concerned with merely practical matters.

The passage begins by identifying a particular point in history: *when the goodness and loving-kindness of God our Saviour appeared* (3:4). Immediately we are reminded that the Christian message is not a religious philosophy but the announcement of an event. As the context makes clear, that event is the earthly ministry of Jesus Christ (mentioned here at the end of 3:6 and previously in 2:14). But it is not only the event as such which is mentioned but also its significance, for we are told that it was the appearance of God's goodness and loving-kindness. God could easily have acted in judgement (which was certainly part of the expectation of John the Baptist when the Messiah came, according to Mt. 3:7-12). Indeed, God's work in Christ *was* in part an act of judgement (on sin and Satan, for example), but that is not its central feature and here the positive side of God's work is emphasized. God acted for the good of his human creatures.

As noted above, Jesus is mentioned in this passage but not till the end of 3:6. The passage begins with the focus entirely on God. It is he who has acted and so it is entirely appropriate that he is the one described here (3:4) as *our Saviour* (as previously in 1:3 and 2:10). The point is reinforced in 3:5 in the words *he saved*, which is the main verb of the whole sentence.

Several aspects of God's work of salvation can be identified here. One can be called the source or basis of our salvation, which is expressed

---

[125] One sentence in *Greek*, that is, though NRSV and NIV both divide into two sentences, as modern translations tend to do with long sentences.

negatively and then positively. The negative side is *not because of any works of righteousness which we had done* (3:5). The reason for this is that no human being is righteous (Rom. 3:10). We can try hard, and perhaps even be relatively good, but in the end we cannot by our own works reach a point at which we can say, 'I am righteous.' This is precisely why God's saving work is necessary.

Fortunately there is a positive side, expressed in the words *but because of his mercy* (3:5). *Mercy* is a favourite word in the PE, occurring in introductory greetings (1 Tim. 1:2, 2 Tim. 1:2) which does not happen in Paul's other letters. The related verb form is found in 1 Timothy 1:13, 16, where the experience of God's mercy summarizes what God has done in Paul's own life. The present passage shows that mercy is not only central to Paul's experience but is a fundamental aspect of the experience of God's salvation in any believer's life.

Another aspect is the process of salvation, the way in which it comes to reality. This is described in terms of what we experience: it is *through the water of rebirth and renewal by the Holy Spirit* (3:5). The translation of these words is quite difficult. To begin with, we should note that the first noun is not literally *water* but *washing* (as NRSV footnote tells us, as well as NIV); it does not necessarily refer to water baptism though many assume that this is the meaning,[126] but it can just as easily refer to an inward and spiritual washing or cleansing.[127]

Larger commentaries will need to be consulted for a proper discussion.[128] We will need to allow some details to remain uncertain, but several things of great significance are clear. These are that the saved person experiences rebirth and renewal, that is, a new life; and that this is the result of the activity of the Holy Spirit. We need to remember the context, especially Paul's focus on practical Christian living, in order to understand properly this rebirth and renewal. It is not just a spiritual experience but a truly new life in the present, a life marked by a changed character brought about by the same Spirit who has been poured out on us.

[126] So Kelly, *Pastorals*, 252.

[127] So Marshall, *Pastorals*, 317-318; Mounce, *Pastorals*, 439-440; Towner, *Timothy-Titus* (2006), 781. Fee, *Timothy-Titus*, 205, agrees, but adds that the language "probably alludes to baptism".

[128] See Knight, *Pastorals*, 341-344; Marshall, *Pastorals*, 316-322; Mounce, *Pastorals*, 441-443, 448-450; Towner, *Timothy-Titus* (2006), 781-784; Witherington, *Commentary*, 158-160.

Though the Spirit has an important role in our experience of salvation, it is still true that God saves, for he is the one who has poured out his Spirit (3:6), something which he has done *richly*, generously, for which we can be truly thankful. Another point which is surely clear from this passage is that this pouring out of the Holy Spirit is not a 'second blessing' experience but part and parcel of a believer's basic conversion experience.

Next the passage speaks of the historical foundation of our salvation: *through Jesus Christ our Saviour*. We have previously observed that the passage is much more about God the Father than about Christ. Indeed, Jesus is not mentioned till now, and nothing specific is said about his work, for example his death on the cross. Yet all that is assumed (having already been mentioned in 2:14), and here we learn of his involvement in the pouring out of the Spirit. In Acts 2:33 says that *Jesus* is the one who has poured out the Spirit, which warns us against making rigid distinctions between the role of the Father and the role of the Son in some aspects. Here it is recognized that the Son was certainly involved: it was *through Jesus Christ*. This at least means that the coming of the Spirit was dependent on the prior work of the Son. If Jesus had not fulfilled his mission, the giving of the Spirit would not have been possible. Another blurring of the roles of Father and Son is seen here in the description of Jesus as *our Saviour* (previously in 1:4 and 2:13). Yes, God saved us, but equally it is the work of Jesus that makes salvation possible.

Finally, we read of the results or blessings of salvation: *so that, having been justified by his grace, we might become heirs according to the hope of eternal life* (3:7). We are not righteous in ourselves, but we are pardoned and acquitted (*justified*) in the sight of God. This is *by his grace*, virtually the same in substance as *according to his mercy* (3:5), and repeating the significant role of grace as explained in 2:11-12. That is our position now in relation to God, but the verse goes a stage further by referring to what still lies ahead, namely our eternal *inheritance* and the *hope* which we have of *eternal life*.

The Roles of the Trinity

There is no need to repeat the details of what has been explained already, especially in the preceding section. But it is rewarding to summarize what these verses say about the roles of Father, Son and Holy Spirit. We can also add material from 2:11-14.

Regarding God the Father, Paul says that God's grace, goodness and love have been revealed (2:11, 3:4), and as the one who has taken this initiative God can appropriately be described as our Saviour (3:4-5; also 1:3, 2:10).

Who is Jesus? Some think of him as only a man, even if perhaps a great man. But this view is inadequate. In many ways the NT shows him to be God. This is usually implied rather than stated directly, but here (2:13) he is specifically called *our great God* (according to the interpretation suggested above).

Jesus' work is also dealt with here: his death and its significance (2:13-14), and also his role in pouring out the Spirit (3:6).

The Holy Spirit is not emphasized in the PE (elsewhere only in 1 Tim. 3:16, 4:1, 2 Tim. 1:14), but 3:5-6 by itself is a very significant passage. It is through the Spirit that we receive new birth and renewal, including the ongoing changing of our character.

Reflection: Defining the Gospel

As a classroom exercise or in a church discussion and study group, it is interesting to see the answers when people are asked to list the essential ingredients of the gospel. Once people begin to offer their suggestions, the whiteboard fills up very quickly. One realizes how many different points can be rightly considered part of the gospel message, but one is also forced to reflect on what is essential and at the heart of the gospel as distinct from what may be considered less central.

In Titus we have two important gospel summaries (2:11-14, 3:4-7) as well as points that can be added from other passages (such as 1:1-3). We can list the following points (at least) from these two main passages. From 2:11-14: the gospel is the working of God's grace; God's grace brings salvation; God's grace trains us for a changed life; we wait for the appearing of Jesus; Jesus is our great God and Saviour; he gave himself to redeem us; he gave himself to purify us for good works. From 3:4-7: the gospel is the working of God's goodness and loving-kindness; God is our Saviour; salvation is not the result of our works; salvation is according to God's mercy; salvation is made effective through the working of the Holy Spirit; the Spirit brings new birth and renewal; God poured out the Spirit; it is through Jesus that the Spirit is poured out; Jesus is our Saviour; God's grace brings justification; the purpose of God's work is to make us heirs with the hope of eternal life. No doubt some of these points can be expressed in different words, but in one form or another, all these things are to be found in these two passages alone.

All this is rather overwhelming. In just eight verses we read about the work of God (the Father), Jesus, and the Holy Spirit. The initiating characteristics of God are described by four different words: grace, goodness, loving-kindness and mercy. The result of it all is expressed by different theological terms: salvation, redemption, purification, new birth, renewal, justification and eternal life. We are told of the effect of the gospel for the present (training us to renounce evil and to do good) and for the future (the hope of Christ's appearing and of eternal life).

So in all this what is the heart of the gospel? One response to this question is that the gospel can be expressed in different ways. There are many different points which can be included, and there is no single, simple summary which suffices for every occasion. That is the reason why in two consecutive chapters of the same letter we have such different statements, because Paul wishes to emphasize different things in different contexts. And that may well be true today. Don't be too quick to judge someone else's gospel preaching simply because they do not use your favourite words.

However, we can go further than this and seek to identify common and essential themes. We suggest at least the following. (1) One is the theme of salvation. Both God and Christ are described as Saviour, and other 'salvation' words occur. This highlights the basic human need of rescue from a serious predicament, a point emphasized also by the words redeem and justify. (2) God's initiative is emphasized (his grace, goodness, and so on), for there is nothing we can do to solve our own problem. (3) The role of Jesus is important. He is described in these verses as saviour and redeemer (though without any clear statement about his death as such). (4) There is a strong emphasis on the importance of a changed life now, and not just some sort of spiritual experience or the discovery of the key to get us into heaven when we die. (5) In no way in contradiction to the previous point is the Christian hope for the future: the appearing of Christ and the hope of eternal life.

What do you think a gospel message should contain? Should all these five points be included every time? What has been omitted from these two passages which you think must be included? Can you find passages of scripture to support your view?

Titus 3:8-15

Titus' Duty

As we come into the second half of the chapter, it is not clear where the paragraph division should be made. NRSV begins a new paragraph in the middle of 3:8 (with the words *the saying is sure* concluding the previous paragraph). NIV includes the whole of 3:8 as the end of the preceding paragraph. An alternative (represented by the UBS[4] and NA[27] editions of the Greek text) is to include 3:8 entirely in the new paragraph, and this makes good sense. Though there can be little doubt that the actual *saying* is the content of 3:4-7, *the saying is sure* can be understood as a suitable introduction to the new paragraph, by reminding Titus of the great significance of the statement just made and thus emphasizing the solemn responsibility he has to *insist on these things*, that is the things which the trustworthy saying asserts.

Thus once again Titus' teaching role is emphasized. This is seen throughout chapter 2 where his responsibility to instruct various groups is clearly defined. That chapter also contains a more general reference to his teaching responsibility (2:13) and this is what we find here in 3:8. The exact translation of the verb *insist* is not clear. NIV similarly has *stress*, but another interpretation is *speak confidently*. Ultimately there is not much difference in the sense, but *speak confidently* sounds a note of assurance in the teaching. Titus is not to speak hesitantly, as if there may be some doubt about what he is saying, but with full confidence. The apostolic teaching which he is to pass on to the churches under his responsibility comes with the authority of Christ and God.

The teaching responsibility must sometimes be exercised in a negative way, by responding forcefully to false teaching. We have previously seen this in 1:13, and we find the same thing in the present paragraph. There are things mentioned in 3:9 which Titus must *avoid*. (For further comment about the *controversies* and other things here, see the section below on "Fruitful and Unfruitful Things".) In part to *avoid* means that Titus must not give them room in his own thinking and understanding. But how is he to respond to those who teach such things? He is not simply to cut them off but rather he must first try to correct them. That is the sense of *after a first and second admonition* (3:10).

This fits with 1:13, which also indicates that an attempt is to be made to correct those who teach what is false. But if this is unsuccessful, decisive action must be taken to *have nothing more to do with anyone who causes divisions* (3:10). We may sometimes be told that we must learn to accept different people with different views, but here it is made clear that there are some people who should *not* be accepted in the Christian fellowship, namely those who threaten the spiritual health and well-being of the other members of the congregation.

The Duty of Every Believer

Returning to 3:8, we can identify not only Titus' duty and responsibility to teach, but also the duty of every believer. A church is not sound simply because the teaching is sound. What is also crucial is that the lives of believers are sound, that is, that they accept the sound teaching and put it into practice in their lives.

It is very easy to take a passage like 3:4-7 and treat it in isolation as a doctrinal statement about God's work of salvation through Christ and through the work of the Spirit. Those verses are indeed a wonderful doctrinal statement, but Paul's purpose here is not simply to give theologically correct instruction. He is reminding Titus of what must be taught in order that the believers *may be careful to devote themselves to good works* (3:8). God's work is a work of bringing *rebirth* and *renewal* (3:5). Its purpose is to create new people who live different lives and who are *zealous for good deeds* (2:14). If this does not happen, there is reason to doubt whether God's work is really being done in a person's life, even if they claim to be a believer. It is a consistent NT theme that true belief can be measured by the visible fruit, with many references in this letter alone to good works (2:7, 14, 3:1, 8, 14), as well as elsewhere (e.g., Mt. 7:20, Gal. 5:6, Eph. 2:10, Jas 2:17). It is important to get the right balance: we are not saved by our good works (3:5) but the faith that saves must definitely be demonstrated by good works.

Fruitful and Unfruitful Things

Throughout the letter to Titus we find contrasts between true and false teaching, true and false teachers, and good and evil deeds, and the same occurs in these final verses of chapter 3. We have already observed the reference to *good works* in 3:8, which are the result of the teaching of the truth. Such good works are described as *excellent and profitable to everyone.* That is a good guideline to evaluate the quality of our lives as believers: does my life bring benefit to others or only to myself? A similar point is made in 3:14, another reference to *good works.* Here the purpose of the works is to *meet urgent needs,* which could include one's own needs but are much more likely to be the needs of others (in that context the needs of Zenas and Apollos would have been the immediate application of the instruction). By acting in this way believers will not be *unproductive* or unfruitful; lives that bear good fruit are characteristic of Jesus' disciples (see Mt. 7:20, Jn 15:2, Gal. 5:22-23).

That is the positive side of the picture. But the passage also presents a negative side, the unfruitfulness of the activity of the false teachers, described as *unprofitable and worthless* (3:9) and as causing *divisions* (3:10). That is because their ministry focuses on *stupid controversies, genealogies, dissensions, and quarrels about the law* (3:9). Most of these words or phrases occur elsewhere in the PE, especially in 1 Timothy, which shows that the same problems were fairly widespread during that period (in Ephesus as well as Crete): *controversies* (1 Tim. 6:4, 2 Tim. 2:23); *genealogies* (1 Tim. 1:4), *dissensions* (1 Tim. 6:4). Disputes regarding the law are not specifically mentioned elsewhere but are suggested by 1 Timothy 1:7.

Thus, not for the first time in the PE, we have here some clear guidance about what sort of teaching is appropriate in the church context and what needs to be avoided.

Paul's Friends and Colleagues

At the time this letter was written Titus was ministering on the island of Crete. Paul wants Titus to come to him (3:12). His plan is to send Artemas or Tychicus to Crete to take Titus' place. This is a little curious, inasmuch as it has been made clear that Titus has important work to do in Crete, and so we wonder why Paul is calling him away from Crete, and this as a matter of some urgency (for *do your best* in 3:12 does not simply mean *do it if you can,* but *hurry to do it*). We may suppose that while the work is important, Titus is not the only one who can do it, and that the instructions given in this letter will apply equally to his replacement after Titus has left Crete.

Artemas is otherwise unknown to us, a reminder of how many details of the NT story we do not know. In contrast Tychicus is relatively well known, being mentioned in Acts 20:4 as one of the party that travelled with Paul to Jerusalem (and described in that passage as *from Asia*, meaning Ephesus or somewhere nearby). At a later time he appears in Colossians 4:7 and Ephesians 6:21 as the bearer of news from Paul (and probably the bearer of those two letters to their respective destinations), and again in 2 Timothy 4:12 as sent by Paul to Ephesus. But even with Tychicus we must admit how little we know about his background and conversion, or about his ministry as a member of Paul's circle of colleagues.

Paul himself has arranged to go to Nicopolis. It is not clear whether he was already at Nicopolis when he wrote these words, but he expected to be there some time soon and he wants Titus to meet him there (3:12). Nicopolis was an important city on the west coast of the Greek mainland.[129] It is likely that Paul normally spent the winter in such a place where there would be opportunity for ministry, during the months when it would be very difficult to travel.

Two other members of Paul's circle are mentioned in 3:13. Once again, one of these is quite unknown (Zenas) and the other much better known. Apollos, from Alexandria in Egypt (Acts 18:24), first appears at Ephesus from where he was intending to travel to Achaea, meaning Corinth (Acts 18:24-28), and then at Corinth (Acts 19:1). He is also mentioned several times in 1 Corinthians. In Acts 19 he is presented as working independently, and he was seen by some at Corinth as a leader in his own right (1 Cor. 1:12). But in Paul's eyes Apollos was not a rival but a labourer in the same work (1 Cor. 3:5-6, 4:6), and here too we find him closely connected with Paul as a colleague.

Again we cannot be certain of the circumstances. Were these two men already in Crete and planning to travel to somewhere else? Or were they about to travel to Crete en route to another place (in which case they could have been the bearers of this letter to Titus)? Either way they need material support. Titus is to *send* them *on their way* with their requirements fully met.

---

[129] Nicopolis, which means 'victory city', was the name of many other ancient towns founded to commemorate a significant victory. Other identifications are less likely. Nicopolis in Macedonia and Nicopolis in Cilicia (the region where Paul's hometown Tarsus was located) have been suggested.

The letter concludes in the normal sort of way with greetings (3:15). Naturally the greetings come from Paul (by implication), but he also mentions those with him. Again our curiosity is aroused to wonder who these were. We can guess that they included other unnamed colleagues and possibly also believers at Nicopolis (or wherever Paul was), but we cannot be more specific than this. The greeting is extended to others, *those who love us in the faith*. This description clearly identifies the Christian context of the letter. The relationship of Paul and his associates with these people in Crete is a faith relationship; it is their common faith in Christ which provides the bond of friendship and fellowship.

The letter is formally addressed to Titus, as we saw at the beginning (1:4) and as is again seen by the word *you* (singular) in the first part of 3:15. But the final word of greeting, *grace be with all of you*, reveals a wider audience, any of the believers in Crete who might happen to hear the reading of the letter or to read it for themselves. Just as 1 Timothy was addressed to Timothy but apparently intended to be heard by the church as a whole, the same is true of this letter to Titus.

2 Timothy

2 Timothy 1:1-18

Paul's Ministry and Circumstances

Paul's second letter to Timothy begins in a familiar sort of way. As in most of his letters (though not all of them, the letters to the Thessalonians, Philippians and Philemon being the exceptions) he begins by describing himself as an *apostle*. He includes a phrase which tells us the authority on which his apostleship rests, namely the *will of God*. And also within his self-description in 1:1 we are told that his apostleship is *for the sake of* (or more literally *according to*, as NIV) *the promise of life that is in Christ Jesus,* or (as we might paraphrase) it is in line with or consistent with that promise. God has not only made the promise but has commissioned Paul to spread the message of this promise. The phrase tells us simultaneously the theological context within which Paul does his work as an apostle and the message he must proclaim. And, we might add, *that* message and no other.

In other respects these opening words are similar to the other two PE, with mention of Paul's apostleship (also 1 Tim. 1:1 and Tit. 1:1) and of the divine authority behind his apostleship (in 1 Tim. 1:1 it is *by the command of God*). The divine authority has a double divine source, for not only does it spring from the will of *God*, but also Paul is an apostle of *Christ*, meaning that he is an official, authorized representative of Christ. The authority of Christ is just as much divine authority as that of God the Father. This point is confirmed by the wording of the actual greeting in 1:2, where *grace, mercy, and peace* are seen to derive equally *from God the Father and Christ Jesus our Lord.*

Another similarity is in the phrase *promise of life* which is roughly parallel to *Christ Jesus our hope* (1 Tim. 1:1) and *the hope of eternal life* (Tit. 1:2), all these phrases reminding the reader of the spiritual blessings available in the gospel. *Promise of life* occurs in 1 Timothy 4:8 also, and *hope of eternal life* in Titus 3:7.

It would be futile to ask why Paul uses different phrases in the three PE to express similar ideas. But the variation does at least show us that the words are not just the mindless repetition of familiar (but meaningless) words. Paul expresses truths that are very familiar to him and dear to his heart, but he does so in a way that shows us that they are fresh and living truths, not merely the words of a formalized greeting.

In all the PE, supposedly addressed to well-known colleagues and indeed friends, Paul finds it necessary to speak of his apostleship, which gives the letters a rather formal and official atmosphere. But that is no doubt exactly what Paul intended, for the letters are not merely personal communications but are intended to give directions for the life of the churches. Though 2 Timothy is generally regarded as the most personal of the three, it too has a wider audience in view. Paul expects that it will be read or heard not only by Timothy but by all the members of the Ephesian church for which Timothy is responsible. Timothy may not need the reminder but it is appropriate that other readers (we included) are reminded that the ultimate authority is not Paul but God.[130]

Moving beyond the introductory description of Paul in 1:1, we find other evidence in this chapter of Paul's circumstances at the time of writing. In contrast to 1 Timothy and Titus, Paul is now in the unhappy situation of being a prisoner (1:8, 16). We will see in chapter 4 that Paul expects this to be his final imprisonment, with death as the outcome (4:6-8). He also mentions his suffering (1:8), though as we see from 1:12, his suffering is not only because he is now a prisoner but because of the ministry entrusted to him, his gospel ministry as *a herald and an apostle and a teacher* (1:11; for this phrase see also 1 Tim. 1:7). In contrast to some modern preachers who constantly inform their hearers of their great successes, Paul knows that gospel ministry (whether inside a prison or outside) involves sharing the suffering and rejection that Christ himself experienced.

Thanksgiving for Timothy

The letter is addressed to Timothy, though as we have noted Timothy is not the only person intended to read or hear it. He is Paul's *child*,

---

[130] See Mounce, *Pastorals*, 463-464. For further suggestions regarding Paul's appeal to his apostleship here, see Towner, *Timothy-Titus* (2006), 440.

another similarity to 1 Timothy, with the minor difference that here he is Paul's *beloved* child but in the earlier letter his *genuine* child (the same word used of Titus in Tit. 1:4). The word *child* is used to describe the spiritual relationship between Paul and Timothy. Paul can also speak of Timothy as his *brother* (in 1 Thess. 3:2, again in a spiritual sense), but here his focus is on his role as the one through whom Timothy came to faith. A few verses later Paul mentions Timothy's natural family, who were certainly very important to him (1:5), but here he reminds Timothy that he belongs to a much larger family and that within this family it is Paul to whom he owes his spiritual birth (not totally and absolutely but in a very significant sense).

The greeting addressed to Timothy is exactly the same as in the first letter (1 Tim. 1:2): *grace, mercy, and peace from God the Father and Christ Jesus our Lord.*

Following the introduction (1:1-2) the letter continues with a word of thanksgiving (1:3). It is God to whom he gives thanks, but Timothy who is the focus of the thanksgiving. There is clearly a deep and very special relationship with Timothy. Paul gives thanks for him and continually prays for him (1:3). He has a deep desire to see Timothy again, not just a wish but something much stronger than that, well expressed by the translation *long to see* (1:4).

This longing is fuelled by the memory of several things. First, there is the memory of Timothy's *tears* (1:4). The circumstances are not identified but it is safe to guess that it was the occasion of a farewell. It may have been the time when Paul left Timothy in Ephesus when he was on his way to Macedonia (1 Tim. 1:3), but we have no way of knowing for certain.[131]

Another thing Paul remembers is Timothy's faith, his *sincere faith* (1:5, as in 1 Tim. 1:5). Mention of Timothy's faith leads to recollection of the same faith in his grandmother Lois and mother Eunice. It is a faith which *lived* in them, an indwelling faith, which tells us that their faith was no mere religious formality but a crucial part of their existence. The English past tense *lived* does not necessarily mean that Lois and Eunice were no longer alive. The Greek tense probably means *took up residence,*[132]

---

[131] According to Mounce, *Pastorals*, 470, this was "most likely their last parting". The suggestion that it refers to the occasion of Acts 20:37 is described as "bizarre" by Marshall, *Pastorals*, 693, and as "a stretch" by Towner, *Timothy-Titus* (2006), 452.

[132] See Marshall, *Pastorals*, 694.

emphasizing the beginning of the experience and without indicating whether it is still the case or not.

We know from the book of Acts that Timothy's mother was a Jew (Acts 16:1), and so we wonder whether the faith of Eunice (and perhaps Lois as well) extends back into her pre-Christian past or is simply her faith as a Christian believer. One way of answering this question is to observe that other examples of the word *faith* in the PE refer to faith in a Christian context (in 2 Timothy, for example, see 1:13, 3:15), and so we might think it is likely to have the same reference here. Indeed it seems unlikely that Paul would speak so positively of Lois and Eunice unless he had knowledge of their acceptance of Jesus as the Messiah. But the matter is not so simple and more can be said.

At this point it is interesting to go back to the parenthesis in 1:3, where Paul describes God as the one *whom I worship with a clear conscience, as my ancestors did*. There is no reason to think that Paul's ancestors had come to believe in Jesus (and in any case only one or at the most two generations earlier than Paul could *possibly* have done so). It is clear that Paul felt a significant continuity with his Jewish past.[133] In fact it was not just his Jewish *past* but his Jewish *present* also, for he remained a Jew, in spite of his life-changing experience on the road to Damascus. In Romans 9-11 he expresses deep anguish over the failure of his fellow Jews to respond positively to Jesus and the gospel message but also confidence that God has a plan for the salvation of the Jews (Rom. 11:26). It is clear that this is not just ethnic loyalty on Paul's part but a deep theological conviction that this was the people God chose (Rom. 11:28). And despite the many failures of the Jewish nation throughout their history, Paul knows that the possibility of a God-pleasing response of faith did not begin only on the day of Pentecost. The classic example is Abraham (Rom. 4), but the NT knows of other, humbler examples of the same among the Jewish people, such as Zachariah and Elizabeth, and Simeon and Anna in Luke 1-2. So although the Jews who have rejected Jesus have made a disastrous choice and cut themselves off from the people of God, this does not invalidate the centuries of faithful worship and service by people like Paul's ancestors and others.

---

[133] Towner, *Timothy-Titus* (2006), 449, points out that *ancestors* need not mean Paul's parents but possibly his Jewish heritage more generally. On the other hand, Johnson, *Timothy*, 337, argues that the language is ambiguous and could easily include reference to Paul's own parents as well as to his broader heritage.

Lois and Eunice could be further examples of the same, people who could be described as worshipping God with a clear conscience, people of faith, and people also (looking ahead to 3:14-15) who had a deep devotion to the scriptures (that is, the books known to us as the Old Testament). In their case the proof of the reality of their faith was their acceptance of the gospel which proclaimed Jesus as the fulfilment of Jewish hopes and aspirations and the only way of salvation.[134]

All this gives us a context within which to interpret the simple word *first* (1:5). If the faith of Lois and Eunice refers only to their *Christian* faith, we might expect that they (rather than Paul) would have led Timothy to faith in Christ. On this understanding how can we account for Paul thinking of himself as Timothy's spiritual father? (A possible but not the easiest reconstruction would be that Lois and Eunice first became Christians, but that soon after and during the same visit of Paul to Lystra Timothy also became a believer. That would allow for Lois and Eunice being *first*, but also for Timothy being Paul's spiritual *child*.) But if Lois and Eunice's faith refers to their ancestral faith as Jews, the problem is removed and it is very obvious that their faith preceded Timothy's, for the simple reason that they were older than he.

This faith dwells in Timothy also, so Paul is convinced (1:5). Naturally we understand that, whatever may have been the historical links with the faith demonstrated by his Jewish ancestors, it is Timothy's faith in Jesus that is of prime importance in the present situation. Although Timothy should not despise the faith of his Jewish ancestors but rather see their life of faith as an example to follow, the revelation of the gospel has shown that it is specifically faith in Jesus which God now requires.

Reflection: Preparation for the Gospel

The comments on 1:3-5 have raised some interesting issues regarding the validity of faith outside a specifically Christian context. Paul speaks positively of the worship offered to God by his ancestors (1:3). "Ancestors" is a very broad description of previous generations without limit. Of those previous generations no more than his parents and grandparents would have had the opportunity to hear the Christian gospel, and yet even these (as far as we know) did not

---

[134] Kelly, *Pastorals*, 157, insists that the faith of Lois and Eunice is "faith in Christ", a little surprising in the light of his previous comment on 1:3 about "the pride Paul takes here in his Jewish religious upbringing" (page 155).

believe in Jesus. Paul is speaking of the worship offered by his Jewish ancestors to the God of the OT. Then almost immediately afterwards, Paul refers to the faith which lived in Timothy's mother and grandmother (1:5), again almost certainly thinking of their faith as Jews in the one true God, something which found expression in their instruction of Timothy during his childhood in the scriptures of the OT (3:14-15). These several verses present a very positive picture of the life of a pious Jew prior to the coming of Christ: they had God's revelation in their scriptures and their worship is viewed as acceptable worship.

This may not be the impression we gain from other parts of the NT. We may think of the negative comments about scribes and Pharisees, and other leaders of the Jews, by John the Baptist and Jesus. We may think of the opposition from the Jews recorded in the book of Acts, as the gospel message is preached in different places. Even Paul speaks quite negatively in a passage such as 1 Thessalonians 2:14-16 (and elsewhere).

Yet these passages record responses to Jewish opposition rather than to the Jews as such or to Jewish religion as such. In fact time and time again the NT presents the earthly ministry of Jesus and the preaching of Jesus by the early church as the fulfilment of OT promises and hopes. The promises made to Abraham and repeated in different ways throughout the OT are seen as fulfilled in Jesus. The God of the OT is the God and Father of our Lord Jesus Christ. The whole Bible presents a single story, to do with God working out his purposes and with Jesus as the one through whom he does so. So the NT does not stand alone but is vitally connected with the OT story and message. This is not the place to expand this theme in detail but it is a fact with which no NT scholar would disagree. Little surprise, therefore, that Paul can speak so positively of his own and Timothy's ancestors, and recall the genuineness of their faith in God, no less genuine than that of their common ancestor Abraham.

In the Indian context there are some who argue that instead of the OT we should use the scriptures of the Indian tradition (that is the Hindu scriptures) as the relevant background to the gospel and leading naturally into the proclamation of Christ as the fulfilment of Indian hopes and aspirations. This approach has a strong emotional appeal, and yet there is a danger of confusion. On the positive side, it is right and proper, and a well-accepted mission practice, to look for points of contact between the gospel and the culture in which the gospel is to be proclaimed. We find Paul doing this when he spoke at Pisidian Antioch (Acts 14:15-17) and especially at Athens (Acts 17:22-31). Though there is disagreement about the details, there are undoubtedly stories and teachings in the Hindu scriptures which similarly provide points of contact, or bridges which can be used to lead from a traditional understanding of reality to the gospel message which we wish to encourage our listeners to consider seriously. Such bridges can be regarded as glimmers of light and pointers to the truth which has been more fully revealed in Christ. The same challenge to find such bridges is present within any cultural context in which it is desired to proclaim the gospel, as many of the early Church Fathers did with the religious and philosophical systems of their own day.

However, confusion arises when it is considered that the Jewish scriptures can simply be replaced by the religious traditions of the dominant culture (in the case of India the scriptures and traditions of Hinduism). The Bible clearly portrays the Jews as God's special people, chosen to fulfil his purposes. Though they failed in much of their God-given task, it was through Jesus, a Jew, a descendant of Abraham (as Paul takes pains to point out in Gal. 3:16, and Matthew also in Matt. 1:1) that those purposes were brought to their potential fulfilment. There is simply no replacement for the OT story nor is it possible to replace the God of the OT with some other god. There is only one collection of scriptures (before Christ) where God has specifically and directly revealed the truth about himself and his purposes, and that is the books of what we call the Old Testament. These books stand as unique, and the Christian gospel cannot be understood outside the framework established by the OT.

The Present Challenges Ahead of Timothy

The strong tradition of faith in Timothy's family provides a foundation for exhorting Timothy regarding his own life and ministry. That is the force of *for this reason* (1:6). The language here might be understood to mean that Timothy has come close to being a backslider, with the translation *rekindle* (NRSV) suggesting that the flame may have gone out. However, that does not seem likely in one described as Paul's *beloved child* (1:2) and one whom to see will bring Paul great *joy* (1:4). And we would expect to sense a greater alarm on Paul's part if this had been the situation with Timothy. A slightly different picture is presented by the translation *fan into flame* (NIV), which suggests more of a gentle exhortation to keep the flame burning brightly, a reminder needed by every Christian worker for it is so easy to slip into patterns which become merely routine.[135]

What requires constant tending and nurturing is the *gift of God* (1:6), a reference in this context to the gift of ministry. This gift is associated with the *laying on of my hands*. This act is associated in other NT passages with recognizing and commissioning someone for ministry (as with Paul

---

[135] Kelly, *Pastorals*, 159, says that "the embers need constant stirring"; see also Mounce, *Pastorals*, 476, for helpful comment.

himself in Acts 13:3), and without any hint of magic it is natural that the same occasion should be seen as the reception of a special divine anointing for the task.

The word *my* in this phrase refers, of course, to Paul, and it is interesting to compare this statement with 1 Timothy 4:14 where it is the laying on of the hands of the *elders* that is identified as the occasion when Timothy received the gift of ministry. It seems highly improbable that there were two separate occasions when Timothy received the same gift,[136] and the most natural understanding is that both Paul and the elders laid hands on Timothy. A possible reason why Paul mentions himself here (rather than the elders) is that he has been focusing on Timothy's deep personal relationship with him and this is another way of reinforcing the point.[137]

The empowering force in Timothy's life is the presence of the Holy Spirit, and as the passage continues Paul speaks of the characteristics of this Spirit (1:7), as a further encouragement to Timothy to pursue his ministry vigorously and enthusiastically. Instead of *spirit*, suggesting our human spirit, *Spirit* (i.e., the Holy Spirit) is better.[138] He begins with a negative statement about what the Spirit is *not*. He is not a Spirit of *fear*. It is possible that Timothy was a timid sort of person (as suggested by 1 Cor. 16:10 and possibly 1 Tim. 4:12) and he needs the encouragement of knowing that he already has within him the resources to overcome such timidity. With this phrase we may compare Romans 8:15 where Paul says that the Spirit is not a *spirit of slavery* to lead us back *into fear*.

Positively Paul speaks of the Spirit's characteristics *of power and of love and of self-discipline*. The relevance of *power* is seen immediately, for it is the *power of God* which is needed to stand firm in the midst of suffering (1:8). Elsewhere, power is mentioned as a feature of a truly godly life (3:5). *Love* is such a fundamental characteristic of the Christian life (see also 1:13, 2:22, 3:10) and such a basic aspect of the

---

[136] However Towner, *Timothy-Titus* (2006), 457-460, considers that two occasions are indicated, the present passage referring to Timothy's conversion. See Marshall, *Pastorals*, 697-698, for comment on the two-occasions view; he himself envisages one occasion only.

[137] So Witherington, *Commentary*, 313.

[138] So Fee, *Timothy-Titus*, 226-227; Towner, *Timothy-Titus* (1994), 160, and *Timothy-Titus* (2006), 460-463; Marshall, *Pastorals*, 698-700; against Mounce, *Pastorals*, 477; Kelly, *Pastorals*, 159. Witherington's question "does the Holy Spirit need to be fanned into flame?" (Witherington, *Commentary*, 314 note 48) is irrelevant, as it is the gift (of ministry) in 1:6 rather than the Spirit which Timothy must rekindle.

Spirit's work (Gal. 5:22) that there is probably no need to find any other reason for its inclusion in this verse. The word translated here *self-discipline* is not used in any other NT passage, but the concept of self-control or self-discipline is seen frequently in the PE (in other Greek words with the same basic stem), though only in this one verse in 2 Timothy. Examples are Titus 2:12, where believers in general are expected to live a self-controlled life, and in reference to the bishop or overseer in 1 Timothy 3:2 and Titus 1:8 (translated in NRSV as *sensible* in one place and *prudent* in the other, but in NIV *self-controlled* in both passages). Our present passage shows that the source of a self-disciplined life is the presence of the Spirit of God. Let Timothy be encouraged to know that he already has great resources and challenged by this knowledge to step out beyond the limitations of his natural timidity to attempt great things for the Lord.

What Paul writes here about the Holy Spirit is relevant to every believer. He speaks of the Spirit as a gift of God to *us* (not only to *you*, Timothy). The gift of the Spirit is especially relevant to Timothy as a Christian leader, but all believers have the same privilege of the presence of this *Spirit of power and of love and of self-discipline*.

The paragraph beginning in 1:8 is linked with what precedes by the word *then* (NIV *so*, or more clearly *therefore*). It is because of the presence of the Spirit that Timothy is not to *be ashamed*. The person who has in his or her life the very presence of the living God need not be ashamed of anyone or anything, and furthermore this same presence provides the power for the believer to stand firm and strong in whatever circumstances.

But there are things of which Timothy may be tempted to be ashamed. One is the *testimony about our Lord*. This is a wonderful thing to talk about among our Christian friends, but in a hostile world we may be tempted to hide the fact that we are committed to him. The context here suggests that it is the Lord's suffering in particular which Timothy may prefer to avoid talking about. Similarly Timothy may prefer to hide the fact that Paul, the Lord's *prisoner*, is his friend and associate. Paul's situation would certainly have been regarded as shameful, to Timothy as well as to Paul, and so it would have been very natural for Timothy to be ashamed of Paul. However, such a response is not appropriate, for what happened to Jesus and Paul, in terms of rejection, suffering and humiliation, is part and parcel of following Christ. The Christian has no option in these matters, and Jesus himself gives a very strong warning to those who are ashamed to follow him in the way of the cross (Mk 8:34-38).

Timothy must also be willing to tread this path. Rather than being ashamed of those aspects of the Christian message which speak of suffering, Paul urges Timothy to *join with me in suffering for the gospel* (1:8). The gospel speaks of wonderful blessing for the believer, and indeed of God's plan for the blessing of all the nations (according to Gal. 3:8 this *is* the gospel). But the gospel is a challenge to many of the attitudes and actions of sinful men and women, and so it often provokes a negative and sometimes an extremely hostile response.

We have seen in 1 Timothy that Timothy has already experienced this, at least in the form of false teaching, which is usually an attempt to present a message more congenial to the thinking and desires of the world around us. So what Paul is saying here is not totally new to Timothy and should not take him by surprise. But the message now seems to be that suffering in more direct and unpleasant forms may lie ahead (as confirmed by 2:3, 3:12), and Timothy needs to come to terms with this possibility in advance.

At the end of 1:8 the reminder comes that the ability to endure suffering is not a matter of our own strength but is possible only in *the power of God*. This phrase takes us back to the earlier reference to the Spirit (1:7), and so assures us that we already have the necessary resources to stand firm even when suffering comes.

Reflection: Going the Distance in Ministry

Paul encourages Timothy with the words "rekindle the gift of God that is within you" (1:6). An exhortation like this tells us that the flame does not automatically stay alight but that it needs to be nurtured or else it will eventually die out.

This of course is the flame of ministry. The young seminary graduate, beginning his or her ministry, does not think about such matters. God has called me, they think, and God will sustain me. This is very true, both in theory and practice, for God's call is the absolutely necessary foundation for ministry, and without God's strength we can do nothing in ministry. Nevertheless, the realities of life soon reveal that this approach will not get us very far. We may admire the zeal of a Henry Martyn and others like him who have expressed a desire to burn out for God, which is what they did, dying at a young age. But Paul does not say let the flame burn out; rather, rekindle it. The challenge for the servant of God is how to keep the flame burning for a lifetime of ministry.

This reminds us that it is a long-distance race we are running. The new theological graduate may begin as if it is a sprint, undertaking every challenge and responding to every request. But you cannot maintain the speed of a sprinter for very long. Yes, hard work is appropriate, but one must learn how to say no as well as yes, or otherwise the burden of everyone's expectations and demands will be overwhelming. The success of a long-distance runner will depend on appropriate preparation, the many things which are not seen by the cheering crowds, and in ministry the same applies, not only the preparation of three or four years of study before beginning full-time ministry, but the continuing preparation of ensuring each day that one is fit to deal with that day's work. In a marathon race one often sees a runner take a cup of water or other nourishment, and in ministry too something similar is needed, perhaps in the form of a regular retreat. Other things are needed, not least turning to God each day in Bible reading and prayer, but also looking after oneself in other ways.

The heading for this reflection is based on the title of a book written by a friend of the author's, a bishop in the Australian Anglican church.[139] Though the book is written for a Western context, Bishop Peter Brain raises issues that are equally relevant in India. One of the book's main points is that a minister must take steps to care for himself or herself, not out of a selfish motivation but simply out of a recognition that ministry is stressful, and therefore survival and fruitfulness in ministry will depend on proper self-protection and nourishment (physical, intellectual, emotional, as well as spiritual).

This is very difficult in India, where a congregation's demands can be constant and often unsympathetic, and a programme of education is urgently needed so that congregations will see the importance of practical strategies to ensure that their minister's flame is regularly rekindled. Denominational leadership will probably have to recognize this need, find ways of promoting healthier attitudes and actions, and help ministers take action to care for themselves adequately. However, this is worth the effort, for the outcome of such a programme will have value not only for the minister, but also for the congregation. It can hardly be good for a congregation to have a minister who has somehow managed to survive, but is merely going through the routines of ministry, with no freshness in his message but only repeating the platitudes which fall automatically, effortlessly and thoughtlessly from his lips.

A Gospel Summary

We have discovered in the other PE several little passages which provide a summary of the gospel or an important part of the gospel (as in 1 Tim. 1:15, 2:5-6, 3:16, Tit. 2:11-14, 3:4-7). These are not so obvious in 2

---

[139] P. Brain, *Going the Distance: How to Stay Fit for a Lifetime of Ministry* (Sydney: Matthias Media, 2004).

Timothy, but there is one other (2:8) which we can add to the present passage (1:9-10).

A number of key points can be identified in 1:9-10. (a) Salvation is God's work, for it is he who *saved us and called us* (1:9). The initiative is his, a point emphasized negatively in the phrase *not according to our works* and positively in *according to his own purpose and grace*. It could hardly be expressed more strongly that we contribute nothing and God does all that is necessary. (b) God's plan has been brought to fulfilment *in Christ Jesus*. In him God's *grace was given to us*. That is not hard for us to grasp, but the phrase *before the ages began* (literally *before eternal times*) takes us well beyond our ability to comprehend (see comment on Tit. 1:2 where the same phrase occurs). What it seems to be saying is that in the mind of God the gift had already been given long before we were ever born and also that in the mind of God the work of Christ had been accomplished before it actually happened in historical time on earth. The words also imply the pre-existence of Christ. Here we have an assurance that God's plan that we should be recipients of his grace is no spur of the moment thought but has the most solid foundation imaginable.

(c) If *before the ages began* implies the prior existence of God's plan to bless us with his grace, it is then made clear that there has also been a revelation of this grace in history (as also in Tit. 1:2). *It has now been revealed* (1:10), the word *now* meaning *in the recent past*, and this recent past means *through the appearing of our Saviour Jesus Christ*. There are passages in which the *appearing* of Christ means his future appearing in judgement (4:1, 8), but here it clearly refers to an appearance that has already occurred, a reference to Jesus' earthly ministry.

The purpose of that appearing is described in two phrases which express a negative and a positive side of the effect of Jesus' work. (d) The negative is that he *abolished death*. Of course, physical death is still a reality, but for the one who believes that Jesus not only died but rose victorious from the dead death has lost its sting. (e) Also he *brought life and immortality to light*. *Life and immortality* are the opposite of death, and describe the positive side of what the believer experiences, partly already during our physical life now on earth and partly in the fact that our physical death is not the end but merely a stage in our eternal existence and our eternal relationship with God.

The Gospel Messenger and His Experience

Paul has spoken about *suffering for the gospel* (1:8) and has described something of the basic content of the gospel (1:9-10) in order to show that it is something worth suffering for. Now he returns to his focus on the gospel messenger (1:11), first speaking about himself and his suffering (1:12) and then (with particular reference to Timothy) giving a reminder of the responsibilities of the one entrusted with the treasure of the gospel (1:13-14).

It is *through the gospel* that *life and immortality* are *brought to light* or revealed. That is to say, the events of Jesus' ministry will have little impact unless they are announced and their significance explained. It is a vitally important message and it must be proclaimed, and Paul recalls his appointment for this purpose, as *a herald and an apostle and a teacher* (1:11; see also 1 Tim. 2:7).

Though it seems paradoxical that the bearer of such a wonderful message should suffer, there are reasons why it is so (as mentioned briefly in the previous section), and Paul is not exempt from suffering (1:12). Yet he is not ashamed to be treated this way (1:12), and in this way he offers himself as an example of what he has urged Timothy to do (1:8). He does not ask anyone else to do what he is not willing to accept for himself.

The reason why he is not ashamed is that he knows God and his power (1:12). He has *put his trust* in God and has learned from experience that God is trustworthy. He therefore has reason to be convinced that God *is able to guard what I have entrusted to him*. The last six words of this translation are an expanded explanation of words which literally mean *my deposit*. The word *deposit* also occurs again in 1:14, referring clearly to the gospel message which God has entrusted to Timothy; and similarly in 1 Timothy 6:20. In those passages the responsibility of guarding falls to Timothy. But here it is God who guards and the deposit is what Paul has deposited (rather than what has been deposited with him, though this is also a grammatically possible interpretation of the phrase).[140]

To what can this refer? It can hardly mean the gospel itself (for the concept of Paul entrusting the gospel to God is bizarre, to say the

---

[140] So Knight, *Pastorals*, 379-380; Marshall, *Pastorals*, 710-711; Mounce, *Pastorals*, 487-488; Towner, *Timothy-Titus* (2006), 475-476; Witherington, *Commentary*, 320. Of the opposite view are Barrett, *Pastorals*, 96-97; Kelly, *Pastorals*, 165-166; Johnson, *Timothy*, 356-357.

least), but it makes good sense to understand it to mean Paul's own life and his life's work.[141] Paul has given himself to God and has lived his life under God's direction, in trust that God is able to take good care of Paul's deposit and in trust that God will use it in ways that will best suit his plan and purpose. Paul is looking ahead to *that day*, the day of judgement (as in 1:18, 4:8) when his life and work will be assessed, and it is the knowledge that God is guarding all that Paul is and does that gives him assurance. (In this explanation we have spoken of Paul's trust in *God*, but it could equally well be *Christ* to whom Paul is referring. Paul does not specify who it is in whom he has believed, and if he had been asked, he may have been happy to say either of the two, or even both.)

Turning the focus away from himself he directs some words of exhortation to Timothy (1:13-14). The central concern is the preservation of Christian truth, described as *the standard of sound teaching* (or more literally *the standard of sound words*, as in 1 Tim. 6:3) and *the good treasure entrusted to you* (or more literally *the good deposit*). There is always room for creative re-expression of the gospel message in ways that will communicate effectively in each specific context, but the basic content of the gospel is not subject to change. The two key verbs here are *hold* (1:13) and *guard* (1:14), both of which point to the need to preserve what has been received, rather than to invent something new. The same point is reinforced by the words *that you have heard from me*, and by the word *deposit* itself, which means the property of someone else which has been entrusted for safe-keeping.

The words *in the faith and love that are in Christ Jesus* (1:13) is the sort of phrase that can easily be regarded as a pious cliché and therefore ignored. Certainly the combination of faith and love is observed in many other places (in 2 Timothy alone in 2:22 and 3:10 also) and virtually the same words as here occur in 1 Timothy 1:14. The link between these words and the rest of the verse is not clear. But it makes good sense to see the phrase as providing the context in which Timothy is to hold fast the true gospel, meaning that Timothy's responsibility is not a mere academic exercise of preserving theological orthodoxy, but he must also demonstrate the

---

[141] Unlikely as it seems to the present author, Towner, *Timothy-Titus* (2006), 476, includes both aspects: "He entrusts the gospel (and by implication the entire Pauline mission) to God."

reality and the practical effect of the gospel in his own life of *faith and love*, both of which are *in Christ Jesus*.

The paragraph finishes with the encouraging reminder that the Christian minister has powerful resources to fulfil his or her responsibilities, in the form of the presence of *the Holy Spirit living in us* (a phrase which recalls Rom. 8:11). As in 1:7 the word *us* indicates that the Spirit's presence is the experience of Christians in general, but this truth obviously has a particular relevance and brings a particular encouragement to the person struggling to uphold the truth of the gospel in a difficult situation.

The Church in Asia

The final verses of the chapter refer to several individuals whose behaviour has had a significant impact on Paul, for good or ill. At first glance we may wonder what this material is doing here, as one might feel that it goes better with the other personal references at the end of the letter (see 4:9-16). However, it fits well as a sequel to the preceding paragraph. An important emphasis in 1:8-14 is the exhortation to Timothy not to be ashamed, either of the Lord or of Paul (1:8), and Paul speaks of his own lack of shame (1:12). Here in the final paragraph Paul adds the example of Onesiphorus, who was not ashamed of Paul's circumstances (1:16), though sadly there are others who cannot be described in the same positive way (1:15). These serve as a reminder to Timothy that, as he seeks to serve God and to stand for the gospel, he cannot expect universal approval and support, even from professing believers.

The paragraph begins with the unhappy comment, *All who are in Asia have turned away from me* (1:15). The word *Asia* does not mean what it means today, including India for example, but refers to the Roman province of that name which was located in western Turkey and of which Ephesus was the capital. In 4:16 Paul speaks of his *first defence*, and this may be the context referred to here. Asia was a long way from Rome, but it is quite likely that his previously loyal colleagues and other Christian brothers and sisters in Asia took fright and were unwilling to be publicly associated with Paul when he was put on trial for his life. Another interpretation is that these were believers from Asia who were present in Rome at the time, who instead of supporting Paul have abandoned him. (We naturally think of Jesus' disciples who deserted him under similar circumstances in Jerusalem.)

Paul specifically names Phygelus and Hermogenes, not otherwise known to us but presumably familiar names to Timothy. A possible reason for mentioning them is that they were people of some importance in the church in Asia and therefore the last people one would expect to take this action. If so, they stand as a warning to Timothy who though a leader was not immune from the temptation to lose courage.

It is not said that these believers have fallen away from the faith. It is Paul personally whom they have deserted. However, there is a fine line between being ashamed of *the testimony about our Lord* (1:8) and of the messenger who bears that testimony. Though Paul draws no conclusions in this passage, he must have wondered whether the failure of people like these to support him also pointed to their doubts concerning the faith itself.[142]

Happily, Paul also has a positive example to point to, Onesiphorus (1:16). (This shows, incidentally, that *all* in 1:15 is not to be interpreted in an absolutely literal sense.[143] Perhaps it means *all who could have been expected to support me* or *all in general*.) Scholars draw attention to two curious features of these comments about Onesiphorus. One is the repetition of the wish (1:16 and 1:18), and the other is the reference to *the household of Onesiphorus* (1:16, as again in 4:19) rather than to Onesiphorus directly. Some draw the conclusion that Onesiphorus was dead,[144] that 1:16 is a prayer for the surviving members of his household, and that 1:18 a prayer for the dead Onesiphorus himself. None of these conclusions is necessary. In 1 Corinthians 1:16 *the household of Stephanas* does not mean

---

[142] So Marshall, *Pastorals*, 717: "it may well have included a rejection of Paul's version of Christian teaching".

[143] *All* has been described as "the sweeping assertion of depression" by N.J.D. White, *The First and Second Epistles to Timothy and the Epistle to Titus*, Expositor's Greek Testament (London: Hodder & Stoughton, 1910), IV, 159, quoted by Marshall, *Pastorals*, 717.

[144] According to Kelly, *Pastorals*, 170, this is "practically certain"; so also Witherington, *Commentary*, 324-326. It is allowed as a possibility by Towner, *Timothy-Titus* (1994), 168, and Mounce, *Pastorals*, 495. But Knight, *Pastorals*, 386, and Marshall, *Pastorals*, 718-719, are not convinced that this conclusion is necessary. See also Towner, *Timothy-Titus* (2006), 482-486, who, after allowing the possibility that Onesiphorus had died, says: "But it is equally possible that he was yet alive, whether away from home, on the way home, or at home. The reference to his household in v. 16 (cf. 4:19) need not exclude a reference to him" (page 484).

the household apart from Stephanas, for Stephanas himself is mentioned in 16:17. So here, the household of Onesiphorus need not imply the other members excluding Onesiphorus but may simply mean Onesiphorus and his household. Even if Onesiphorus is dead, the words of 1:18a are in the form of a wish (not a prayer), surely an appropriate thing to wish for any Christian friend, alive or dead.[145] It may have been included as a spontaneous play on the word *find*: as Onesiphorus *found* Paul (1:17), may he also *find* mercy from the Lord (1:18).[146]

There are several reasons for Paul's positive thoughts about Onesiphorus. One is his general kindness to Paul (note the word *often*), presumably in Ephesus as well as in Rome. Another is his response to Paul's imprisonment to which shame would not be a surprising reaction, but on the contrary he *was not ashamed of my chain*. Thirdly, far from being ashamed he went out of his way to locate Paul in his imprisonment (1:17). We do not know why Onesiphorus was in Rome. It was not necessarily for the primary purpose of visiting Paul but could have been business or some other reason. Nevertheless, once in Rome he took great pains to search for Paul whose place of imprisonment was obviously not common knowledge. Fourthly, he has performed many other acts of service in Ephesus (1:18), as Timothy well knows; in other words his ministry has not only been for Paul's benefit but has served the needs of many others.

The two wishes in this passage (verse 16 and verse 18) are not identical. The second focuses specifically on the day of judgement (the same phrase *on that day* is found in 1:12, 4:8), whereas the first may very well be a prayer for the Lord's mercy in their present circumstances. Certainly *mercy* is seen as a potential blessing in the present (as in the greetings in 1:2 and 1 Tim. 1:2) and is not only for the final day. Another detail in the second prayer is the repetition of *the Lord*. Many regard the first as a reference to Jesus and the second God,[147] but if that is what Paul intended, one can think of several other ways he could have made the point more clearly. Perhaps the repetition is nothing more than a

---

[145] So Marshall, *Pastorals*, 720; Mounce, *Pastorals*, 497.

[146] So Johnson, *Timothy*, 361.

[147] So Kelly, *Pastorals*, 170; Fee, *Timothy-Titus*, 238; Marshall, *Pastorals*, 720; Mounce, *astorals*, 496; Witherington, *Commentary*, 325. Towner, *Timothy-Titus* (2006), 484, also allows this possibility, but points to 4:8 as evidence that the second *Lord* in our present passage may refer to Christ.

way of emphasizing the point that it is the Lord's privilege to show mercy as he wishes, which no one else can demand or assume. To Paul it probably made little difference whether the reader should think of *the Lord* as referring to Jesus or to God. In 1:2 both are described as the source of mercy.

Reflection: Shame

Three times in this chapter Paul speaks about not being ashamed (1:8, 12, 16). This raises a topic which has become prominent in NT scholarship in the last decade or so, a result of recognizing that most of the people in the NT story belonged to cultures where honour and shame played a major part in daily life. The basic idea is that a person's behaviour is largely determined by what brings honour and what avoids shame, not only honour and shame for the individual but honour and shame for one's family and society in general: we do what brings honour to ourselves and those who are significant in our lives and we avoid doing what brings shame to the same people. This hardly needs to be explained for readers in India where this principle is very well accepted and understood. The problem is that it is so well understood that it may operate mostly at a subconscious level, meaning that many Indians probably do not often think about how much this deep-rooted attitude influences our behaviour.

The NT presents a different principle of ethical behaviour, the principle of right and wrong as determined by the will of God. This may sometimes clash with the honour and shame principle, as in a situation where a person may tell a lie in order to avoid the shame of a certain action becoming known; for example, they may deny cheating in an exam because to admit cheating will cause shame. For the people of the God who never lies (Tit. 1:2) lying is wrong (so also is cheating, of course), but avoiding shame may be a stronger influence which decides how we will respond.

Nevertheless, the shame culture was very much part and parcel of the world in which Paul and Timothy lived, and as Paul wrote to Timothy he would have been very conscious of the powerful attraction of avoiding actions which might cause shame. For a Christian there were many possible causes of shame. Timothy is urged not to be ashamed of the gospel message (the testimony about our Lord, 1:8) which could easily have been seen as something shameful (a message about a crucified criminal). Jesus warned of the temptation to be ashamed of him (Mk 8:38), a temptation which Paul was proud to say he had avoided (Rom. 1:16).

Timothy is also urged not to be ashamed of Paul (1:8), as it was obviously a potential source of very great shame to be known as an associate of a prisoner. He mentions Onesiphorus as an example of one who was not ashamed of Paul's status as a prisoner (1:18), and the positive way in which he speaks about Onesiphorus indicates that his reaction was not something to be assumed. Indeed it was probably because Paul was a source of shame that all in Asia had turned away from him (1:15).

Suffering might be another source of shame, inasmuch as it suggests failure rather than success, and Paul vigorously asserts that despite his sufferings he is not ashamed (1:12).

One of the challenges for the early Christians was the need to redefine what brings honour and shame, and the same is likely to be true for us today. Our definitions are naturally provided by our own culture. Indian culture tells us that honour comes from being recognized as great, but within the Christian community into which we have been called we need to learn that it is an honour to become like a child and to serve. Indian culture tells us that the acquiring of many possessions will increase our honour, but within the Christian community we are taught the relatively small value of money and possessions. In the eyes of the world (that is, our culture and society) it is a shameful thing to be associated with the foolishness of the gospel (1 Cor. 1:18), but the same thing is honour in the eyes of God.

There is nothing automatically wrong in seeking what is honourable and avoiding what is shameful. But the important question is: whose definition of what is honourable and what is shameful do we accept? Are they the definitions given by God or those of the unbelievers around us? These two definitions are not the same thing.

2 Timothy 2:1-13

Timothy's Duties

Chapter 2 continues Paul's appeal to Timothy to be faithful in the exercise of the ministry entrusted to him. We recall the direct commands of chapter 1 on this same theme (1:6, 8, 13, 14) and this is again the focus of the instructions here, especially in the first paragraph (2:1-7).

However, before the instructions about Timothy's specific responsibilities, Paul takes him back to the foundations. He reminds him of the need to be strong and even more important of the source of the strength that is available to him. Other examples of the verb used here speak of *the Lord* strengthening his servants (4:17, 1 Tim. 1:12) or of being strong *in the Lord* (Eph. 6:10), but here it is *grace* which Timothy is encouraged to see as his source of strength. As in Titus 2:11-12, grace is seen not only as the source of salvation but as the source of life-changing power for the believer. It is grace that is *in Christ Jesus*, available to us because of the work of Christ and our relationship with him. Grace provides gifts which are totally undeserved. It is a familiar truth that the gift of salvation is available only on the basis of grace, but it is also grace alone which makes possible the presence of God through his Spirit in a believer's life. This is the source of power of which Paul reminds Timothy here. Spiritual power is not a second blessing but part of the basic package, an outflowing of the work of Christ which opens the floodgates of grace.

Thus strengthened Timothy must fulfil his responsibilities in ministry. Two areas are identified here. In the first place he must safeguard the teaching he has heard from Paul and pass it on to others (2:2). Paul speaks about *what you have heard from me* but then also says *through many witnesses*. It is not clear how the witnesses fit into the picture. Much of what Timothy learned must have come directly from Paul. Unlike us today, Timothy had the privilege of direct contact with Paul and did not need others to report Paul's teaching to him. Perhaps the sense is that Timothy's knowledge of Paul's teaching is supported and confirmed by many others who had also heard Paul speak.[148]

The concern expressed in 2:2 links naturally with 1:13, where also Paul is anxious for Timothy to keep a firm hold on the apostolic teaching. But Timothy's own grasp of this teaching is only the first step and here the concern is taken several steps further. Paul looks to the generations to come and realizes that there must be an unbroken transmission of gospel truth. In all this we can identify two responsibilities which Timothy is expected to fulfil. (a) He must hold firmly to the truth, no doubt finding fresh ways to express it as may be appropriate to his own context but at the same time neither adding to its substance nor subtracting anything of importance. (b) He must identify others to whom this truth can be safely entrusted. These are described as *faithful people* (not *males* as NIV *faithful*

---

[148] This is essentially the explanation offered by most commentators; all acknowledge the difficulty of the phrase.

men could be misunderstood to imply), people whose first necessary quality is trustworthiness or reliability. Their other necessary ability is that they *will be able to teach others also*. Paul does not identify these people; that is Timothy's task, as indeed it remains the duty of Christian leaders in each generation, the necessary method for preserving the truth of the gospel. It only needs one broken link in the chain to provide the opportunity for false teaching, or at the very least an unbalanced understanding of the gospel, to arise.

The second focus here is the call to be prepared to suffer (2:3). This repeats the exhortation given in 1:8 (using exactly the same Greek verb). The translation *share in suffering* probably implies sharing with Paul (as made specific in NRSV translation of 1:8 *join with me in suffering*). Timothy is not being asked to do something unique. Suffering is an experience of believers in general (Rom. 8:17), part of what it means to take up the cross as one follows Jesus (Mk 8:34). But it especially applies to the Christian leader who is expected to be an example of the Christian life. In this context the metaphor of the soldier is particularly relevant, for no soldier expects a life of comfort, convenience and security. The Christian life is a fight to be fought (1 Tim. 1:18, Eph. 6:10-17). The Christian experience can be described in other ways, for example by focusing on the many blessings available to the believer. Nevertheless to overlook the element of struggle or to do everything possible to avoid suffering would be to distort the Christian life and indeed to fail to be a disciple of Jesus Christ. Paul encourages the somewhat timid Timothy (1:7) to share the suffering that inevitably comes in one form or another.

Reflection: Guarding the Deposit

In 2:2 Timothy is given the responsibility of entrusting the message to others. The verb entrust could also be translated "hand over" or "deposit", and it is closely related to the noun "treasure" (NIV "deposit"). This occurs in 1:14 in the instruction "guard the good deposit", similar to 1 Timothy 6:20 (which is the same except that it lacks the word "good").

This is a picture from the banking industry. A bank can operate successfully only if it has a good reputation for reliability. Only gamblers will deposit their money in a high-risk institution, but banks cannot afford to operate at high risk. We know that a financial system can run into serious difficulties or even collapse, but normally when we deposit money into our bank account we fully expect that it will be safeguarded - used to increase the bank's profits, but used sensibly and as safely as possible, so that when we want to make a withdrawal, the bank will have the funds to repay us.

That is how Paul pictures the gospel. It is something we hold in trust from God. It is not ours but God's. We do not invent it. We have no right to change it (by addition or subtraction). We are called to use it to build God's kingdom (as a bank uses our deposited money), and this may require finding fresh ways of expressing and explaining it for the sake of communicating it to our target audience. But ultimately it is something to guard, which means to preserve it intact.

A further responsibility is mentioned in 2:2, the duty to pass it on to the next generation of leaders and teachers. Again the emphasis is on faithful transmission, inasmuch as Timothy is to pass on what he has heard from Paul. Again, the point is that it is not Timothy's duty to create the message but to preserve it and pass it on.

This is no less the responsibility of today's church in India: to preserve and pass on the gospel for the glory of God and the benefit of future generations. It is possible to take this solemn responsibility very lightly. We easily forget the struggle of the church in the first generation to define the gospel (for example, whether or not circumcision was a requirement), or in the second century to deal with the threat of Gnosticism, or in the following centuries to provide adequate understandings of the Trinity or the person and work of Christ. Vigilance is continually required to preserve the truth of the gospel. In our own context one of the greatest threats is from preachers who want to tell us that the gospel is God's promise of success and wealth. In the face of such teaching how many of our faithful church-attending people are equipped to know what is right and what is wrong? If the answer is 'not as many as should be', that is probably a symptom that guarding the deposit is not a high priority on the agenda of our church leaders.

As a footnote to this comment, some have felt that this emphasis on safeguarding what has been handed down is evidence that the PE come from a later period where rigid doctrine and a strict orthodoxy have replaced the theological creativity of the earliest period of the church. However, right from the beginning there was a concern for truth and acceptance of the traditions (e.g., Gal. 1:6-7, 1 Cor. 15:3, Rom. 6:17). There has never been room in the church for playing loose with the truth of the gospel.

Soldier, Athlete and Farmer

The remaining half of the first paragraph continues the same exhortation with the use of three striking metaphors. The first makes further use of the comparison of Christian ministry with the life of the soldier (2:4), and then the athlete (2:5) and the farmer (2:6) are also used to illustrate aspects of ministry.

The main point made here about the soldier (2:4) is the importance of total commitment and discipline. A soldier cannot be distracted by non-military matters and get himself *entangled in everyday affairs*. He is focused on one thing only and that is *to please the enlisting officer*. We might think that it is the commanding officer rather than the enlisting officer whom the soldier seeks to please, but probably Paul is assuming that in his context these are one and the same person.[149]

Is Paul saying that a pastor (or other Christian worker) should work full-time in ministry and avoid any other form of labour? It is unlikely that he is laying down such detailed and specific rules. To understand it that way would be to press the metaphor beyond its intended application. The point is the priority of the pastor's commitment to his or her ministry. Other tasks may also be necessary (indeed, we know that Paul himself worked at his trade), but the priority is to remember that one has been enlisted for Christian ministry and to please the enlisting officer, in this case the Lord Jesus Christ himself.

An athlete must participate in the competition *according to the rules* (2:5), or else he or she will be disqualified. For example, if a sprinter runs outside the marked lane, there is an automatic disqualification. How does this apply to Christian ministry? What rules does Paul refer to? A person working within the framework of a church denomination or other Christian organisation is required to follow the rules set by that body but that is not what Paul means here. The rules are much more probably the basic principles of ministry that should be the basis for any ministry of leadership in the church. In the immediate context the focus has been on two things: (a) holding fast to and passing on the truth, and (b) being prepared to suffer (see 2:2-3). Whatever other tasks might fall to a Christian leader in their specific context, basic principles like these must never be forgotten. A leader has no authority to rewrite the principles of ministry clearly set forth in scripture.[150]

---

[149] This explanation is implied by Knight, *Pastorals*, 393-394; Marshall, *Pastorals*, 729.

[150] It is pointed out that many ancient athletic contests had strict rules regarding preparation. Kelly, *Pastorals*, 175-176, for example, suggests that this is the point of emphasis here. But if it is necessary to choose between the rules of preparation and the rules of participation, it is surely the latter with which Paul is concerned; so Mounce, *Pastorals*, 510.

Paul also refers here to the *crown* received by the athlete. In the ancient athletic contests the winner of a competition received a laurel wreath as the prize of victory (a perishable and temporary reward as is noted in 1 Cor. 9:25). This is another detail of the metaphor which should not be pressed beyond its intended meaning. In the athletic contest there could be only one winner, but Christian ministry is not a competition - though to listen to the boasting of some, one might begin to think that it is. In this contest the aim is not to win but to finish well, as Paul claims to have done in 4:7 (see comments on that verse). In this contest *all* can be crowned with the reward of the judge's approval, "Well done, good and faithful servant" (Mt. 25:21).

The third metaphor here is that of the farmer (2:6). The first and most obvious point here is that a successful farmer is a hard worker (as NIV most clearly translates): without hard work there is little or no fruit. A church leader similarly must work hard, as is also indicated in 1 Timothy 4:10 and 5:17 (where the same verb is used as here, though differently translated in those verses in NRSV and NIV). This is a constantly needed reminder for the Christian leader who is often not directly accountable to anyone else on a daily basis. No one knows what the pastor does and it is easy to fall into the temptation to be lazy, appearing on Sundays and fulfilling one's public duties but perhaps wasting a lot of time the rest of the week.

There is also a comment about such a farmer enjoying the fruit of his labour in the form of *the first share of the crops*. Even if this did not always happen (as in the case of farmers who worked someone else's land), Paul suggests that this is their moral right. There seems to be an implied promise of reward for those in ministry, but he does not say enough to tell us what sort of reward he has in mind. It could be the reward of material support (see 1 Tim. 5:17), or it could be some sort of spiritual reward. In the latter case it could be either the reward of seeing the fruit of one's labours in changed lives now or the eternal reward to be received in heaven. With all these uncertainties it is wise not to put too much weight on this aspect of the picture of the farmer. Indeed, it is possible that this is an incidental detail in the picture, with the main emphasis on the need for the farmer and those involved in Christian ministry to work hard in their God-given tasks.[151]

---

[151] This conclusion is supported by Marshall, *Pastorals*, 730; Mounce, *Pastorals*, 510. But Towner, *Timothy-Titus* (2006), 495, and Witherington, *Commentary*, 330, see the reward as a significant focus.

Following the three metaphors, the paragraph finishes with the encouragement to *think over what I say* (2:7). The metaphors use pictures familiar to Timothy from his cultural context, but he will need to reflect on their meaning and work out how to apply them to his own specific situation. The same encouragement needs to be taken seriously by every reader of scripture, along with the assurance that as we engage in such reflection *the Lord will give understanding in all things*.

The Gospel

In this letter Paul has twice already reminded Timothy to safeguard and pass on the truth of the gospel (1:13-14, 2:2) and once already he has provided a brief summary of some of the basics of the gospel (1:9-10). Another statement of the gospel is given here (2:8), not a complete explanation but only a summary.

We may identify three points. (a) The gospel is about Jesus. The words *remember Jesus Christ* may seem almost quaint, since Timothy is not likely to have forgotten Jesus. But it is a way of expressing the truth that Jesus is the heart of the gospel message. Christian leaders make pronouncements on all sorts of subjects (social issues, for example), often without mentioning Jesus at all, but a simple statement like this brings us back to necessary basics. (b) Jesus rose from the dead. Reference to the resurrection reminds us that Jesus died, and part of the gospel is that Jesus died for our sins (1 Cor. 15:3). However, the resurrection is important in its own right, for without Jesus' resurrection there is no gospel. Without his resurrection there is no victory over death or eternal life. (c) Jesus is a descendant of David. This draws attention to his role as Messiah (Mt. 1:1, Mk 10:47-48, Rom. 1:3) and to the fulfilment in Jesus of the promise to David that his kingdom will have no end (2 Sam. 7:12-16, Lk. 1:32-33). It is this Jesus Timothy must remember, the one who has risen victorious over death and whose kingdom is eternal. *That is my gospel*, says Paul, and so it must be Timothy's gospel also. He must remember this Jesus, not only for his own encouragement but also as the gospel to be passed on to others.

As we read on we can again see similarities with chapter 1. There Paul's statement of the gospel (1:9-10) was linked with the theme of suffering immediately before and immediately after (1:8, 11-12). The main point was that the gospel is such a wonderful message that there is no shame in suffering for it (the theme of shame being mentioned in 1:8 and 1:12). Now again the subject of the gospel is immediately followed by mention of Paul's suffering (2:9) and endurance (2:10). He is even treated as *a criminal*, and is imprisoned, *chained* (2:9). This is the result of human opposition to the gospel and Paul can do nothing to prevent that (unless he stops preaching the gospel). But it is implied again that the gospel is worth this suffering. There is a delightful contrast between Paul being chained and the impossibility of the word of God being chained (2:9). This is well illustrated by many passages in the book of Acts, such as Paul's situation in Rome where the gospel of the kingdom is proclaimed *with all boldness and without hindrance* (Acts 28:31), although Paul is under house arrest at the time, and even more dramatically at Philippi where Paul and Silas' imprisonment does not prevent the conversion of the jailer following the earthquake (Acts 16:25-34).

So Paul says that he is willing to suffer for the sake of *the elect*, those God has chosen (2:10). The result is worth the suffering, for what is at stake is the offer of *salvation* and *eternal glory*. And just in case Timothy may have forgotten, he is reminded again that this salvation is *in Christ Jesus* (2:10); there is no other name by which we can be saved (Acts 4:12).

Though Paul speaks of his own gospel ministry and his own experience of suffering, it is quite clear that his concern is for Timothy and others. This is a message for Timothy to take to heart, and equally a message to be heeded by all whom God has called to be among the *faithful people who will be able to teach others also* (2:2). We are entrusted with a glorious message, focusing on the person and work of the Lord Jesus Christ. It is a message (we need to remember) which will provoke opposition in an ungodly world, but the suffering is worthwhile in view of the benefits which the gospel brings.

Reflection: Once Again - What is the Gospel?

This topic has been raised already in the reflections on Titus 3, under the heading "Defining the Gospel". There we noted how many different points can be included within what seem to be simple gospel summaries, and we also attempted to identify what might be considered to be at the heart of the gospel. 2 Timothy provides some further fuel for the same fire, with two important statements to consider (1:9-10 and 2:8).

The shorter and simpler of the two is 2:8, which contains one point with two sub-headings. The main point is Jesus Christ, and the two things said about him are that he has been raised from the dead and that he is descended from David. Paul says very simply "that is my gospel". So the gospel as defined in this verse is Jesus, his resurrection and messiahship. Naturally enough, there is great scope to expand all of this, and it needs to be expanded and explained much more fully in order to be understood by a modern hearer. Nevertheless, this statement stands as a very plain reminder that the gospel is the message about Jesus. It would be interesting to do a survey of the preaching in your church over a period of three or six months, and to ask how often the sermon contains a significant focus on Jesus and a significant explanation of some aspect of his life and work. That would be an excellent test of whether your church really is a gospel-proclaiming church. If you are the pastor, look back over your own messages over the past few months. If you are normally a listener rather than the preacher, this may be something which you can raise with your pastor - but, please, in a sensitive way.

In chapter 1 we have a longer and rather different summary (1:9-10). In the commentary five points were identified in this passage and there is no need to repeat them here. But several summary observations may be made. (a) The gospel is the message of God's act of salvation. This is emphasized in several ways: God is the subject of the verbs "saved" and "called"; the irrelevance of our own works is mentioned; God's grace is of central importance. It is interesting to note that not one of these points is mentioned in 2:8. (b) But linking more closely with 2:8, we see that Jesus occupies a place of fundamental importance: it is in him that God's grace operates; he is our Saviour; he is the one who abolished death and brought life and immortality to light. (c) Salvation is more than simply going to heaven at the end of our earthly existence but includes a new experience of life (now in the present as well as future), as expressed in the statement about Christ's work at the end of 1:10 as well as in the description that God has called us with a holy calling, a calling to be holy people (1:9).

So again - what is a true definition of the gospel? As we have opportunity to explain the gospel, the details may vary from one situation to another. But there are some essentials, not least the central significance of Jesus and his work.

A Sure Saying

2:11-13 contain a *saying* that is *sure* (2:11), the only one in 2 Timothy following the three in 1 Timothy (1:15, 3:1, 4:9) and one in Titus (3:8). The first question to ask is how it fits in the context. It is introduced abruptly, without any stated connection with what Paul has been saying, and this opens the possibility that it is nothing more than a separate statement, with little or no relation to the context. Such a conclusion could be drawn from translations which make 2:11-13 a separate paragraph (such as NIV). On the other hand, NRSV includes this section with the preceding verses as part of the same paragraph, suggesting that Paul is continuing the same theme. This is a much more satisfactory approach.

This is confirmed when we observe that the first two lines of the saying deal with the issue of Christian suffering: dying with Christ (2:11) and enduring (2:12). This explains why Paul uses this saying here (though the saying covers more than this theme). It is another way of making the point, by means of an already familiar saying, that Christian suffering is not a futile exercise. Paul has already said the same in 2:10. Now again he says that suffering is not the end of the story, for the one who has died with Christ (that is, every believer) will also live with him, and the one who endures suffering will also share his reign. The same points are made elsewhere in Paul's letters (see Rom. 6:8, 8:17).

All this reinforces the encouragement which Paul seeks to give Timothy as a Christian minister that suffering is not something to be avoided, even if from a natural point of view it is not something to be sought or desired. We can expect that following Christ will bring suffering and when it happens it is to be seen as evidence that we are truly his disciples (see Mt. 10:25, Lk. 6:40, Jn 13:16, 15:20).

But as well as this encouragement, the sure saying contains something more in the remaining lines. One side of the coin is dying with Christ and enduring suffering, which leads to glory and blessing. But the other side of the coin is what happens to the one who denies him. The saying provides the same warning that Jesus himself gave, that the Son of Man will be ashamed of the one who is ashamed of him (Mk 8:38).

The implications of denying Christ or faithlessness are continued in the final portion of the saying (2:13). We may prove to be *faithless*, but Christ *remains faithful*. Some understand this to mean that despite our unfaithfulness to him he remains faithful to us and forgives whatever we do.[152] This is an unlikely interpretation, for it virtually contradicts the previous line of the saying unless we make a subtle distinction between denial and faithlessness (and nothing in the context suggests such a distinction). More likely it is a warning against expecting cheap

---

[152] So Kelly, *Pastorals*, 180-181; Towner, *Timothy-Titus* (1994), 180; Mounce, *Pastorals*, 517-518.

forgiveness, as if it does not matter what we do for we can always be sure that God will forgive. That line of argument was strongly denied in Romans 6 (especially verses 1, 15). In that same letter Paul wrote, *What if some were unfaithful? Will their unfaithfulness nullify the faithfulness of God?* (3:3). The faithfulness of God (in Romans) or of Christ (in 2 Timothy 2:13) is not a reference to faithfulness to *us*, no matter what, but faithfulness to the *divine plan and purpose*.[153] Understood thus, the present verse is really a warning against thinking that we are indispensable to God's purposes. He will faithfully fulfil his purposes even if we go the other way, the way of denial and faithlessness.

So for Timothy, and for us, there is a choice: either faithfully walking with Christ in the way of the cross with the glorious prospect of life, or being unfaithful and denying him and reaping the dreadful consequences. There is really no choice here at all.

2 Timothy 2:14-26

False Teaching and Its Antidote

The new paragraph begins (2:14) with the instruction to *remind them of this*. The verse is very general, with the word translated *this* referring broadly to the instruction of the preceding verses, and with no specific audience mentioned. NRSV uses the pronouns *them* (twice) and *they*, but none of these words occur in the Greek (which is literally *call these things to mind, warning not to dispute about words*). We soon discover that there is a problem of false teaching in the background (2:16-18), but at the beginning of the paragraph Paul is more concerned with the general nature of Timothy's ministry, which should focus on the truth about Jesus and identify with him despite the suffering which this will bring. Whether or not there is a specific problem to deal with, true pastoral ministry will always recall these things.

People sometimes think that Paul's major concern is theology, but that is a very one-sided impression. The teaching of theology by Paul

---

[153] So Marshall, *Pastorals*, 742: "Christ remains faithful to his cause." Also Knight, *Pastorals*, 406-407, who considers that 2:13a refers "to temporary unfaithfulness and not to unbelief".

always serves the purpose of exhorting God's people to make the right response to God (which should be so, one might suggest, wherever theology is taught). So it has been in this chapter. That is why Paul so strongly objects to *wrangling over words* (2:14) as an end in itself (which, sadly, theological discussion can sometimes become). A few verses later he condemns *profane* (NIV *godless*) *chatter* (2:16), and also *stupid and senseless controversies* (2:23). All these things are negative, ruining the hearers (2:14), producing impiety (2:16) and breeding quarrels (2:23).

From all this we might be tempted to draw the conclusion 'less talk and more action'. Yet that too would be a one-sided response, for the same paragraph contains Paul's exhortation to Timothy to be *a worker who has no need to be ashamed, rightly explaining the word of truth* (2:15). The misuse of words does not mean that words should be avoided. The gospel itself is a word, *the word of truth*. But the context makes it clear that the gospel is more than a word, in the sense that it is more than just something we talk about; it is also something to be put into practice. The truth which the gospel brings has much to say about the way we live our lives, and if someone's life is not changed, we may doubt whether that person has truly heard or responded to the gospel.

Paul's immediate concern is the way Timothy exercises his ministry. The phrase *word of truth* has major implications, for it makes clear that one must distinguish between truth and error. The Christian minister must constantly check that what he or she is saying is the truth, that it is God's word which is being proclaimed not one's own. Then also this word needs to be *rightly explained* (NRSV) or *carefully handled* (NIV). The exact sense of the single Greek word used here is not clear, partly because it is quite a rare word. Scholars debate whether it refers primarily to the teaching of correct doctrine or to the life of the minister needing to be consistent with the truth. One might suggest that both these aspects are relevant to the context, with a concern for correct doctrine seen in the statement about Jesus (2:8) and in the false teaching about the resurrection (2:18), but also a concern about putting gospel truth into practice in following Jesus in the path of suffering on the way to glory (2:11-12). A true ministry of the *word of truth* requires a careful balance of these different elements.[154]

---

[154] For discussion of this rare Greek word *orthotomeo*, translated here *rightly explaining*, see Marshall, *Pastorals*, 748-749; Mounce, *Pastorals*, 524-525.

There is a particular problem in the background, associated with two men named Hymenaeus and Philetus (2:17). One may suppose that Hymenaeus is the same man as mentioned in 1 Timothy 1:20 (though this cannot be proved); there is no other reference to Philetus. These men *have swerved from the truth* (2:18), their particular mistake being the claim that *the resurrection has already taken place*. They were not saying that there is no resurrection at all (a false teaching referred to in 1 Cor. 15:12), but that there is no *further* resurrection in the future. Paul teaches elsewhere that we are already raised with Christ (e.g., Rom. 6:4, Col. 3:1), and it is possible that false conclusions had been drawn from that teaching.[155] But the believer's ultimate experience of salvation is fundamentally connected with a future resurrection, and it is not surprising to learn that by denying this these false teachers were *upsetting the faith of some* (2:18).

God's Firm Foundation

In the face of such problems we might become discouraged, possibly thinking that God's work is being threatened and will be ruined. But Paul gives an assurance that *God's firm foundation stands* (2:19). The image is of an ancient building, which often had inscriptions in the stone work. God's work, more specifically his church,[156] is pictured as a building, protected by a seal in the form of two inscriptions which are derived from OT passages.

The first is *The Lord knows those who are his* (from Num. 16:5). The point is that even in a context of false teaching, where there is a danger of people going astray and abandoning the truth of the gospel, God protects his own people. The second is *Let everyone who calls on the name of the Lord turn away from iniquity* (loosely based on Num. 16:26 and Isa. 26:13). Again, this needs to be understood against the background of false teaching, in which there are some who teach what is false and do what is unrighteous but God's true people take his name and remain separate from iniquity. The fact that there are people like this is proof

---

[155] According to Mounce, *Pastorals*, 539, "the prevailing philosophical dualism and incipient Gnosticism" may also have been influences underlying this false teaching.

[156] So Marshall, *Pastorals*, 755, who says this is the view of most scholars. Also Witherington, *Commentary*, 338: "the true people of God are in view." Mounce, *Pastorals*, 528, sees the focus to be more on individuals.

that God is at work and that the building he has constructed is strong and remains standing.

At 2:20 both NRSV and NIV commence a new paragraph, which may be a little misleading. In fact the house metaphor continues from the previous verse, and it may be better to think of 2:19-21 as a separate paragraph or sub-section, with the common factor being the image of a house. Now, however, it is not the building as such but the equipment used inside the building which is the focus. Paul observes that a large house contains many types of vessels, *some for special use, some for ordinary* (2:20). The point is not that within God's household there is a wide range of gifts and ministries (which is certainly true, as shown by 1 Cor. 12), but an encouragement to believers to aim to be *special utensils* (2:21). All believers, whatever their specific gifts, can become *dedicated and useful to the owner of the house* (God) and *ready for every good work*. The necessary condition is that they *cleanse themselves of the things I have mentioned*. It is only those who turn away from false teaching and evil living who can be useful vessels. Otherwise, it is implied, they remain *ordinary* vessels and not particularly useful to the owner.[157]

Timothy's Spiritual Growth

Timothy himself must strive to be one of the *special utensils* described in 2:21, and Paul now directly addresses Timothy and applies the points to him. The words apply equally to all Christian ministers.

Paul exhorts Timothy from both a negative and a positive perspective: *shun ... pursue* (2:22). The same contrast (with exactly the same Greek words) occurs in 1 Timothy 6:11. He must *shun youthful passions*. Timothy's relative youthfulness has been mentioned in 1 Timothy 4:12 (see comments on that verse). But one does not need to be young to be tempted by youthful passions (or *desires* NIV). Things that are characteristic of younger and immature people have no place in the life of a person like Timothy. So, turning away from these he must *pursue* the positive Christian virtues that are listed here: *righteousness, faith, love, and peace*. Most of these are commonly referred to in lists of desirable characteristics, and in fact the first three come in the parallel instruction

---

[157] Kelly, *Pastorals*, 187, thinks the point is that the orthodox believer must avoid "his unworthy brethren", which seems to go further than the text suggests, as well as being in conflict with 2:24-26.

of 1 Timothy 6:11. On the other hand, *peace* occurs here only in the PE (apart from the introductory greeting of each letter), and is particularly relevant in the context of the instructions which follow immediately (see the following section). Such positive characteristics are the true mark of *those who call on the Lord* and evidence of a *pure heart* (2:22), these words being similar to the second of the inscriptions in 2:19 and describing the people whose lives bear witness to the firmness of the foundation of God's building. Timothy must make sure he is included in this number.

Dealing with Opponents

The final verses of the paragraph (2:23-26) remind Timothy of the problems which have arisen in the church and Paul gives directions how Timothy should respond to them.

The problem of *stupid and senseless controversies* (2:22) has been mentioned elsewhere in the PE (as in 1 Tim. 1:6, 6:4, Tit. 3:9); a few verses earlier Paul has spoken about *wrangling over words* (2:14). Such things have negative effects: here *quarrels,* and elsewhere *speculations* (1 Tim. 1:4). We might say that they generate a lot of heat but not much light. Timothy is to avoid getting entangled in such fruitless debates: he must *have nothing to do with* them.

Instead of being *quarrelsome* he must be *kindly to everyone* and *an apt teacher* (2:24). The teaching role has been stressed elsewhere, in the ministry of the overseer (1 Tim. 3:2, Tit. 1:9) and the elder (1 Tim. 5:17). The same is said here of *the Lord's servant,* not Timothy alone but anyone in a position of responsible leadership in God's church. Naturally teaching will always have a positive element (in the strengthening of believers to understand more of the truth), but here the major focus is on the role of the teacher in relation to false teachers: he is to *correct opponents with gentleness* (2:25). Thus, when Timothy is instructed to *have nothing to do with the controversies* promoted by the false teachers, it does not mean that he is to have nothing to do with the false teachers. Rather, he is encouraged to interact with them and seek to correct their errors.

These letters strongly oppose any teaching which deviates from the apostolic testimony to the truth of the gospel. There is no place in the church for such teaching, but yet there remains room for a positive approach to those who teach what is false. They are not simply to be excommunicated (a relatively easy response), but Timothy is given the more challenging task of trying to help them see the error of their ways. *Perhaps* in the goodness of God *they will repent and come to know the truth* (2:25). The final verse of the chapter speaks of them *being held captive by him* [the devil] (2:26), a description which may not appeal to some sophisticated modern readers, but in fact it is a charitable interpretation of the situation, in the sense that these people are portrayed as not necessarily promoting their own ideas but as instruments in the hands of a stronger power. It may be possible through patient teaching of the truth to help them *escape from the snare of the devil*, and the Christian teacher should look for opportunities to correct the errors of others.[158]

2 Timothy 3:1-9

Difficulties of the Last Days

The new chapter begins by referring to the *last days* (3:1). It might seem natural to think of this expression as describing a period immediately before Jesus' coming in glory. But the NT provides a broader perspective, by describing in this way not only those particular days in the future but also the time between Jesus' ministry on earth and his second coming (Acts 2:17, Heb. 1:2, 2 Pet. 3:3). The present age is the last days. From this perspective we can say that from the time of the apostles till now all who have believed in Jesus have lived in the last days.[159]

So the last days are in fact now (now for us and now in Paul's time also). Even ignoring other NT passages we can see this in the present paragraph, where 3:5-7 especially make it clear that Paul is talking about things that are happening now.[160]

---

[158] In the final phrase there is a hidden difficulty. In English *him* and *his* both appear to refer to the devil, but the use of different pronouns in Greek make it possible that they do not have the same reference. Thus an alternate interpretation is to place *having been held captive by him (the devil)* in parentheses, with *to do his (God's) will* explaining the purpose of helping someone escape from the devil's snare; so Johnson, *Timothy*, 403. For discussion of the possibilities, see Marshall, *Pastorals*, 767-768.

[159] So Knight, *Pastorals*, 428-429; Towner, *Timothy-Titus* (1994), 190-191, and *Timothy-Titus* (2006), 553-554; Marshall, *Pastorals*, 771; Mounce, *Pastorals*, 543.

[160] Kelly, *Pastorals*, 193, though describing the last days as "the period just before the Parousia and the end of the present age" also recognizes that Paul is speaking about present realities.

These *last days*, he says, will produce *distressing times* (3:1). Paul has already experienced this truth in his own life, for *all who are in Asia have turned away from me* (1:15), *Demas has deserted me* (4:10) and *Alexander the coppersmith did me great harm* (4:14). The distressing times are further exemplified by the presence of people characterized by the sins mentioned in 3:2-4. This list contains eighteen items which provide a very unpleasant picture of human life. It is difficult to identify any particular pattern or framework in the list but in general it speaks of human self-centredness. This is specifically stated in the first item (*lovers of themselves*) and is implied throughout. It deals with human self-centredness in the obsession with the so-called good life (*lovers of money, profligates, lovers of pleasure*), in the focus on oneself and one's own importance (*boasters, arrogant, swollen with conceit*), in the mistreatment of others (*abusive, disobedient to their parents, ungrateful, inhuman, implacable, slanderers, brutes, haters of good, treacherous, reckless*), and not least in their wrong attitude and relationship to God (*unholy,* and not *lovers of God*).

It is reasonable to ask why these things should be presented as characteristic of the *distressing times* of the *last days*. Are they not merely aspects of human sinfulness which are seen in every generation? It is possible that Paul means that these things will be seen in a greater measure in the last days. Or the clue may be in 3:5, for there it is seen that Paul is not only talking about unbelievers in general but also of some in the church, people *holding to the outward form of godliness but denying its power*. If someone is observing the outward forms, with an appearance of being a godly person, he or she certainly wants to be thought of as a genuine member of the community of faith. To think that people characterized by the evil ways listed in 3:2-4 could consider themselves godly persons comes as a disturbing possibility. Even more disturbing is the possibility that others within the Christian community might be fooled by the outward pretence and fail to see the reality of such a person's life.

The passage makes it clear that outward form is not enough and that true godliness includes spiritual power, the power of God's Spirit to enable the believer to do God's will. That means a changed life, the opposite to the sort of life described in 3:2-4. The evidence of godliness is a godly *life* and not just a superficial *appearance* of godliness.

More About False Teachers

In the Ephesus context of 2 Timothy, Paul is not merely concerned about general issues or vague possibilities, or a potential problem at some time in the future, but about real people actually influencing the life of the church at Ephesus, for the specific instruction is given to *avoid them* (3:5). He has already referred to false teachers in chapter 2. Timothy's proper response is to avoid their teaching and their methods (2:14, 16-18, 23). On the other hand, he should try to correct them (2:25-26). How does that instruction relate to the present command to *avoid them*, for it is surely difficult to avoid and correct at the same time? Possibly chapter 3 refers to a different level of false teaching, more dangerous than that described in chapter 2 and so requiring a different level of response, though there is no hint of that in the text. Perhaps a better suggestion is that a commonsense interpretation rather than a strictly logical one is in order, and that Paul's concern is that Timothy should make every effort to remove the influence of such people from the congregation, refusing to allow them opportunities to peddle their teaching and urging believers who are at risk to avoid contact with them, without necessarily cutting himself off entirely from such contact.

Nothing is said about the actual content of the teaching of these people. Paul has put the spotlight on the evil lives of the false teachers and that is perhaps sufficient reason to regard their influence as extremely dangerous. It is that influence which is described in the following verses (3:6-7). The language here could easily be interpreted as extremely anti-feminist and it is certainly not flattering to women. At the same time, one should not dismiss out of hand the possibility that Paul is giving a factual description (even if in terms which we might hesitate to use today); that is to say, it was women of perhaps a lower social and educational level who were the unfortunate targets of the false teachers and they simply did not have the capacity to resist. It is also possible that the words of 3:7 (*always being instructed* but not able to *arrive at a knowledge of the truth*) are less a description of the mental ability of these women than of the nature of the false teaching. The reason they cannot arrive at a knowledge of the truth is that the false teachers are not teaching the truth. In fact the following verse clearly tells us that these people are *of corrupt mind and counterfeit faith* and *oppose the truth* (3:8). This is a more satisfactory explanation, for the NT perspective is that the gospel has the power to communicate to all, however limited their education might be.

It is common for false teachers (in today's context members of sects, for example) to target people whose faith is weak. Whatever one may think or feel about the language used in 3:6-7 it should not be forgotten that there are people vulnerable to false teaching. This serves as a major challenge to the churches, not only to protect such people from hearing false teaching but more positively to equip them to be able to withstand it.

The false teachers are compared with *Jannes and Jambres* (3:8). According to Jewish tradition they were two of Pharaoh's magicians who opposed Moses when he appeared before Pharaoh to demand the release of the Israelites from Egypt. They are not mentioned in the OT narrative.[161] Why exactly Paul chooses to use them as an example is not fully explained here. Perhaps the word *opposed* is our best clue: they opposed God's appointed representative Moses, in a similar manner (it is implied) to the way the false teachers at Ephesus were treating Timothy, God's representative in his own generation.

The statement *they will not make much progress* (3:9) is added as an assurance to Timothy in his leadership of a church under threat. Such an assurance may be based on 2:19, *the Lord knows those who are his*, a strong statement of the sovereign will and purposes of God and of God's hand of protection over his people. Yet such an assurance should never provide grounds for complacency in the church. However true it is that *their folly will become plain to everyone*, it may take some time for this to happen and much damage can be done in the meantime. Church leaders must never sit back and simply assume that God will take care of his people, for God has appointed shepherds of the flock as his agents in that great task.

2 Timothy 3:10-17

Good Examples for Timothy

The negative examples of the previous verses are now replaced by good and positive examples, first the example of Paul himself. Timothy has *observed* Paul's life (3:10-11), the verb here meaning something like *study*

---

[161] Further information about Jannes and Jambres may be found in Marshall, *Pastorals*, 778-779; Mounce, *Pastorals*, 547-548; Johnson, *Timothy*, 407-408; Towner, *Timothy-Titus* (2006), 563-564.

at close range;[162] it is stronger than *know* (NIV). Timothy has had a close acquaintance with Paul, so that he knows from personal experience and observation what sort of person Paul is and what sort of life he has led as a servant of Christ. We may wonder how the references to *Antioch* and *Iconium* (3:11) fit in this context, for we may assume that Paul is here referring to the events recorded in Acts 13 and 14 which actually took place *before* he reached Timothy's home town of Lystra. But no doubt the events that took place in those places became so well known in Lystra and probably so much part of family conversation in Timothy's home that it was not much different from Timothy being present and observing them for himself. In any case Paul does not mean that Timothy had observed every detail of Paul's life, but simply that he had known him long enough and closely enough to know the facts of Paul's life and to have an intimate acquaintance with his character and lifestyle.

The list of his characteristics which he offers to Timothy as an example begins with *teaching,* an appropriate emphasis in view of the concern which Paul has already expressed about false teachers and false teaching. *Conduct* is a general description of how Paul lived his life. When he speaks of his *aim in life,* he clearly reveals that his life had purpose and direction and was not merely an aimless reaction to whatever circumstances happened to arise. The following four characteristics (*my faith, my patience, my love, my steadfastness*) are virtues which we find elsewhere in this letter, so that when Paul encourages Timothy to demonstrate these in his own life (for example, faith and love in 2:22, patience in 4:2, steadfastness in 2:12), he is only being asked to follow the example he has already seen in Paul.

As the list continues in 3:11, we see that Paul is not speaking only of what we might call the victorious Christian life. On the contrary, Paul's example includes *persecutions* and *suffering.* This last word is actually plural (*sufferings*), as in NIV. A literal translation here is *sufferings, the sorts of things which happened to me in Antioch, in Iconium, in Lystra.* He does not mean the events in these places only (as NRSV suggests), but he specifically mentions them as being particularly familiar to Timothy, as examples of sufferings which befell him in many places. The verse finishes on a triumphant note, a reminder to Timothy of what he must surely have known already, that *the Lord rescued me from them all.* To be

---

[162] Witherington, *Commentary,* 356.

rescued from them does not mean not having to undergo such things but being preserved in the midst of them and being brought through them. That does not always mean being rescued from the physical results of opposition and persecution, for Paul anticipated his own death in the near future (4:6-8).

In 3:12 he specifically says that a way of life which genuinely follows Christ will inevitably involve such experiences, not only for Paul or for a Christian leader like Timothy, but for *all who want to live a godly life in Christ Jesus*. This is an implied warning to Timothy: if all followers of Christ will be persecuted, he can hardly expect to be the one exception. It is also a repetition of the call to *suffer for the gospel* (1:8) *like a good soldier of Jesus Christ* (2:3). This is especially necessary in a situation when *wicked people and impostors will go from bad to worse* (3:13), a specific example of the *distressing times* of the *last days* mentioned in 3:1. The word translated *impostors* could have the general sense of *swindlers* or *cheats*, but it literally means *sorcerers*, possibly a reference back to Jannes and Jambres in 3:8. Even if the false teachers Timothy must deal with are not literally sorcerers,[163] Paul could easily have regarded them as sorcerers or magicians in a metaphorical sense, bewitching their hearers with false teaching, false claims and false promises.

By contrast, Timothy is not to be deceived by such people but must continue in his convictions (3:14), that is, *in what you have learned and firmly believed*. Timothy's convictions are strengthened by remembering their source and so Paul also says *knowing from whom you learned it*. He is not referring to himself but to Timothy's own family, as the following verse confirms when it speaks of the knowledge Timothy has gained *from childhood* (3:15).

We have already seen the influence in Timothy's life of his mother Eunice and his grandmother Lois, for in 1:5 Paul speaks of the faith that was present in their lives. Though this probably means faith in God in a general sense (rather than specifically faith in Jesus), it is in principle the same thing, as indeed in the life of Abraham whose faith was reckoned to him as righteousness (Gen. 15:6, Rom. 4:9). So Timothy had already seen faith demonstrated in the lives of Eunice and Lois, so that when he

---

[163] It is possible but not necessary to see here a reference to involvement in magic arts; see Kelly, *Pastorals*, 200; Marshall, *Pastorals*, 786; Towner, *Timothy-Titus* (2006), 578-579; Witherington, *Commentary*, 358.

heard the gospel through Paul's preaching in Lystra he was good soil ready to receive the message about Jesus.

Reflection: Aims in Life

Paul speaks in 3:10 of his "aim in life". These three English words represent a single Greek word which in different contexts can be translated plan or purpose. It may refer to a specific plan in a particular situation, such as the plan of the sailors to reach the harbour called Phoenix (Acts 27:13). Another passage refers to a more general purpose of life, as in Barnabas' exhortation to the believers in Antioch (Acts 11:23). Here in 2 Timothy it also refers to something to do with Paul's life in general.

The standard Greek dictionary provides the definition "that which is planned in advance" (BDAG). The two key elements are "planning" and "in advance". It has been observed that planning is often not done well in India. For the Commonwealth Youth Games in Pune in 2008, a large sum of money was allocated for the beautification of the city (such as roadworks, cleaning and painting). It was reported that some of these works were still being done many months after the games were over. This was not a case of corruption. The intention and desire to present an attractive face to the visiting athletes and spectators were there but the ability to plan and co-ordinate was lacking or possibly the ability to plan early enough to ensure that the work was completed in time.

The phrase 'chalta hai' is not uncommon in India. Things will happen eventually in their own good time. But often that is not true. The city of Pune was not ready for the games. The 'chalta hai' mentality is a form of fatalism more appropriate to some other religious faiths. There is an opposite extreme, often observed in the West, where every moment of one's life must be spent in a measurably profitable way and one can be made to feel very guilty about time that is said to be 'wasted'.

Between these two extremes the Bible gives examples which provide a better pattern to follow. One is Jesus, who certainly had time to spend with people but did not allow people to set the agenda of his life. His life had purpose, in general the purpose of serving (Mk 10:45) and in particular the purpose of bringing his ministry to a climax in Jerusalem (Lk. 9:51). On a day to day basis he had his priorities. One day he determined to spend time in prayer and then engage in preaching ministry (Mk 1:35-39), and not even the urgent demands of Peter and the crowds stopped him from doing this.

Or we might think of Paul. He likewise planned his ministry (and indeed the activities of many others as we will see in the comments on 2 Tim. 4), but he was flexible enough to make adjustments if the plans did not work out (Acts 15:36, 16:6-8, Rom. 1:11-13, 15:22-25). He speaks of his ambition in ministry (Rom. 15:20) and was concerned not to run aimlessly (1 Cor. 9:26).

Most of the passages mentioned above deal with ministry-related goals (the topic of a reflection on 1 Timothy 1), but Paul's words here also say something about life in general. Why do I live my life? Is it merely to survive from one day to the next, or do I have a more significant reason to live? What do I aim to achieve this year? How do I plan to improve my performance (in studies, business, role in family, involvement in Christian ministry, and so on)? What specific goals have I set so that at the end of the year (or the end of the month or whatever period is appropriate) I will be able to measure my success or otherwise? 'Chalta hai' is fine if we think God wants our life just to drift along aimlessly. But such an attitude is hard to justify biblically.

The Holy Scriptures

Here Paul mentions another aspect of the family influence on Timothy. As a natural part of life in a Jewish home (even though only partly Jewish, according to Acts 16:1) the scriptures would have been read, and so, Timothy is reminded, *from childhood you have known the sacred writings* (3:15). When Paul wrote this letter to Timothy the 'New Testament' did not exist, and so the reference here is not to the Bible as we know it today, but the books of the *Hebrew* Bible, the 'Old Testament'. But even so, Paul claims that these writings *are able to instruct you for salvation through faith in Christ Jesus*. Though the OT does not speak specifically of Christ, it nevertheless points to him and to the salvation that is available through faith in him. This is a common NT perspective. Jesus himself set the example when he said, *Everything written about me in the law of Moses, the prophets, and the psalms must be fulfilled* (Lk. 24:44). Paul speaks of *the gospel of God, which he promised beforehand through his prophets in the holy scriptures* (Rom. 1:2), and of *the righteousness of God through faith in Jesus Christ* as something which has been *attested by the law and the prophets* (Rom. 3:21-22). On the day of Pentecost Peter explained the incredible event that had taken place by saying that *this is what was spoken through the prophet Joel* (Acts 2:16). Many similar examples could be given.

This leads to perhaps the best known words of this letter, the statement about the inspiration and the value of scripture (3:16-17). The phrase *all scripture* is virtually the same as *the sacred writings* (3:15). In the context of Paul's time it can only mean the books of the Old Testament.

In the course of time the Christian church came to see that other books also should be regarded as having the status of *sacred writings*, namely the books of our New Testament, and naturally the statement here about the books of the Old Testament applies equally to the books of the New Testament (even though that was not what Paul had in mind at the time of writing).

All scripture, he says, is *inspired by God*. This phrase, one word in Greek, means literally *God-breathed*.[164] Though this is the literal translation, we need not understand the phrase in a literalistic sense, as if God in heaven produced a big breath which somehow wafted into the books of the Bible. However, we do need to give the phrase serious content. At the very least it says that what we read in the Bible comes from God. It is not that God's message is merely *in* the Bible, or that the Bible merely *contains* God's message, but that the Bible *is* God's message. It is not possible to say that one passage comes from God but that another passage does not, especially if it is a passage which we do not like. Rather, *all scripture* or *every scripture*[165] is inspired.

Nowhere in the Bible is any explanation given about how inspiration works. It is clear that the books of the Bible are also human productions. Each book was written in a language familiar to writer and readers, and within a particular historical and cultural context. There is no hint that the books were produced through some sort of direct divine dictation (except for some sections such as the words of the Ten Commandments). Nevertheless, even if we do not understand the exact process, the books are also God's books, bearing the message and the words which he intends.

For this reason, Paul says, scripture is *useful* (3:16), and he then mentions four areas of usefulness. First, it is useful for *teaching* (again first in the list, as we observed in 3:10), for knowledge of the truth. It is useful for *reproof*, for drawing attention to errors of understanding and wrong behaviour. It is useful for *correction*, for setting the one who has gone wrong (the person who has been reproved) on the right path. And

---

[164] For useful discussion of the Greek adjective *theopneustos* and the concept of inspiration, see Marshall, *Pastorals*, 793-794; Mounce, *Pastorals*, 565-566.

[165] Though scholars spill much ink discussing these options (e.g., Marshall, *Pastorals*, 792; Mounce, *Pastorals*, 566; Towner, Timothy-Titus (2006), 585-588), it does not seem to make much difference which of these two translations we adopt.

finally, it is useful for *training in righteousness*, not only for dealing with problems when they arise but as a guidebook to be used proactively to show the right way to respond to God and walk in his way.

The purpose of scripture and of its use in these four ways is summarized in 3:17. Here we read of *everyone who belongs to God*. The literal translation of these words is *man of God* (as in NIV). The same phrase occurs in 1 Timothy 6:11 where it specifically describes Timothy. In the Greek translation of the OT, the phrase refers to leaders such as Moses and David, but it is also used to describe God's people more generally. This background suggests that the phrase here is particularly relevant to Timothy as a leader in the church but also that the words of 3:17 cannot be limited to leaders only. The stated purpose of the proper use of scripture applies to all believers.

That purpose includes becoming *proficient*. That word alone does not tell us much but the last words of the verse explain what sort of proficiency Paul has in mind. It is being proficient so as to be *equipped for every good work*. (The NIV *thoroughly equipped* combines the two words *proficient* and *equipped* into one phrase.) As throughout the PE, we find here a very practical concern. Scripture is not merely a source book for theological information or philosophical speculation. Its purpose is to change people's lives. The intention that the believer's life should be characterized by good works is expressed in very similar phrases earlier in the letter (2:21) and in Titus 3:1. Paul would not have thought it possible for someone to be a Christian in a merely intellectual or cultural sense.

This final phrase of the chapter brings us back to the central issue here. We are reminded that Paul has a practical outcome in mind and is not merely giving doctrinal instruction. The focus of the whole paragraph (3:10-17) is the encouragement to Timothy to *continue in what you have learned and firmly believed* (3:14). Timothy is reminded that his present convictions have a very solid foundation. They are based on the word of the living God himself, reinforced by the examples he has seen in the lives of his mentor Paul and his beloved mother and grandmother. With these words Paul has thoroughly prepared the way for the final exhortations of the next chapter.

Reflection: Value and Use of Scripture

An earlier reflection (on 1 Timothy 4) focused our attention on the significant place of the reading of scripture in the context of public worship. Here in 2 Timothy 3:16-17 we go back to even more fundamental matters related to the Bible. The passage begins by affirming the inspiration of scripture (here by the use of the adjective "God-breathed"). Volumes have been written on this doctrine, and these few paragraphs are not the place to try to explain or defend that doctrine. Nor is this the place to justify applying this statement to the books of our New Testament (as well as to the Old Testament books which are what the verse originally had in mind).

Though Paul affirms the inspiration of scripture, the emphasis here is on its practical use. This arises from the authority of scripture as inspired and therefore coming as God's message to us. As mentioned in the commentary, the two aspects of scripture as the productions of human authors and as the word of God need to be held in balance. Neither should be ignored if we wish to come to a correct understanding of a passage. The scholar tends to focus on the human element (attempting to understand a passage in its original context), whereas the preacher tends to focus on the divine element (attempting to bring a message from God to the congregation). Both aspects are in fact essential: the classroom and the scholarly book would be enriched by a greater awareness of the divine authority of the text that is being studied, and the Sunday sermon would be enriched if the preacher took more time to understand the words of the passage in its human context. However, one might suggest that the logical priority should be given to the divine origin and authority of scripture, for that is what gives the Bible its enduring usefulness. Scripture is not just human reflections (as are the words you are now reading) but the eternal word of God.

3:16 mentions four areas of usefulness, which need little explanation: teaching, reproof, correction and training in righteousness. The phrases are certainly applicable to a believer's private use of the Bible, but the immediate context is Timothy's responsibility in his ministry. First, he is to use the scriptures to teach the truth. At a number of places in this book we have raised the question whether the regular ministry of our churches in India (that is, primarily, the Sunday sermon) can be described as teaching, which is clearly what Paul assumes to be necessary and fundamental for the healthy life of a congregation (and the individual members of it).

The other phrases underline the point which we have also seen many times in the PE that the ministry of Timothy or Titus or any other leader is not just an academic exercise. Teaching of the truth has a far deeper purpose than merely imparting theological expertise. Hence we read of reproof and correction. If teaching is often absent, it is even more likely that reproof and correction will also be absent. Be suspicious of the preacher who never says anything negative. Negative things do sometimes need to be said: errors of understanding, sinful actions and habits, do occur and need to be pointed out. Some have an inner feeling that our ministry must always be encouraging and never draw attention to the dark side of a person's life. That approach may appear to be loving and sensitive, but to overlook sin can hardly be a loving response. Of course there are some pastors who delight in pointing out such things, usually from the pulpit where they are beyond contradiction. Yes, there is a place in the Sunday sermon to speak about sin and judgement, but usually the best way to deal with these matters is at a personal level. The pastor who lacks the courage to speak to an individual face to face but rebukes him or her from the pulpit (not directly by name, though everyone knows who he means) may need to be rebuked himself. Also it should not be forgotten that reproof must be followed by correction. It is never sufficient to point out the fault; the essential next step is to help the person get back on track.

The final phrase points to the ultimate purpose: training in righteousness, explained further in 3:17 and especially by the phrase "equipped for every good work". That may remind us of Titus 2:12 where we read of the training role of God's grace, leading to the same result. Putting the two passages together, we can say that it is through the proper understanding and application of the Bible that this training will take place. The Bible is clearly not a book for academic study alone, or even worse a book to be kept on the shelf and not read at all.

2 Timothy 4:1-5

Timothy's Motives

Paul does not expect to live much longer. He was not an extremely old man (perhaps about 60 years of age) but he faced the prospect of execution by the Roman authorities at some time in the foreseeable future. This expectation is clearly indicated in 4:6 and in these circumstances he gives his final instructions to Timothy (4:1-5).

The opening words of the paragraph (4:1) are a way of reminding Timothy that the commission entrusted to him does not merely come from a human source. Paul issues a solemn *charge* (as in NIV, or as in NRSV, *I solemnly urge you*), *in the presence of God and of Christ Jesus.* As we see elsewhere in the PE, Christ is placed on the same level as God the Father. The divine status of Christ is confirmed by the statement that he *is to judge the living and the dead,* though Paul's purpose is not so much to give Timothy a theological lesson about the person of Christ as to remind him that he will be among those required to give an account on the day of judgement. The point is reinforced in an even stronger way in the words *in view of his appearing and his kingdom,* for Christ will return in glory and his status as king revealed.

Such a charge should motivate Timothy to press on in the midst of whatever difficulties he may have to face and to fulfil the responsibilities which are summarized in the following verses. Indeed every minister of the gospel needs to be reminded regularly of this solemn truth that his or her ministry is conducted in the presence of the almighty God and his exalted Son, and so the priority in ministry must be to please God and seek his approval rather than the approval of human masters and judges (see 1 Cor. 4:1-5, Gal. 1:10, 1 Thess. 2:4).

Timothy's Duties

Nine commands are directed towards Timothy in 4:2-5 (five in verse 2 and four in verse 5). This information might lead us to expect instruction about a wide variety of tasks in ministry, but it is striking to observe that most of them relate to one general responsibility, namely Timothy's speaking role. All except two of the commands (*be sober* and *endure suffering* in verse 5) relate directly or indirectly to the matter of his words and his message.

The instructions begin with *proclaim the message* (4:2), where the word *message* is literally *word* (as in NIV), a shorthand way of describing the Christian message (as in 2:9, 15, Tit. 1:3, though these other passages all add some further description, such as *word of truth* in 2:15). This command summarizes what is at the heart of Paul's concern, which is that the apostolic tradition should continue to be faithfully passed on, the same concern which we have seen in 2:2 and elsewhere. The task is to *proclaim* this word, this verb calling to mind the role of a public herald making an announcement which has been entrusted to him by a recognized authority. In the same way Timothy is a herald with such a responsibility; the *word* of the Christian message is an announcement to be given with the authority of God.

Timothy is to attend to this task *whether the time is favourable or unfavourable* (4:2). This translation is an interpretation of the phrase *in season and out of season* (NIV). It could be understood to refer to times which are convenient or inconvenient for Timothy, but the main point is more likely to relate to the convenience of the hearers. Students in the schools of rhetoric were taught to identify times when hearers would be most ready to listen to and be persuaded by their arguments;[166] this was nothing less than plain commonsense. But here Timothy is told *not* to wait for such moments. We may be a long time waiting for hearers to be ready to hear the gospel, but rather than wait we are to create opportunities for gospel ministry whether people seem likely to be ready to listen or not. The message is too important and the need is too urgent to wait for what might seem like a time when the hearer seems likely to respond positively. This does not rule out applying the point to the preacher also, for if the convenience of the hearer is not to be allowed to decide the matter, even less can the preacher use his or her own personal convenience as a criterion to determine whether and when to proclaim the word.

The following commands express different aspects of the ministry of proclaiming the word: *convince, rebuke, and encourage* (4:2). These commands speak of the application of the word (in both negative and positive ways) to the congregation and thus remind us that the ministry of the word is much more than academic exposition or the giving of theological information. They are also a reminder that proclaiming the word is not only preaching the gospel to the unconverted. Believers need to continue to hear the word as the only reliable way to stay on the Christian path.

The final phrase of 4:2 describes the manner and means of performing this ministry. The manner is *with the utmost patience*, for, as every pastor knows, a spiritual lesson is not learned and accepted the first time it is taught. Perseverance and much repetition is needed. The means is *teaching*. Thus, the verse begins with proclamation and ends with teaching. These are ultimately not two different things but merely different perspectives on the same thing.

Paul speaks in 4:3-4 of the context in which Timothy is called to carry out his work. When he writes that *the time is coming when people will not put up with sound doctrine* (4:3), he gives a good example of the sort of *unfavourable time* referred to in 4:2. Such people will find *teachers*

---

[166] Towner, *Timothy-Titus* (2006), 600-601; Witherington, *Commentary*, 364.

to suit their own desires (4:3) which sadly will mean that they will no longer be *listening to the truth* (4:4). Even then it will be Timothy's duty to proclaim the word, as far as it is possible to do so, but the more immediate reason for mentioning this coming time is that Timothy should use every available opportunity for proclamation now, before that coming time actually arrives.

Returning to direct instructions to Timothy (4:5), Paul says *always be sober*, not only literally (though that is important too) but more particularly in a metaphorical sense, "free fr[om] every form of mental and spiritual drunkenness" (BDAG). This is in contrast, one may assume, with the lack of sobriety evidenced by the false teachers and their followers who allow themselves to come under the influence of *myths* (4:4). The instruction to *endure suffering* repeats what has been said already (1:8, 2:3), following the example of Paul himself (2:9), and is particularly relevant in view of the description of the *distressing times* of the *last days* described in chapter 3. He is to *do the work of an evangelist*, not necessarily in the limited context of preaching to the unconverted but referring generally to the task of gospel proclamation. This, we have seen, is appropriate for believers and unbelievers alike, and gives Timothy the same task as Paul himself who was called to proclaim the gospel (1 Cor. 1:17, 9:16) but whose gospel ministry had a very broad focus.[167] Finally comes the encouragement to *carry out your ministry fully*, which may be understood in a general sense to refer to whatever tasks fall within Timothy's responsibility but in the context of this paragraph has special reference to the various aspects of the ministry of the word.

Reflection: Communicating the Truth

One can hardly read two or three paragraphs of the PE without being aware of the major emphasis on teaching, and we have drawn attention to this a number of times. It is hardly a coincidence that this theme appears again in the last chapter of Paul's last letter, as part of his final legacy, we might say. So in 4:2 we find the words "proclaim", "be persistent", "convince", "rebuke", "encourage", "teaching"; in 4:3-4 a focus on the importance of sound teaching

---

[167] Knight, *Pastorals*, 457, limits the reference to evangelism in a narrow sense; so also, apparently, Towner, *Timothy-Titus* (1994), 205-206, though in his 2006 commentary he recognizes that "it may be artificial to distinguish rigidly between proclamation to the church and to those outside the faith" (page 600). Others recognize a wider sense; e.g., Barrett, *Pastorals*, 117; Marshall, *Pastorals*, 804; Witherington, *Commentary*, 366.

and the truth; and finally in 4:5 the instruction to do the work of an evangelist (or, in more general terms, engage in gospel proclamation). There is no risk of Timothy missing the point. There is a message to be communicated and Timothy must see that he fulfils his responsibility to do so.

In all this it is easy to make the mistake of thinking that the emphasis is on the process. We may have a concept of preaching which means one person standing and delivering an oration for 20 or 30 minutes - or 50 or 60. One person speaks, the rest seem to be listening, and we think that is what is required on every occasion. Even in a small meeting of 10-15 people in a private home, someone is identified as 'the speaker' and he or she may feel it necessary to follow a formal monologue style of delivery and even stand to deliver the message, for this (and this alone) is understood to be proper proclamation. The Indian mentality tends to favour what is formal and structured rather than the informal and less structured.

The present author does not wish to belittle that style of presentation. In fact he has many files full of messages delivered in exactly that way. But we miss the point if we think that is Paul's major concern in a passage like this. The main focus is not on the process or the manner of presentation but on the content and substance. This is seen in the emphasis on sound teaching and the truth. Paul does not simply want Timothy to speak (many unsuitable people are willing to do that, as verse 3 tells us), but to speak the truth.

As we think about Paul's ministry, we realize that in addition to the many times in which he preached a formal sermon (as we might describe it) he used other methods of communication. In Thessalonica he argued with the Jews, explaining and proving his claims about Jesus (Acts 17:2-3). In Beroea, his next place of ministry, we read that the Jews examined the scriptures to test Paul's claims (Acts 17:11), and it is hard to imagine that Paul was not present as part of the discussion. In Corinth his ministry again included arguing his case and trying to convince (Acts 18:4), and it is hard to imagine a merely passive audience. The impression in each of these cases is a situation of lively interaction, discussion, argument and counter argument.

In the PE also there have been hints that communicating the truth is much more than delivering a formal sermon. One context that is mentioned several times is dealing with opponents who teach what is false. Warning such a person (Tit. 3:10) could well be a public action in the presence and hearing of others as witnesses, but correcting an opponent with the purpose of encouraging them to return to the truth (2 Tim. 2:25) would be much more appropriately done privately in an informal manner. It is not only false teachers who need to be rebuked (2 Tim. 3:16), and though rebuke in general terms can be done from the pulpit, rebuke of an individual guilty of a particular offence is most effectively done privately and informally.

There are three issues, the first two of fundamental importance. One is the content of the communication. There are many messages in Christian meetings which may be assessed as wonderful pieces of oratory but which fail the test of communicating the word of God. The latest fad in pop-psychology is not the word of God. Even a faithful believer's testimony is not the word of God. Such things may be used to illustrate and illuminate a verse or passage of scripture but in themselves are not the word of God. We need to remember that the word of God is not just whatever may come into the mind of the preacher (however great that preacher's reputation may be), but "the sound teaching that conforms to the glorious gospel of the blessed God" (1 Tim. 1:11). That is the test of content.

The second matter is that this content must be communicated with authority and without compromise. The truth of the gospel is not for us to decide. It is something already given in trust, as it was long ago entrusted to Paul (1 Tim. 1:11), to Timothy (2 Tim. 1:14) and by Timothy to others (2 Tim. 2:2). We do not decide by majority vote to add anything or subtract anything. Our task is to communicate it faithfully.

The third issue is also important though without the same fundamental significance. That is the method of communication. We have observed that the delivery of a monologue is not the only style observed in the pages of the NT. If the aim is to communicate, then we need to find the most appropriate means of communication. In small groups, discussion is an option, as long as that does not become a mere sharing of personal thoughts which are all accepted as equally correct; there needs to be a competent leader who has the skill to deal gently with error and point the group in the right direction. But despite the dangers of the method, more effective learning is likely to take place in a context where people actively participate rather than merely being expected to be passive listeners. Even in church it is possible to use other methods beyond the traditional sermon, including the use of technology (as is already done in some churches in India). The duty of church leadership is not just to see that the Sunday service takes place and that it includes a sermon. The duty is to see that the word of truth is communicated in the most effective ways possible - and indeed not only in the Sunday service. Here is a worthwhile item for the agenda of your next church committee meeting.

2 Timothy 4:6-8

Paul's Future

Paul now speaks of his own death (4:6), though it requires some care to see exactly what he means. There seem to be two stages. The first is expressed by the words *I am already being poured out as a libation*. This is already happening - not his death but a preliminary. A libation was a drink-offering (such as wine) which was not the actual sacrifice but accompanied the sacrifice. Paul pictures himself as such an offering, perhaps referring to his present trials and difficulties which clearly point to death not far away.[168] Then at the end of the verse he speaks directly of his death, *my departure*, as relatively close. It is not that the time *has come* (as in NRSV and NIV) but that it is "about to occur" (BDAG); we might say it is just around the corner. The instruction to Timothy to come and join him (4:9, 21) assumes that Paul anticipates at least some passage of time. His death is not so close that the date has been marked on the calendar but rather that the writing is on the wall and Paul knows that his death will be the outcome of the present circumstances.

Even though Paul is not yet dead, and indeed has not yet stopped working (see comments on 4:11, 13 below), he can speak of successfully fulfilling his own responsibilities: *I have fought the good fight, I have finished the race, I have kept the faith*. These phrases can be understood to refer in a general way to living the Christian life. But in the context of his exhortations to Timothy to fulfil his ministry responsibilities there is almost certainly a more specific meaning: he has completed his tasks in ministry.

In the light of all this he can look forward confidently to receiving from the Lord (Jesus, as in 4:1) the *crown of righteousness* (4:8). The exact significance of this phrase has been much debated. Partly it depends on the meaning we give to the word *righteousness* itself. If it means *righteous behaviour*, the crown is the reward for righteous behaviour. But if it refers to one's status as a person accepted by God, the crown *is* that status and relationship which though experienced already will be more fully enjoyed *on that day*, the day of judgement.[169] It is not an exclusive crown,

---

[168] So Witherington, *Commentary*, 368: "the language is not about sacrifice, but rather the events that accompany sacrifice and death, and it may well presage these other events". Towner, *Timothy-Titus* (2006), 610, likewise recognizes the distinction between the libation and the actual sacrifice but also notes the very close connection between the two and comments that "the metaphor with its allusion to wine may well intend to evoke the imagery of Paul's blood (i.e., his life) being poured out".

[169] Kelly, *Pastorals*, 210, and Johnson, *Timothy*, 432, argue for the first possibility, but Knight, *Pastorals*, 461, and Towner, *Timothy-Titus* (1994), 207, for the second, though in his 2006 commentary Towner is less certain: "best not to distinguish too rigidly between these options" (pages 615-616). The latter position is supported by Marshall, *Pastorals*, 809 ("Probably both ideas should be combined ... The crown connotes righteousness but is granted to those who are righteous"), and Witherington, *Commentary*, 370 ("It could be either").

reserved for apostles and other great ones, but is for *all who have longed for* (literally *loved*, as NIV) *his appearing* (4:8), that is, for all committed Christian people.

We should not make the mistake of reading this paragraph (4:6-8) as an entirely new and separate section. It is closely connected with what has gone before. Timothy has been charged to carry out serious and significant responsibilities. Paul's comments about himself are not merely the wandering reminiscences of an old man but serve two positive purposes in this context. (a) They provide an example. Timothy must live the Christian life and fulfil his responsibilities in ministry just as Paul has done. (b) They stress the urgency of the matter. Paul will not be around to lead the work and offer support and guidance, and so Timothy must step up to the mark and do what is required without hesitation.

2 Timothy 4:9-22

Paul's Situation

The final paragraphs of the letter include a number of personal references, as in most of Paul's letters (in Titus, for example, though not in 1 Timothy). It is tempting to consider these as of little importance and to skip over them quickly, but to do so would be to deprive ourselves of some important information about the last period of Paul's life.

The letter has already revealed that Paul is a prisoner (1:8, 16), and that he expects to die in the foreseeable future (4:6), even if not immediately. In this final passage he mentions his *first defence* (4:16), meaning the first stage of his present trial (rather than a previous trial such as may have taken place after the end of the Acts narrative).[170] Clearly that *first defence* led to no result, for he has not yet been found guilty and punished nor has he been acquitted and released. Despite having no human help, he had experienced the Lord's presence, so much so that he can speak of being *delivered from the mouth of the lion* (4:17). Though not released from prison

---

[170] So most recent commentators, e.g., Towner, *Timothy-Titus* (1994), 211; Mounce, *Pastorals*, 594-595; Witherington, *Commentary*, 380. For a simple explanation of the legal process, see Kelly, *Pastorals*, 218. For fuller discussion of the options, see Towner, *Timothy-Titus* (2006), 635-649.

and from the threat of death, he had been delivered thus far and enabled to use the opportunity to testify to the gospel.

However he is still in prison and does not expect to be acquitted. For that reason he wants his friends and colleagues to come to him. He asks Timothy to come (4:9), and when he comes to bring Mark as well (4:11); and not only Mark but also some of his personal items including *the cloak that I left with Carpus at Troas* (4:13). The reason for that particular request is that winter is near. In the words *do your best to come before winter* (4:21), we glimpse something of Paul's desperate circumstances. Clearly he does not expect any favours from his Roman guards.

Paul's Disappointment

Perhaps the best known verse in this final chapter of Paul's last letter is 4:7: *I have fought the good fight, I have finished the race, I have kept the faith.* These words give an impression of a triumphant Paul, ready to face whatever lies ahead and with absolute satisfaction at what he will leave behind. That is part of the picture, but if we focus exclusively on this verse we will receive a false impression of the overall situation.

The comment above at the end of the previous section has raised the issue of Paul's desperate situation. He is in severe physical need and obviously fears for his health if Timothy cannot reach him before winter arrives.

There are also other details which reveal a somewhat desperate and disappointed Paul. Some of these have come to light in earlier chapters of the letter. *All who are in Asia have turned away from me*, he has said (1:15). The same thing has happened in Rome, where *all deserted me*, he says, at the time of his first defence (4:13). It was not absolutely true that he had no sympathetic support in Rome, for in 4:21 he sends greetings from some of the believers there. But in the context of an official trial before the imperial authorities, it is not hard to guess that potential supporters melted away in fear. The wish *may it not be counted against them* (4:16) suggests that Paul feels a measure of sympathy even in the midst of his disappointment. At the present time *only Luke is with me* (4:11); others in Rome were with him in a more remote sense but Luke alone had the courage to stay with Paul.

In this catalogue of disappointments, Paul singles out two men for special mention. The first is Demas who, *in love with this present world, has deserted me* (4:10). Demas is known to us from references elsewhere. In Colossians 4:14 he and Luke send greetings to the Colossians. In Philemon 24 Paul describes him as a *fellow-worker*. He was clearly part of Paul's inner circle of friends and colleagues, and this increases Paul's pain in the present circumstances. Paul's expectation is that the true servant of God will not be ashamed of the gospel but will be willing to suffer for it. That was his exhortation to Timothy in 1:8, and clearly he expected the same of Demas. Instead, Demas apparently found *Thessalonica* (4:10) a safer place than Rome under these circumstances.

When it is said that Demas was *in love with this present world* (4:10), it is debated whether he had turned away from the gospel as such or had only abandoned Paul. Though the verse speaks of abandoning *me*, Paul, it is worth noting the interesting contrast between Demas who *loved* the present world and others who *love* the appearing of Jesus (4:8). The same Greek verb is used in both verses and the implication seems clear enough that Demas has failed to love what a true believer should love, for otherwise he would not have taken the action which he has.

The other major disappointment has been *Alexander the coppersmith* (4:14; perhaps better *metalworker*, NIV). This is quite likely to be the same Alexander mentioned in 1 Timothy 1:20, one of those who have *suffered shipwreck in the faith*, and whom Paul has *turned over to Satan*; the identification is supported by the information that *he strongly opposed our message* (4:15). If it is the same man, it is not hard, with a little imagination, to guess that he reacted negatively to Paul's treatment on that occasion and harboured a desire for revenge. In such a context it has been reasonably suggested that the *great harm* which he did to Paul (4:14) was to provide information or lodge a complaint which led to Paul's arrest.[171] Furthermore, it is quite likely that this happened at *Troas* (4:13), which would explain why Paul left his *cloak* and *the books* there. Paul warns that Timothy *must beware of* Alexander (4:15), which shows that even here in these final verses Paul is not only thinking of his own personal setbacks but is concerned about the situation which Timothy faces at Ephesus where Alexander may continue to exercise influence.

---

[171] So Mounce, *Pastorals*, 593; Towner, *Timothy-Titus* (2006), 631; Witherington, *Commentary*, 379. Marshall accepts this as a possibility but suggests that because of our ignorance of the circumstances a less specific interpretation is preferable (Marshall, *Pastorals*, 822).

These several references give a rather different picture than the impression one might receive from 4:7 alone. It is not a happy situation. Paul is naturally disappointed on a personal level, as he remembers people like Demas with whom he had worked closely as a trusted colleague as well as the lack of support from others in his hour of need. But it is much more than a personal issue. It is the situation in the churches which concerns him most. The general desertion of Paul (1:15, 4:11, 16) points to an unwillingness to suffer for the gospel, and even Timothy is in danger from this temptation, as we have seen several times throughout the letter. Paul may well be satisfied about his personal performance (4:7), but he comes towards the end of his ministry and the end of his life with grave concerns for the future. This lends weight and urgency to his appeal to Timothy, an appeal (we may think) which bore fruit, for in a later NT book we learn that Timothy underwent imprisonment (Heb. 13:23); he proved to be willing to suffer for the gospel and to continue in gospel ministry.

Paul's Strategies

One of the remarkable features of the final verses is that they reveal a Paul who is still very much involved in ministry. He is planning the movements of others and indeed he is still working himself, despite his imprisonment and his strong expectation that he is not likely to be released and that the end of his life is in sight.

Regarding his own activity, the instruction to Timothy to bring Mark is linked with the reason that Mark is *useful in my ministry* (4:11). It is hardly likely that he wants Mark to make such a journey merely to wash his clothes or do some other menial, mundane task.[172] We may not be able to say exactly what *ministry* Paul has in mind, but almost certainly it is gospel-focused activity of some sort. Perhaps a hint is given in the request for *the books, and above all the parchments* (4:13), for if Mark is the same person as the author of the second Gospel and was already by this time beginning to show literary interests and skills, it may have been this gift which Paul wanted to utilize in his own ministry. It is natural that Paul would have wished to continue reading and writing.

---

[172] So Marshall, *Pastorals*, 817; Towner, *Timothy-Titus* (2006), 625-626. But Kelly, *Pastorals*, 214, favours the idea of "personal service".

But whatever exactly Paul had in mind, he had certainly not given up but had ministry matters very much in mind, despite the uncertainties of his own personal circumstances.

It is also not possible to say exactly what Paul means when he speaks of the *books* and the *parchments*, and in fact it is even difficult to know whether he refers to two groups of items or only one; in the latter case *the books, namely the parchments* would be the translation. A common suggestion is that some may be copies of some OT books, but it is not likely to be the whole OT which would be a very bulky collection. It is also possible that Paul had personal notebooks. It would be of great interest to know what sorts of books and notes Paul carried with him on his journeys. Travel was tiring and often dangerous, and only items of vital importance would be carried as extra baggage. As with many other details of NT history, there is much in this area which we simply do not know.

As well as his own work, Paul continues to plan and direct and take interest in the work of his friends and colleagues, who are ministering in different places. *Crescens has gone to Galatia* (4:10). This may be the area known from Paul's earlier ministry (Acts 13-14) and his letter to those churches. But the same name applied to Gaul (modern France), and in fact some early scribes, understanding the passage to refer to Gaul, have changed *Galatia* to *Gallia*. We have no other information about Crescens, but his name is Latin, and it is possible (if nothing more) that Paul planned a missionary outreach to Gaul during or soon after his ministry in Spain and sent Crescens (a Roman?) for this purpose. In later tradition Crescens was claimed as a bishop in Gaul. Of course there are many guesses in such a reconstruction, but what fascinating possibilities are suggested about the early (possibly first) preaching of the gospel in that land. If only we knew.[173]

Titus has gone *to Dalmatia* (4:10). Here we are on firmer ground in trying to reconstruct the picture. In Titus 3:12 Paul had requested Titus to join him at Nicopolis on the west coast of Greece, and assuming that he did so, it is not hard to envisage that he later travelled further along the same coast in a north-westerly direction. Dalmatia was some distance in that direction, on the way to Illyricum where Paul had been involved in gospel ministry (Rom. 15:19).

---

[173] For discussion of the possibilities mentioned here, see Kelly, *Pastorals*, 213.

Tychicus has been sent to *Ephesus* (4:12). This was Tychicus' home area (Acts 20:4) and other references to him in relation to this general area are found in Ephesians 6:21 and Colossians 4:7, as the bearer of those letters and the bringer of news about Paul. In Titus 3:12 Tychicus was mentioned as one of the possible replacements for Titus on Crete. The fact that Tychicus is now being sent to Ephesus (we may guess to take the place of Timothy who is asked to join Paul) may suggest that it was not Tychicus but Artemas whom Paul decided to send to Crete. In any case these references add up to an impressive picture of a valuable member of Paul's team, capable of being entrusted with several significant tasks.

We know nothing more about *Carpus* (4:13), who may simply have been a resident of *Troas* (rather than one of Paul's colleagues) and a member of the congregation which existed there, known to us from Acts 20:6-12.

Greetings are sent (4:19) to some of the believers in Ephesus: *Prisca* (in some passages written in the longer form *Priscilla*) and *Aquila*, well known from several passages in Acts (18:2, 18, 26) and Paul's other letters (Rom. 16:3, 1 Cor. 16:19), and the *household of Onesiphorus* (as in 1:16).[174]

Erastus is *in Corinth* (4:20). Erastus is a name found elsewhere. In Romans 16:23 he is identified as *the city treasurer* of Corinth and the mention of Corinth in our present text makes it likely that it is the same Erastus in both passages. Acts 19:22 mentions Erastus and Timothy as *two of his [Paul's] helpers*, and this could be a third reference to the same man. The role of city treasurer was not a permanent office and Erastus could easily have given time to assist Paul in whatever ways may have been possible or suitable. The fact that he is mentioned now as having *remained* in Corinth perhaps implies that Timothy was aware that he had not always been restricted to that city.

Trophimus is *in Miletus* (4:20). Elsewhere he is described as from *Asia* (Acts 20:4), more specifically as an *Ephesian* (Acts 21:29). Possibly therefore Timothy wondered why Trophimus was not now in Ephesus and Paul here supplies the reason: he was *ill*. Little is known of this man, except that he was in Paul's travelling party (Acts 20:4), almost certainly as one of the authorized representatives of the churches taking to Jerusalem the money Paul had collected in the Gentile churches.

---

[174] See comments on 1:16 about whether this means Onesiphorus and his household, or the household excluding Onesiphorus (whom some suggest was dead).

The other names in 4:21 are those of believers in Rome who send greetings to Timothy. These are *Eubulus, Pudens, Linus and Claudia*. Of these one name of special interest is Linus, who by tradition was bishop of Rome following Peter.[175] Along with them *all the brothers and sisters* join in sending greetings. The sense of belonging to the fellowship of the wider church was apparently much stronger then than it usually is today (even though, as we have seen, these believers were not able to assist Paul at his first defence).

Paul's Hope

In the previous paragraph Paul has mentioned his hope of future recognition, the *crown of righteousness* which he will receive from the Lord Jesus (4:8). In the last half of the chapter he has given plenty of evidence of the unreliability of human help, but again has testified to his experience of the Lord's presence and strength (4:17, at the time of the first defence), which have enabled him to proclaim the message even in that unpromising situation. He describes this picturesquely and metaphorically as being *rescued from the lion's mouth* (4:17).

This gives him further confidence as he faces the future (4:18). *The Lord will rescue me*, he says, which is not an expectation of release from prison or acquittal at the end of his trial but rescue of a different kind. It is not being rescued from having to go through difficult times or even rescue from death, but being protected spiritually within such experiences, with the end result that the Lord will *save me for his heavenly kingdom*. This is Paul's ultimate hope and the reason for the doxology which acknowledges that to the Lord belongs *the glory for ever and ever*.

This is not only Paul's experience but that of every true believer. This point has been expressed in 4:8 (*to all who have longed for his appearing*) and is the theme again in the final verse of the letter, as he expresses the wish for Timothy that *the Lord be with your spirit* (4:22). This wish is directed specifically to Timothy (for the word *your* is singular), but in the last phrase, *grace be with you*, the pronoun *you* is plural. So the final greeting is in effect addressed to all the congregation, a reminder that the Lord's presence and blessing is not for the elite (whoever they may be) but for all God's people. Praise be to God!

[175] The tradition is not unanimous about who succeeded Peter; see Marshall, *Pastorals*, 830.

Reflection: Partnership and Perseverance in Ministry

When Paul writes to the Philippians he gives thanks for their partnership in the gospel (Phil. 1:5). The practical demonstration of such partnership is often seen in the closing words of his letters, and not least in this chapter, the last that he is known to have written.

There is no doubt that Paul was someone with remarkable gifts and great strength of character. He could be very determined, as we see on the occasion when he and Barnabas had a difference of opinion and parted company (Acts 15:36-41). It would be easy to conclude that Paul was a dictatorial individualist. Perhaps there were occasions when that might have been a reasonable description. But there is much more to Paul than that, and the stronger impression is that he was a team player. We might want to call it a team with a very strong and dominant captain-coach, but however that may be there was nearly always a team associated with Paul as he conducted his ministry.

Paul's ability to attract others to join him in co-operative effort is dramatically illustrated at the end of 2 Timothy. There are at least ten who are mentioned as fellow-workers in some sense (Crescens, Titus, Luke, Mark, Tychicus, and Timothy himself; probably Prisca and Aquila, Erastus and Trophimus should be included); from the final verses of Titus we could add the names of Artemas, Zenas and Apollos. Despite his circumstances, which had caused many to separate themselves from him, he can still count on the assistance of these men (and one woman).

One problem of teams in ministry is that jealousies easily arise. India is not exempt from this universal problem. The older man feels threatened by the younger, or sometimes the opposite applies where a younger man who is the team leader is unable to cope with an older, experienced person being part of the team. The skilled musician makes those who lack musical talent feel inadequate. The eloquent preacher earns applause which other members of the team envy. Many other similar things could be mentioned.

The point is that teamwork in ministry is usually much more difficult in reality than we might wish. We agree that teams are a better way to fulfil the ministry of a church or organization, but it requires people of maturity to make teams work well. Many times the problem is avoided by restricting the team to members of the family, and so what is announced as a Christian ministry is often just a family business in which outsiders are not welcome. As in so many other ways, Paul sets an outstanding example here.

The final matter worth pondering is Paul's perseverance. Although he says, "I have finished the race," that was not quite true. He was in prison under close guard and we would have forgiven him if he had actually given up, if he had said that there was nothing more for him to do, nothing which he could do in those circumstances. But on the contrary these verses show him doing all that he could despite the limitations. He is still vitally interested in the well-being of his churches and involved in organizing different people to look after the interests of the churches in different places (not only Timothy in Ephesus). He even wants his books, in contrast to those who leave their books behind when they finish seminary. Circumstances change and opportunities change, but the genuine minister of the gospel will be committed to the cause of the gospel till the end of his or her life. That was true of Paul. That is Paul's challenge to us. It continues to be a challenge to those who serve Christ in India, and the health of the church in India will be directly related to the persevering commitment of those who claim to be servants of the church's Lord.